Mometrix
TEST PREPARATION

MoGEA

(081)
Secrets Study Guide
Part 2 of 2

Dear Future Exam Success Story

First of all, **THANK YOU** for purchasing Mometrix study materials!

Second, congratulations! You are one of the few determined test-takers who are committed to doing whatever it takes to excel on your exam. **You have come to the right place.** We developed these study materials with one goal in mind: to deliver you the information you need in a format that's concise and easy to use.

In addition to optimizing your guide for the content of the test, we've outlined our recommended steps for breaking down the preparation process into small, attainable goals so you can make sure you stay on track.

We've also analyzed the entire test-taking process, identifying the most common pitfalls and showing how you can overcome them and be ready for any curveball the test throws you.

Standardized testing is one of the biggest obstacles on your road to success, which only increases the importance of doing well in the high-pressure, high-stakes environment of test day. Your results on this test could have a significant impact on your future, and this guide provides the information and practical advice to help you achieve your full potential on test day.

Your success is our success

We would love to hear from you! If you would like to share the story of your exam success or if you have any questions or comments in regard to our products, please contact us at **800-673-8175** or **support@mometrix.com**.

Thanks again for your business and we wish you continued success!

Sincerely,
The Mometrix Test Preparation Team

Need more help? Check out our flashcards at:
http://mometrixflashcards.com/MoGEA

Copyright © 2022 by Mometrix Media LLC. All rights reserved.
Written and edited by the Mometrix Exam Secrets Test Prep Team
Printed in the United States of America

TABLE OF CONTENTS

NATURAL SCIENCES 1
   BIOLOGY 1
   ECOLOGY 12
   GEOLOGY 15
   EARTH SCIENCE AND WEATHER 22
   SPACE SCIENCE 25
   SAFETY AND EQUIPMENT 28
   SCIENTIFIC INQUIRY AND REASONING 34
   HISTORY AND IMPACT OF SCIENCE 40
   SOCIAL STUDIES SKILLS 44

SOCIAL AND BEHAVIORAL SCIENCES 51
   U.S. HISTORY 51
   WORLD HISTORY 61
   U.S. GOVERNMENT AND CITIZENSHIP 66
   UNITED STATES POLITICAL SYSTEMS 73
   ECONOMICS 79
   GEOGRAPHY 82
   CULTURAL STUDIES 92

HUMANITIES AND FINE ARTS 95
   VISUAL ARTS 95
   MUSIC 101
   PERFORMING ARTS 110
   WORLD LITERATURE 116
   LITERARY PERIODS AND MOVEMENTS 120
   PUBLIC SPEAKING 123

UNIFIED, COHERENT, AND EFFECTIVE WRITING 125
   THE WRITING PROCESS 125
   OUTLINING AND ORGANIZING IDEAS 127
   WRITING STYLE AND FORM 133
   MODES OF WRITING 137
   RESEARCH WRITING 142

MOGEA PRACTICE TEST 146
   COMMUNICATIONS 146
   MATHEMATICAL SCIENCES 154
   NATURAL SCIENCES 159
   SOCIAL AND BEHAVIORAL SCIENCES 163
   HUMANITIES AND FINE ARTS 168
   WRITING PROMPT 170

ANSWER KEY AND EXPLANATIONS 171
   COMMUNICATIONS 171
   MATHEMATICAL SCIENCES 173
   NATURAL SCIENCES 176

SOCIAL AND BEHAVIORAL SCIENCES	178
HUMANITIES AND FINE ARTS	180

HOW TO OVERCOME TEST ANXIETY — 182
CAUSES OF TEST ANXIETY — 182
ELEMENTS OF TEST ANXIETY — 183
EFFECTS OF TEST ANXIETY — 183
PHYSICAL STEPS FOR BEATING TEST ANXIETY — 184
MENTAL STEPS FOR BEATING TEST ANXIETY — 185
STUDY STRATEGY — 186
TEST TIPS — 188
IMPORTANT QUALIFICATION — 189

THANK YOU — 190

ADDITIONAL BONUS MATERIAL — 191

Natural Sciences

Biology

SUBFIELDS OF BIOLOGY

There are a number of subfields of biology:

- **Zoology** – The study of animals
- **Botany** – The study of plants
- **Biophysics** – The application of the laws of physics to the processes of organisms and the application of the facts about living things to human processes and inventions
- **Biochemistry** – The study of the chemistry of living organisms, including diseases and the pharmaceutical drugs used to cure them
- **Cytology** – The study of cells
- **Histology** – The study of the tissues of plants and animals
- **Organology** – The study of tissues organized into organs
- **Physiology** – The study of the way organisms function, including metabolism, the exchange of matter and energy in nutrition, the senses, reproduction and development, and the work of the nervous system and brain
- **Genetics** – The study of heredity as it relates to the transmission of genes
- **Ethology** – The study of animal behavior
- **Ecology** – The study of the relationship of living organisms to their environments

CLASSIFICATION OF LIFE FORMS

All living creatures can be classified into one of three domains and then into one of six kingdoms:

- Domain Bacteria
  - **Kingdom Eubacteria**—single celled prokaryotes with little internal complexity, contains peptidoglycan. Members have just one chromosome, reproduce asexually, may have flagella, and are very simple in form.
- Domain Archaea
  - **Kingdom Archaebacteria**—single celled prokaryotes with little internal complexity, does not contain peptidoglycan. Members have just one chromosome, reproduce asexually, may have flagella, and are very simple in form.
- Domain Eukarya
  - **Kingdom Protista**—single celled eukaryotes with greater internal complexity than Bacteria or Archaea. They have a true nucleus surrounded by a membrane that separates it from the cytoplasm. Most are one-celled and have no complex tissues like plants.
  - **Kingdom Fungi**—single celled or multicellular with considerable variation and complexity. Members have no chlorophyll, so they don't make their own food like plants. They reproduce using spores. Fungi are made up of filaments called hyphae that, in larger fungi, can interlace to form a tissue called mycelium.

- **Kingdom Plantae**—multicellular with great variation and complexity, rigid cell walls. This group consists of organisms that have chlorophyll and make their own food. Plants have differentiated tissues and reproduce either sexually or asexually.
- **Kingdom Animalia**—multicellular with much variation and complexity, cell membrane. This group consists of organisms that move around and have to feed on existing organic material.

> **Review Video: Kingdom Animalia**
> Visit mometrix.com/academy and enter code: 558413
>
> **Review Video: Kingdom Fungi**
> Visit mometrix.com/academy and enter code: 315081
>
> **Review Video: Kingdom Plantae**
> Visit mometrix.com/academy and enter code: 710084

CHARACTERISTICS OF INVERTEBRATES

Invertebrates are animals with no internal skeletons. They can be divided into three groups:

1. **Marine Invertebrates** – Members of this group live in oceans and seas. Marine invertebrates include sponges, corals, jellyfish, snails, clams, octopuses, squids, and crustaceans, none of which live on the surface.
2. **Freshwater Invertebrates** – Members of this group live in lakes and rivers. Freshwater invertebrates include worms on the bottom, microscopic crustaceans, and terrestrial insect larvae that live in the water column, but only where there is no strong current. Some live on the surface of the water.
3. **Terrestrial Invertebrates** – Members of this group live on dry ground. Terrestrial invertebrates include insects, mollusks (snails, slugs), arachnids, and myriapods (centipedes and millipedes). Terrestrial invertebrates breathe through a series of tubes that penetrate into the body (trachea) and deliver oxygen into tissues. Underground terrestrial invertebrates are generally light-colored with atrophied eyes and no cuticle to protect them from desiccation. They include worms that live underground and in caves and rock crevices. This group also includes insects such as ants that create colonies underground.

CHARACTERISTICS OF VERTEBRATE GROUPS

The **vertebrates**, animals with an internal skeleton, are divided into four groups:

1. **Fish** – This group is the most primitive, but is also the group from which all other groups evolved. Fish live in water, breathe with gills, are cold-blooded, have fins and scales, and are typically oviparous, which means they lay eggs. Fish typically have either cartilaginous skeletons (such as rays and sharks) or bony skeletons.
2. **Amphibians** – The skin of animals in this group is delicate and permeable, so they need water to keep it moist. Amphibians are oviparous. The young start out in water with gills, but the adults use lungs.
3. **Reptiles and birds** – The skin of animals in this group has very hard, horn-like scales. Birds have exchanged scales for feathers. Reptiles and birds are oviparous, although birds care for their eggs and reptiles do not. Members have a cloaca, an excretory and reproductive cavity that opens to the outside. Reptiles are cold-blooded, but birds are warm-blooded.

4. **Mammals** – These are the most highly evolved vertebrates. Mammals have bodies covered with fur; are warm-blooded; are viviparous, meaning they give birth to live young which are fed with milk from female mammary glands; and are tetrapods (four-legged). Most live on the ground (except whales and dolphins) and a few fly (bats).

HUNTERS AND PREY ANIMALS

The interaction between **predators** and their **prey** is important to controlling the balance of an ecosystem. **Hunters** are **carnivorous** animals at the top of the ecological pyramid that eat other animals. Hunters tend to be territorial, leaving signs to warn others to stay out or risk a fight. Hunters are equipped to capture with claws, curved beaks, spurs, fangs, etc. They try to use a minimum amount of energy for each capture, so they prey upon the more vulnerable (the old, ill, or very young) when given a choice. Predators never kill more than they can eat. Some hunters have great speed, some stalk, and some hunt in groups. **Prey** animals are those that are captured by predators for food. They are usually **herbivores** further down the ecological pyramid. Prey animals have special characteristics to help them flee from predators. They may hide in nests or caves, become totally immobile to escape detection, have protective coloration or camouflage, have warning coloration to indicate being poisonous, or have shells or quills for protection.

LIFE PROCESSES THAT ALL LIVING THINGS HAVE IN COMMON

Living things share many **processes** that are necessary to survival, but the ways these processes and interactions occur are highly diverse. Processes include those related to:

- **Nutrition** – the process of obtaining, ingesting, and digesting foods; excreting unused or excess substances; and extracting energy from the foods to maintain structure.
- **Transport** (circulation) – the process of circulating essential materials such as nutrients, cells, hormones, and gases (oxygen and hydrogen) to the places they are needed by moving them through veins, arteries, and capillaries. Needed materials do not travel alone, but are "piggybacked" on transporting molecules.
- **Respiration** – the process of breathing, which is exchanging gases between the interior and exterior using gills, trachea (insects), or lungs.
- **Regulation** – the process of coordinating life activities through the nervous and endocrine systems.
- **Reproduction and growth** – the process of producing more of one's own kind and growing from birth to adulthood. The more highly evolved an animal is, the longer its growth time is.
- **Locomotion** (in animals) – the process of moving from place to place in the environment by using legs, flight, or body motions.

ORGANISMS THAT INTERFERE WITH CELL ACTIVITY

Viruses, bacteria, fungi, and other parasites may infect plants and animals and interfere with normal life functions, create imbalances, or disrupt the operations of cells.

- **Viruses** – These enter the body by inhalation (airborne) or through contact with contaminated food, water, or infected tissues. They affect the body by taking over the cell's protein synthesis mechanism to make more viruses. They kill the host cell and impact tissue and organ operations. Examples of viruses include measles, rabies, pneumonia, and AIDS.
- **Bacteria** – These enter the body through breaks in the skin or contaminated food or water, or by inhalation. They reproduce rapidly and produce toxins that kill healthy host tissues. Examples include diphtheria, bubonic plague, tuberculosis, and syphilis.

- **Fungi** – These feed on healthy tissues of the body by sending rootlike tendrils into the tissues to digest them extracellularly. Examples include athlete's foot and ringworm.
- **Parasites** – These enter the body through the skin, via insect bites, or through contaminated food or water. Examples include tapeworms, malaria, or typhus.

HYDROCARBONS AND CARBOHYDRATES

Carbon is an element found in all living things. Two types of carbon molecules that are essential to life are hydrocarbons and carbohydrates. **Hydrocarbons**, composed only of hydrogen and carbon, are the simplest organic molecules. The simplest of these is methane, which has one carbon atom and four hydrogen atoms. Methane is produced by the decomposition of animal or vegetable matter, and is part of petroleum and natural gas. **Carbohydrates** are compounds made of hydrogen, carbon, and oxygen. There are three types of these macromolecules (large molecules):

1. **Sugars** are soluble in water and, although they have less energy than fats, provide energy more quickly.
2. **Starches**, insoluble in water, are long chains of glucose that act as reserve substances. Potatoes and cereals are valuable foods because they are rich in starch. Animals retain glucose in their cells as glycogen, a special type of starch.
3. **Cellulose**, composed of glucose chains, makes up the cells and tissues of plants. It is one of the most common organic materials.

> **Review Video: Basics of Hydrocarbons**
> Visit mometrix.com/academy and enter code: 824749

LIPIDS, PROTEINS, AND NUCLEIC ACIDS

Besides hydrocarbons and carbohydrates, there are three other types of carbon molecules that are essential to life: lipids, proteins, and nucleic acids. **Lipids** are compounds that are insoluble or only partially soluble in water. There are three main types: fats, which act as an energy reserve for organisms; phospholipids, which are one of the essential components of cell membranes; and steroids such as cholesterol and estrogen, which are very important to metabolism. **Proteins** are complex substances that make up almost half the dry weight of animal bodies. These molecules contain hydrogen, carbon, oxygen, and other elements, chiefly nitrogen and sulfur. Proteins make up muscle fibers and, as enzymes, act as catalysts. **Nucleic acids** are large molecules (polymers) composed of a large number of simpler molecules (nucleotides). Each one has a sugar containing five carbons (pentose), a phosphorous compound (phosphate group), and a nitrogen compound (nitrogenated base). Nucleic acids facilitate perpetuation of the species because they carry genetic information as DNA and RNA.

CELL

The **cell** is the basic organizational unit of all living things. Each piece within a cell has a function that helps organisms grow and survive. There are many different types of cells, but cells are unique to each type of organism. The one thing that all cells have in common is a **membrane**, which is comparable to a semi-permeable plastic bag. The membrane is composed of phospholipids. There are also some **transport holes**, which are proteins that help certain molecules and ions move in and out of the cell. The cell is filled with a fluid called **cytoplasm** or cytosol. Within the cell are a variety of **organelles**, groups of complex molecules that help a cell survive, each with its own unique membrane that has a different chemical makeup from the cell membrane. The larger the cell, the more organelles it will need to live.

> **Review Video: Difference Between Plant and Animal Cells**
> Visit mometrix.com/academy and enter code: 115568
>
> **Review Video: An Introduction to Cellular Biology**
> Visit mometrix.com/academy and enter code: 629967
>
> **Review Video: Cell Structure**
> Visit mometrix.com/academy and enter code: 591293

NUCLEUS AND MITOCHONDRIA IN EUKARYOTIC CELLS

Eukaryotic cells have a nucleus, a big dark spot floating somewhere in the center that acts like the brain of the cell by controlling eating, movement, and reproduction. A **nuclear envelope** surrounds the nucleus and its contents, but allows RNA and proteins to pass through. **Chromatin**, made up of DNA, RNA, and nuclear proteins, is present in the nucleus. The nucleus also contains a nucleolus made of RNA and protein. **Mitochondria** are very small organelles that take in nutrients, break them down, and create energy for the cell through a process called cellular respiration. There might be thousands of mitochondria depending on the cell's purpose. A muscle cell needs more energy for movement than a cell that transmits nerve impulses, for example. Mitochondria have two membranes: a **cover** and the **inner cristae** that folds over many times to increase the surface work area. The fluid inside the mitochondria, the matrix, is filled with water and enzymes that take food molecules and combine them with oxygen so they can be digested.

> **Review Video: Mitochondria**
> Visit mometrix.com/academy and enter code: 444287
>
> **Review Video: Cellular Energy Production**
> Visit mometrix.com/academy and enter code: 743401
>
> **Review Video: Cell Functions**
> Visit mometrix.com/academy and enter code: 883787

CHLOROPLASTS OF PLANT CELLS

Chloroplasts, which make plants green, are the food producers of a plant cell. They differ from an animal cell's mitochondria, which break down sugars and nutrients. **Photosynthesis** occurs when the energy from the sun hits a chloroplast and the chlorophyll uses that energy to combine carbon dioxide and water to make sugars and oxygen. The nutrition and oxygen obtained from plants makes them the basis of all life on earth. A chloroplast has two membranes to contain and protect the inner parts. The **stroma** is an area inside the chloroplast where reactions occur and starches are created. A **thylakoid** has chlorophyll molecules on its surface, and a stack of thylakoids is called a granum. The stacks of sacs are connected by **stromal lamellae**, which act like the skeleton of the chloroplast, keeping all the sacs a safe distance from each other and maximizing the efficiency of the organelle.

PASSIVE AND ACTIVE TRANSPORT

Passive transport within a cell does not require energy and work. For example, when there is a large concentration difference between the outside and the inside of a cell, the pressure of the greater concentration, not energy, will move molecules across the lipid bilayer into the cell. Another example of passive transport is osmosis, which is the movement of water across a membrane. Too much water in a cell can cause it to burst, so the cell moves ions in and out to help equalize the amount of water. **Active transport** is when a cell uses energy to move individual molecules across the cell membrane to maintain a proper balance. **Proteins** embedded in the lipid bilayer do most of the transport work. There are hundreds of different types of proteins because they are specific. For instance, a protein that moves glucose will not move calcium. The activity of these proteins can be stopped by inhibitors or poisons, which can destroy or plug up a protein.

> **Review Video: Passive Transport: Diffusion and Osmosis**
> Visit mometrix.com/academy and enter code: 642038

MITOTIC CELL REPLICATION

Mitosis is the duplication of a cell and all its parts, including the DNA, into two identical daughter cells. There are five phases in the life cycle of a cell:

1. **Prophase** – This is the process of duplicating everything in preparation for division.
2. **Metaphase** – The cell's different pieces align themselves for the split. The DNA lines up along a central axis and the centrioles send out specialized tubules that connect to the centromere. The centromere has two strands of a chromosome (condensed DNA) attached to it.
3. **Anaphase** – Half of the chromosomes go one way and half go another.
4. **Telophase** – When the chromosomes get to the side of the cell, the cell membrane closes in and splits the cell into two pieces. This results in two separate cells, each with half of the original DNA.
5. **Interphase** – This is the normal state of the cell, or the resting stage between divisions. During this stage, the cell duplicates nucleic acids in preparation for the next division.

> **Review Video: Mitosis**
> Visit mometrix.com/academy and enter code: 849894
>
> **Review Video: Cellular Division: Mitosis and Meiosis**
> Visit mometrix.com/academy and enter code: 109813

MICROBES

Microbes are the smallest, simplest, and most abundant organisms on earth. Their numbers are incalculable, and a microscope is required to see them. There is a huge variety of microbes, including bacteria, fungi, some algae, and protozoa. Microbes can be harmful or helpful.

Microbes can be **heterotrophic** (eat other things) or **autotrophic** (make food for themselves). They can be solitary or colonial, sexual or asexual. Examples include mold, a multi-cellular type of fungus, and yeasts, which are single-celled (but may live in colonies). A **mushroom** is a fungus that lives as a group of strands underground called hyphae that decompose leaves or bark on the ground. When it reproduces, it develops a mushroom whose cap contains spores. **Mold** is a type of zygote fungi that reproduces with a stalk, but releases zygospores. **Good bacteria** can be those that help plants absorb the nitrogen needed for growth or help grazing animals break down the cellulose in plants. Some **bad bacteria** are killed by the penicillin developed from a fungus.

ROOTS, STEMS, AND LEAVES

Roots are structures designed to pull water and minerals from soil or water. In large plants such as trees, the roots usually go deep into the ground to not only reach the water, but also to support and stabilize the tree. There are some plant species that have roots above ground, and there are also plants called epiphytes that live in trees with their roots clinging to the branches. Some roots, like carrots and turnips, serve as food. Roots are classified as **primary** and **lateral** (like a trunk and branches). The **apical meristem** is the tip of a root or shoot that helps the plant increase in length. **Root hairs** are fuzzy root extensions that help with the absorption of water and nutrients. The majority of the plant above ground is made up of the stems (trunk and branches) and leaves. **Stems** transport food and water and act as support structures. **Leaves** are the site for photosynthesis, and are connected to the rest of the plant by a vascular system.

Gymnosperms, Cycads, and Conifers

Gymnosperms are plants with vascular systems and seeds but no flowers (flowers are an evolutionary advancement). The function of the seed is to ensure offspring can be produced by the plant by providing a protective coating that lets the plant survive for long periods until it germinates. It also stores food for the new plant to use until it can make its own. Seeds can be spread over a wide area. **Cycads** are sturdy plants with big, waxy fronds that make them look like ferns or palms. They can survive in harsh conditions if there is warm weather. For reproduction, they have big cones located in the center of the plant. The female plant grows a fruit in the middle of the stem. **Conifers** are trees that thrive in northern latitudes and have cones. Examples of conifers are pine, cedar, redwood, and spruce. Conifers are evergreens because they have needles that take full advantage of the sun year-round. They are also very tall and strong because of the chemical substance xylem in their systems.

Angiosperms

Angiosperms are plants that have flowers. This is advantageous because the plant's seeds and pollen can be spread not only by gravity and wind, but also by insects and animals. Flowers are able to attract organisms that can help pollinate the plant and distribute seeds. Some flowering plants also produce fruit. When an animal eats the fruit, the plant seeds within will be spread far and wide in the animal's excrement. There are two kinds of angiosperm seeds: monocotyledons (monocots) and dicotyledons (dicots). A **cotyledon** is the seed leaf or food package for the developing plant. **Monocots** are simple flowering plants such as grasses, corn, palm trees, and lilies. They always have three petals on their flowers, and their leaves are long strands (like a palm frond). A **dicot** has seeds with two cotyledons, or two seed leaves of food. Most everyday flowers are dicots with four or five petals and extremely complex leaves with veins. Examples include roses, sunflowers, cacti, and cherry trees.

Arthropods

Arthropods have a number of unique characteristics:

- They have an **exoskeleton** (outside instead of inside).
- They **molt**. As the arthropod grows, it must shed its old shell and grow a new one.
- They have several **legs**, which are jointed.
- Their advanced **nervous systems** allow for hunting, moving around, finding a mate, and learning new behaviors for adaptation.
- They develop through **metamorphosis**. As arthropods develop, they change body shape. There are two types of metamorphosis:
    - *Complete* – The entire body shape changes. An example is butterflies, which change from worm-like larvae to insects with wings.
    - *Gradual* – The arthropod starts off small with no wings, and then molts and grows wings. Example: Grasshoppers.

Arthropods include spiders, crustaceans, and the enormous insect species (26 orders) called uniramians. Ranging from fleas to mosquitoes, beetles, dragonflies, aphids, bees, flies, and many more, uniramians have exoskeletons made of chitin, compound eyes, complex digestive systems, and usually six legs. This group is extremely diverse. Some can fly, some have toxins or antennae, and some can make wax, silk, or honey.

REPTILES

One group of vertebrates is the **reptile**. This group includes:

- **Crocodilia** – This is a group of reptiles that can grow quite large, and includes alligators and crocodiles. Normally found near the water in warmer climates, Crocodilia might be more closely related to birds than other reptiles.
- **Squamata** – This is the order of reptiles that includes snakes and lizards. Snakes are special because they have no legs and no ears. They feel vibrations, smell with their tongues, have specialized scales, and can unhinge their jaws to swallow prey that is larger than they are. Like snakes, lizards have scales, but they differ in that they have legs, can dig, can climb trees, and can grab things.
- **Chelonia** – This is the order of reptiles that includes turtles and tortoises. It is a special group because its members have shells. Different varieties live in forests, water, and deserts, or anywhere the climate is warm enough. They also live a long time, up to hundreds of years. Turtles are typically found near water and tortoises on land, even dry areas.

REPRODUCTION IN MAMMALS

When classified according to how they reproduce, there are three types of mammals:

1. **Monotremes** are rare mammals that lay eggs. These were the first mammals, and are more closely related to reptiles than other mammals. Examples include the duck-billed platypus and the spiny anteater.
2. **Marsupials** are special mammals. They give birth to live young, but the babies mature in pouches, where they are carried and can feed on milk. Many are found in Australia. The isolation of this island continent prevented placental mammals from taking hold. Examples of marsupials include kangaroos, possums, and koalas.
3. **Placental mammals** give birth from the females' placenta to live young. The young may be able to walk immediately, or they may need to be carried. They are still dependent on parental care for at least a short time. Placental mammals are the dominant form of mammals. Members of this group include cetaceans such as whales and dolphins, which are mammals that evolved but returned to the ocean.

RESPIRATORY SYSTEM

The **respiratory system** exchanges gases with the environment. Amphibians exchange gases through their moist skin, and fish use gills, but mammals, birds, and reptiles have lungs. The human respiratory system is made up of the nose, mouth, pharynx, trachea, and two lungs. The purpose of the respiratory system is to bring oxygen into the body and expel carbon dioxide. The respiratory system can inhale viruses, bacteria, and dangerous chemicals, so it is vulnerable to toxins and diseases such as pneumonia, which causes the lungs to fill with fluid until they cannot take in enough oxygen to support the body. **Emphysema**, often caused by smoking tobacco, destroys the tissues in the lungs, which cannot be regenerated. The respiratory system interacts with the **digestive system** in that the mouth and pharynx are used to swallow food and drink, as well as to breathe. It interacts with the circulatory system in that it provides fresh oxygen through blood vessels that pass through the lungs. This oxygen is then carried by the circulatory system throughout the body.

> **Review Video: Respiratory System**
> Visit mometrix.com/academy and enter code: 783075

SKELETAL SYSTEM

The human body has an **endoskeleton**, meaning it is inside the body. It is made up of bones instead of the hard plate of exoskeletons or fluids in tubes, which comprise the hydrostatic system of the starfish. The purpose of the skeleton is to support the body, provide a framework to which the muscles and organs can connect, and protect the inner organs. The skull protects the all-important brain and the ribs protect the internal organs from impact. The skeletal system interacts with the muscular system to help the body move, and softer cartilage works with the calcified bone to allow smooth movement of the body. The skeletal system also interacts with the circulatory system in that the marrow inside the bones helps produce both white and red blood cells.

> **Review Video: Skeletal System**
> Visit mometrix.com/academy and enter code: 256447

NERVOUS SYSTEM

The **nervous system** is divided into two parts: the **central nervous system** (brain and spinal cord) and the **peripheral nervous system** (a network of billions of neurons of different types throughout the entire body). The neurons are connected end to end, and transmit electrical impulses to each other. **Efferent neurons** send impulses from the central system to the limbs and organs. **Afferent neurons** receive sensory information and transmit it back to the central system. The nervous system is concerned with **senses and action**. In other words, it senses something and then acts upon it. An example is a predator sensing prey and attacking it. The nervous system also automatically senses activity inside the body and reacts to stimuli. For example, the first bite of a meal sets the whole digestive system into motion. The nervous system **interacts** with every other system in the body because all the tissues and organs need instruction, even when individuals are not aware of any activity occurring. For instance, the endocrine system is constantly working to produce hormones or adrenaline as needed.

> **Review Video: The Nervous System**
> Visit mometrix.com/academy and enter code: 708428

GENETICS, GENES, AND CHROMOSOMES

Genetics is the science devoted to the study of how characteristics are transmitted from one generation to another. In the 1800s, Gregor Mendel discovered the three laws of heredity that explain how genetics works. Genes are the hereditary units of material that are transmitted from one generation to the next. They are capable of undergoing mutations, can be recombined with other genes, and can determine the nature of an organism, including its color, shape, and size. **Genotype** is the genetic makeup of an individual based on one or more characteristics, while phenotype is the external manifestation of the genotype. For example, genotype determines hair color genes, whereas phenotype is the actual color of the hair observed. **Chromosomes** are the structures inside the nucleus of a cell made up primarily of deoxyribonucleic acid (DNA) and proteins. The chromosomes carry the genes. The numbers vary according to the species, but they are always the same for each species. For example, the human has 46 chromosomes, and the water lily has 112.

> **Review Video: Gene & Alleles**
> Visit mometrix.com/academy and enter code: 363997
>
> **Review Video: Genetic vs. Environmental Traits**
> Visit mometrix.com/academy and enter code: 750684
>
> **Review Video: Chromosomes**
> Visit mometrix.com/academy and enter code: 132083

MENDEL'S CONTRIBUTIONS TO GENETICS

Johann Gregor Mendel is known as the father of **genetics**. Mendel was an Austrian monk who performed thousands of experiments involving the breeding of the common pea plant in the garden of his monastery. Mendel kept detailed records including seed color, pod color, seed type, flower color, and plant height for eight years and published his work in 1865. Unfortunately, his work was largely ignored until the early 1900s. Mendel's work showed that genes come in pairs and that dominant and recessive traits are inherited independently of each other. His work established the law of segregation, the law of independent assortment, and the law of dominance.

DARWIN'S CONTRIBUTIONS TO THE THEORY OF EVOLUTION

Charles Darwin's theory of evolution is the unifying concept in biology today. From 1831 to 1836, Darwin traveled as a naturalist on a five-year voyage on the *H.M.S. Beagle* around the tip of South America and to the Galápagos Islands. He studied finches, took copious amounts of meticulous notes, and collected thousands of plant and animal specimens. He collected 13 species of finches each with a unique bill for a distinct food source, which led him to believe, due to similarities between the finches, that the finches shared a common ancestor. The similarities and differences of fossils of extinct rodents and modern mammal fossils led him to believe that the mammals had changed over time. Darwin believed that these changes were the result of random genetic changes called mutations. He believed that mutations could be beneficial and eventually result in a different organism over time. In 1859, in his first book, *On the Origin of Species*, Darwin proposed that natural selection was the means by which adaptations would arise over time. He coined the term "natural selection" and said that it is the mechanism of evolution. Because variety exists among individuals of a species, he stated that those individuals must compete for the same limited resources. Some would die, and others would survive. According to Darwin, evolution is a slow, gradual process. In 1871, Darwin published his second book, *Descent of Man, and Selection in Relation to Sex*, in which he discussed the evolution of man.

> **Review Video: Darwin's Contributions to Theory of Evolution**
> Visit mometrix.com/academy and enter code: 898980

CONTRIBUTION TO GENETICS MADE BY ALFRED HERSHEY AND MARTHA CHASE

Alfred Hershey and Martha Chase did a series of experiments in 1952 known as the **Hershey-Chase experiments**. These experiments showed that deoxyribonucleic acid (DNA), not protein, is the genetic material that transfers information for inheritance. The Hershey-Chase experiments used a bacteriophage, a virus that infects bacteria, to infect the bacteria *Escherichia coli*. The bacteriophage T2 is basically a small piece of DNA enclosed in a protein coating. The DNA contains phosphorus, and the protein coating contains sulfur. In the first set of experiments, the T2 was marked with radioactive phosphorus-32. In the second set of experiments, the T2 was marked with radioactive sulfur-35. For both sets of experiments, after the *E. coli* was infected by the T2, the *E. coli* was isolated using a centrifuge. In the first set of experiments, the radioactive isotope (P-32) was found in the *E. coli*, showing that the genetic information was transferred by the DNA. In the second set of experiments, the radioactive isotope (S-35) was not found in the *E. coli*, showing that the genetic information was not transferred by the protein as was previously thought. Hershey and Chase conducted further experiments allowing the bacteria from the first set of experiments to reproduce, and the offspring was also found to contain the radioactive isotope (P-32) further confirming that the DNA transferred the genetic material.

Ecology

AUTOTROPHS, PRODUCERS, HERBIVORES, CARNIVORES, OMNIVORES, AND DECOMPOSERS

Energy flows in one direction: from the sun, through photosynthetic organisms such as green plants (producers) and algae (autotrophs), and then to herbivores, carnivores, and decomposers. **Autotrophs** are organisms capable of producing their own food. The organic molecules they produce are food for all other organisms (heterotrophs). **Producers** are green plants that manufacture food by photosynthesis. **Herbivores** are animals that eat only plants (deer, rabbits, etc.). Since they are the first animals to receive the energy captured by producers, herbivores are called primary consumers. **Carnivores**, or secondary consumers, are animals that eat the bodies of other animals for food. Predators (wolves, lions, etc.) kill other animals, while scavengers consume animals that are already dead from predation or natural causes (buzzards). **Omnivores** are animals that eat both plants and other animals (humans). **Decomposers** include saprophytic fungi and bacteria that break down the complex structures of the bodies of living things into simpler forms that can be used by other living things. This recycling process releases energy from organic molecules.

ABIOTIC FACTORS AND BIOTIC FACTORS

Abiotic factors are the physical and chemical factors in the environment that are nonliving but upon which the growth and survival of living organisms depends. These factors can determine the types of plants and animals that will establish themselves and thrive in a particular area. Abiotic factors include:

- Light intensity available for photosynthesis
- Temperature range
- Available moisture
- Type of rock substratum
- Type of minerals
- Type of atmospheric gases
- Relative acidity (pH) of the system

Biotic factors are the living components of the environment that affect, directly or indirectly, the ecology of an area, possibly limiting the type and number of resident species. The relationships of predator/prey, producer/consumer, and parasite/host can define a community. Biotic factors include:

- Population levels of each species
- The food requirements of each species
- The interactions between species
- The wastes produced

HOW PLANTS MANUFACTURE FOOD

Plants are the only organisms capable of transforming **inorganic material** from the environment into **organic matter** by using water and solar energy. This transformation is made possible by chloroplasts, flat structures inside plant cells. **Chloroplasts**, located primarily in leaves, contain chlorophyll (the pigment capable of absorbing light and storing it in chemical compounds), DNA, ribosomes, and numerous enzymes. Chloroplasts are surrounded by a membrane. The leaves of plants are the main producers of oxygen, which helps purify the air. The **chlorophyll** in chloroplasts is responsible for the light, or luminous, phase of photosynthesis. The energy it absorbs breaks down water absorbed through the roots into hydrogen and oxygen to form ATP molecules that store energy. In the dark phase, when the plant has no light, the energy molecules are used to attach carbon dioxide to water and form glucose, a sugar.

Producers, Consumers, and Decomposers

The **food chain**, or food web, is a series of events that happens when one organism consumes another to survive. Every organism is involved in dozens of connections with others, so what happens to one affects the environment of the others. In the food chain, there are three main categories:

- **Producers** – Plants and vegetables are at the beginning of the food chain because they take energy from the sun and make food for themselves through photosynthesis. They are food sources for other organisms.
- **Consumers** – There are three levels of consumers: the organisms that eat plants (primary consumers, or herbivores); the organisms that eat the primary consumers (secondary consumers, or carnivores); and, in some ecosystems, the organisms that eat both plants and animals (tertiary consumers, or omnivores).
- **Decomposers** – These are the organisms that eat dead things or waste matter and return the nutrients to the soil, thus returning essential molecules to the producers and completing the cycle.

> **Review Video: Food Webs**
> Visit mometrix.com/academy and enter code: 853254

System of Classification for Living Organisms

The main characteristic by which living organisms are classified is the degree to which they are **related**, not the degree to which they resemble each other. The science of classification is called **taxonomy**. This classification is challenging since the division lines between groups is not always clear. Some animals have characteristics of two separate groups. The current system of taxonomy involves placing an organism into a **domain** (Bacteria, Archaea, and Eukarya), and then into a **kingdom** (Eubacteria, Archaeabacteria, Protista, Fungi, Plantae, and Animalia). The kingdoms are divided into phyla, then classes, then orders, then families, and finally genuses and species. For example, the family cat is in the domain of eukaryotes, the kingdom of animals, the phylum of chordates, the class of mammals, the order of carnivores, the family of felidae, and the genus of felis. All species of living beings can be identified with Latin scientific names that are assigned by the worldwide binomial system. The genus name comes first, and is followed by the name of the species. The family cat is *felis domesticus*.

> **Review Video: Biological Classification Systems**
> Visit mometrix.com/academy and enter code: 736052

Properties That Contribute to Earth's Life-Sustaining System

Life on earth is dependent on:

- All three states of **water** – gas (water vapor), liquid, and solid (ice)
- A variety of forms of **carbon**, the basis of life (carbon-based units)
- In the atmosphere, carbon dioxide, in the forms of methane and black carbon soot, produces the **greenhouse effect** that provides a habitable atmosphere.
- The earth's **atmosphere and electromagnetic field**, which shield the surface from harmful radiation and allow useful radiation to go through.

- The **earth's relationship to the sun and the moon**, which creates the four seasons and the cycles of plant and animal life.
- The combination of **water, carbon, and nutrients** that provides sustenance for life and regulates the climate system in a habitable temperature range with non-toxic air.

Geology

EARTH SYSTEM SCIENCE

The complex and interconnected dynamics of the continents, atmosphere, oceans, ice, and life forms are the subject of **earth system science**. These interconnected dynamics require an interdisciplinary approach that includes chemistry, physics, biology, mathematics, and applied sciences in order to study the Earth as an integrated system and determine (while considering human impact and interaction) the past, present, and future states of the earth. Scientific inquiry in this field includes exploration of:

- Extreme weather events as they pertain to a changing climate
- Earthquakes and volcanic eruptions as they pertain to tectonic shifts
- Losses in biodiversity in relation to the changes in the earth's ecosystems
- Causes and effects in the environment
- The sun's solar variability in relation to the earth's climate
- The atmosphere's increasing concentrations of carbon dioxide and aerosols
- Trends in the earth's systems in terms of changes and their consequences

TRADITIONAL EARTH SCIENCE DISCIPLINES

Modern science is approaching the study of the earth in an integrated fashion that sees the earth as an interconnected system that is impacted by humankind and, therefore, must include social dimensions. Traditionally, though, the following were the earth science disciplines:

- **Geology** – This is the study of the origin and structure of the earth and of the changes it has undergone and is in the process of undergoing. Geologists work from the crust inward.
- **Meteorology** – This is the study of the atmosphere, including atmospheric pressure, temperature, clouds, winds, precipitation, etc. It is also concerned with describing and explaining weather.
- **Oceanography** – This is the study of the oceans, which includes studying their extent and depth, the physics and chemistry of ocean waters, and the exploitation of their resources.
- **Ecology** – This is the study of living organisms in relation to their environment and to other living things. It is the study of the interrelations between the different components of the ecosystem.

GEOLOGICAL ERAS

Geologists divide the history of the earth into units of time called **eons**, which are divided into **eras**, then into **periods**, then into **epochs** and finally into **ages**. Dates are approximate of course, and there may be variations of a few million years. (Million years ago is abbreviated as Ma.) Some of the most commonly known time periods are:

- **Hadean Eon** – About 4.5 to 3.8 billion years ago
- **Archaean Eon** – 3.8 to 2.5 billion years ago
- **Proterozoic Eon** – 2.5 billion to 542 Ma
- **Phanerozoic Eon** – 542 Ma to the present
  - **Paleozoic Era** – 542 Ma to 251 Ma
    - **Cambrian Period** – 542 to 488 Ma
    - **Ordovician Period** – 488 to 443 Ma
    - **Silurian Period** – 443 to 416 Ma
    - **Devonian Period** – 416 to 359 Ma

- ❖ Carboniferous Period – 359 to 290 Ma
- ❖ Permian Period – 290 to 252 Ma
- o Mesozoic Era – 252 to 65 Ma
  - ❖ Triassic Period – 252 to 200 Ma
  - ❖ Jurassic Period – 200 to 150 Ma
  - ❖ Cretaceous Period – 150 to 65 Ma
- o Cenozoic Era – 65 Ma to the present
  - ❖ Paleogene Period – 65 to 28 Ma
  - ❖ Neogene Period – 28 to 2 Ma
  - ❖ Quaternary Period – about 2 Ma to the present

DEVELOPMENT OF LIFE ON EARTH ACCORDING TO TIME PERIODS

The **evolution** of life on earth is believed to have occurred as follows:

- Igneous rocks formed. (Hadean Eon)
- The continents formed. (Archaean Eon)
- The first multi-cellular creatures such as hydras, jellyfish, and sponges appeared about 600 Ma.
- Flatworms, roundworms, and segmented worms appeared about 550 Ma.
- Moss, arthropods, octopus, and eels appeared. (Cambrian Period)
- Mushrooms, fungi, and other primitive plants appeared; sea animals began to use calcium to build bones and shells. (Ordovician Period)
- Fish with jaws appeared. (Silurian Period)
- Fish developed lungs and legs (frogs) and went on land; ferns appeared. (Devonian period)
- Reptiles developed the ability to lay eggs on land and pine trees appeared. (Carboniferous Period)
- Dinosaurs dominated the land during the Triassic and Jurassic Periods.
- Flying insects, birds, and the first flowering plants appeared; dinosaurs died out. (Cretaceous Period)
- Mammals evolved and dominated; grasses became widespread. (50 Ma)
- Hominids appeared more than 2 Ma.

HYDROSPHERE AND HYDROLOGIC CYCLE

The **hydrosphere** is anything on earth that is related to water, whether it is in the air, on land, or in a plant or animal system. A water molecule consists of only two atoms of hydrogen and one of oxygen, yet it is what makes life possible. Unlike the other planets, earth is able to sustain life because its temperature allows water to be in its liquid state most of the time. Water vapor and ice are of no use to living organisms. The **hydrologic cycle** is the journey water takes as it assumes different forms. Liquid surface water evaporates to form the gaseous state of a cloud, and then becomes liquid again in the form of rain. This process takes about 10 days if water becomes a cloud. Water at the bottom of the ocean or in a glacier is not likely to change form, even over periods of thousands of years.

> **Review Video: Hydrologic Cycle**
> Visit mometrix.com/academy and enter code: 426578

AQUIFERS

An **aquifer** is an underground water reservoir formed from groundwater that has infiltrated from the surface by passing through the soil and permeable rock layers (the zone of aeration) to a zone of saturation where the rocks are impermeable. There are two types of aquifers. In one, the water is under pressure (**confined**) as the supply builds up between layers of impermeable rocks and has to move back towards the surface, resulting in a spring or artesian well. The second type of aquifer is called "**unconfined**" because it has room to expand and contract, and the water has to be pumped out. The highest level of the aquifer is called the water table. If water is pumped out of the aquifer such that the water table dips in a specific area, that area is called a cone of depression.

BIOSPHERE

Biosphere is the term used by physical geographers to describe the living world of trees, bugs, and animals. It refers to any place where life exists on earth, and is the intersection of the hydrosphere, the atmosphere, the land, and the energy that comes from space. The biosphere includes the upper areas of the atmosphere where birds and insects can travel, areas deep inside caves, and hydrothermal vents at the bottom of the ocean.

Factors that affect the biosphere include:

- The **distance and tilt** between the earth and the sun – This produces temperatures that are conducive to life and causes the seasons.
- **Climate, daily weather, and erosion** – These change the land and the organisms on and in it.
- Earthquakes, tornadoes, volcanoes, tsunamis, and other **natural phenomena** – These all change the land.
- **Chemical erosion** – This changes the composition of rocks and organic materials.
- **Biological erosion** – This is bacteria and single-celled organisms breaking down organic and inorganic materials.

ECOLOGICAL SYSTEM AND BIOME

An **ecological system**, or ecosystem, is the community of all the living organisms in a specific area interacting with non-living factors such as temperature, sunlight, atmospheric pressure, weather patterns, wind, types of nutrients, etc. An ecosystem's development depends on the energy that passes in and out of it. The boundaries of an ecosystem depend on the use of the term, whether it refers to an ecosystem under a rock or in a valley, pond, or ocean.

A **biome** is a general ecosystem type defined by the plants and animals that live there and the local climate patterns. Examples include tropical rainforests or savannas, deserts, grasslands, deciduous forests, tundra, woodlands, and ice caps. There can be more than one type of biome within a larger climate zone. The transition area between two biomes is an ecotone, which may have characteristics of both biomes.

EROSION

Erosion is the process that breaks down matter, whether it is a rock that is broken into pebbles or mountains that are rained on until they become hills. Erosion always happens in a downhill direction. The erosion of land by weather or breaking waves is called **denudation**. **Mass wasting** is the movement of masses of dirt and rock from one place to another. This can occur in two ways: **mechanical** (such as breaking a rock with a hammer) or **chemical** (such as pouring acid on a rock to dissolve it). If the material changes color, it indicates that a break down was chemical in nature. Whatever is broken down must go somewhere, so erosion eventually builds something up. For example, an eroded mountain ends up in a river that carries the sediment towards the ocean, where it builds up and creates a wetland or delta at the mouth of the river.

CLIMATES

Scientists have determined the following different types of **climates**:

- Polar (ice caps)
- Polar (tundra)
- Subtropical (dry summer)
- Subtropical (dry winter)
- Subtropical (humid)
- Subtropical (marine west coast)
- Subtropical (Mediterranean)
- Subtropical (wet)
- Tropical (monsoon)
- Tropical (savannah/grasslands)
- Tropical (wet)

Several factors make up and affect climates. These include:

- Temperature
- Atmospheric pressure
- The number of clouds and the amount of dust or smog
- Humidity
- Winds

The moistest and warmest of all the climates is that of the tropical rainforest. It has daily convection thunderstorms caused by the surface daytime heat and the high humidity, which combine to form thunderclouds.

> **Review Video: Climates**
> Visit mometrix.com/academy and enter code: 991320

LAYERS OF THE EARTH

The earth has several distinct **layers**, each with its own properties:

- **Crust** – This is the outermost layer of the earth that is comprised of the continents and the ocean basins. It has a variable thickness (35-70 km in the continents and 5-10 km in the ocean basins) and is composed mostly of alumino-silicates.
- **Mantle** – This is about 2900 km thick, and is made up mostly of ferro-magnesium silicates. It is divided into an upper and lower mantle. Most of the internal heat of the earth is located in the mantle. Large convective cells circulate heat, and may cause plate tectonic movement.
- **Core** – This is separated into the liquid outer core and the solid inner core. The outer core is 2300 km thick (composed mostly of nickel-iron alloy), and the inner core (almost entirely iron) is 12 km thick. The earth's magnetic field is thought to be controlled by the liquid outer core.

COMPOSITION OF EARTH'S ATMOSPHERE
The earth's **atmosphere** is 79% nitrogen, 20% oxygen, and 1% other gases. The oxygen was originally produced almost entirely by algae-type plants. The atmosphere has four layers:

- **Troposphere** – This is the layer closest to the earth where all weather takes place. It is the region that contains rising and falling packets of air. Air pressure at sea level is 0.1 atmospheres, but the top of the troposphere is about 10% of that amount.
- **Stratosphere** – In this layer, air flow is mainly horizontal. The upper portion has a thin layer of concentrated ozone (a reactive form of oxygen) that is largely responsible for absorbing the sun's ultraviolet rays.
- **Mesosphere** – This is the coldest layer. Temperatures drop to -100°C at the top.
- **Thermosphere** – This is divided into the lower ionosphere and the higher exosphere. This layer is very thin and has many ionized atoms with a net electrical charge. The aurora and Van Allen Belts are here. This layer also absorbs the most energetic photons from the sun and reflects radio waves, enabling long distance radio communication.

> **Review Video: Earth's Atmosphere**
> Visit mometrix.com/academy and enter code: 417614

PALEONTOLOGY
Paleontology is the study of prehistoric plant and animal life through the analysis of **fossil remains**. These fossils reveal the ecologies of the past and the path of evolution for both extinct and living organisms. A historical science, paleontology seeks information about the identity, origin, environment, and evolution of past organisms and what they can reveal about the past of the earth as a whole. Paleontology explains causes as opposed to conducting experiments to observe effects. It is related to the fields of biology, geology, and archaeology, and is divided into several sub-disciplines concerned with the types of fossils studied, the process of fossilization, and the ecology and climate of the past. Paleontologists also help identify the composition of the earth's rock layers by the fossils that are found, thus identifying potential sites for oil, mineral, and water extraction.

DETERMINING THE ORDER IN WHICH GEOLOGIC EVENTS OCCURRED USING THE ROCK RECORD
The **Law of Superposition** logically assumes that the bottom layer of a series of sedimentary layers is the oldest, unless it has been overturned or older rock has been pushed over it. In addition, since **igneous intrusions** can cut through or flow above other rocks, these other rocks are older. For example, molten rock (lava) flows out over already present, older rocks. Another guideline for the rock record is that **rock layers** are older than the folds and faults in them because the rocks must exist before they can be folded or faulted. If a rock contains **atomic nuclei**, reference tables of the half-lives of commonly used radio isotopes can be used to match the decay rate of known substances to the nuclei in a rock, and thereby determine its age. Ages of rocks can also be determined from **contact metamorphism**, the re-crystallization of pre-existing rocks due to changes in physical and chemical conditions, such as heat, pressure, and chemically active fluids that might be present in lava or polluted waters.

MATCHING ROCKS AND GEOLOGIC EVENTS IN ONE PLACE WITH THOSE OF ANOTHER
Geologists physically follow rock layers from one location to another by a process called "walking the outcrop." Geologists walk along the outcropping to see where it goes and what the differences and similarities of the neighboring locations they cross are. Similar rock **types** or **patterns** of rock layers that are similar in terms of thickness, color, composition, and fossil remains tell geologists

that two locations have a similar geologic history. Fossils are found all over the earth, but are from a relatively **small time period** in earth's history. Therefore, fossil evidence helps date a rock layer, regardless of where it occurs. **Volcanic ash** is a good time indicator since ash is deposited quickly over a widespread area. Matching the date of an eruption to the ash allows for a precise identification of time. Similarly, the **meteor impact** at the intersection of the Cretaceous and Tertiary Periods left a time marker. Wherever the meteor's iridium content is found, geologists are able to date rock layers.

SEQUENCING THE EARTH'S GEOLOGIC HISTORY FROM THE FOSSIL AND ROCK RECORD

Reference tables are used to match specimens and time periods. For example, the fossil record has been divided into time units of the earth's history. Rocks can therefore be dated by the fossils found with them. There are also reference tables for dating plate motions and mountain building events in geologic history. Since humans have been around for a relatively short period of time, **fossilized human remains** help to affix a date to a location. Some areas have missing **geologic layers** because of erosion or other factors, but reference tables specific to a region will list what is complete or missing. The theory of **uniformitarianism** assumes that geologic processes have been the same throughout history. Therefore, the way erosion or volcanic eruptions happen today is the same as the way these events happened millions of years ago because there is no reason for them to have changed. Therefore, knowledge about current events can be applied to the past to make judgments about events in the rock record.

REVEALING CHANGES IN EARTH'S HISTORY BY THE FOSSIL AND ROCK RECORDS

Fossils can show how animal and plant life have changed or remained the same over time. For example, fossils have provided evidence of the existence of dinosaurs even though they no longer roam the earth, and have also been used to prove that certain insects have been around for hundreds of millions of years. Fossils have been used to identify four basic eras: **Proterozoic**, the age of primitive life; **Paleozoic**, the age of fishes; **Mesozoic**, the age of dinosaurs; and **Cenozoic**, the age of mammals. Most ancient forms of life have disappeared, and there are reference tables that list when this occurred. Fossil records also show the evolution of certain life forms, such as the horse from the eohippus. However, the majority of changes do not involve evolution from simple to complex forms, but rather an increase in the variety of forms.

MOUNTAINS

A **mountain** is a portion of the earth that has been raised above its surroundings by volcanic action or tectonic plate movement. Mountains are made up of igneous, metamorphic, and sedimentary rocks, and most lie along active plate boundaries. There are two major mountain systems. The **Circum-Pacific** encircles the entire Pacific Ocean, from New Guinea up across Japan and the Aleutians and down to southern South America. The **Alpine-Himalaya** stretches from northern Africa across the Alps and to the Himalayas and Indonesia. **Orogeny** is the term for the process of natural mountain formation. Therefore, physical mountains are orogens. **Folded mountains** are created through the folding of rock layers when two crustal plates come together. The Alps and Himalayas are folded mountains. The latter was formed by the collision of India with Asia. **Fault-block mountains** are created from the tension forces of plate movements. These produce faults that vertically displace one section to form a mountain. **Dome mountains** are created from magma pushing up through the earth's crust.

VOLCANOES AND VOLCANIC MOUNTAINS

Volcanoes are classified according to their activity level. An **active** volcano is in the process of erupting or building to an eruption; a dormant volcano has erupted before and may erupt again someday, but is not currently active; and an **extinct** volcano has died out volcanically and will not erupt ever again. Active volcanoes endanger plant and animal life, but lava and ash add enriching minerals to the soil. There are three types of volcanic mountains:

- **Shield volcanoes** are the largest volcanic mountains because of a repeated, viscous lava flow from small eruptions over a long period of time that cause the mountain to grow.
- **Cinder cone volcanoes**, or linear volcanoes, are small in size, but have massive explosions through linear shafts that spread cinders and ash around the vent. This results in a cone-shaped hill.
- **Composite volcanoes** get their name from the mix of lava and ash layers that build the mountain.

SUBDIVISIONS OF ROCK

The three major subdivisions of rock are:

- **Igneous** (magmatites) – This type is formed from the cooling of liquid magma. In the process, minerals crystallize and amalgamate. If solidification occurs deep in the earth (plutonic rock), the cooling process is slow. This allows for the formation of large crystals, giving rock a coarse-grained texture (granite). Quickly cooled magma has a glassy texture (obsidian).
- **Metamorphic** – Under conditions of high temperature and pressure within the earth's crust, rock material melts and changes structure, transitioning or metamorphosing into a new type of rock with different minerals. If the minerals appear in bands, the rock is foliated. Examples include marble (unfoliated) and slate (foliated).
- **Sedimentary** – This is the most common type of rock on earth. It is formed by sedimentation, compaction, and then cementation of many small particles of mineral, animal, or plant material. There are three types of sedimentary rocks: clastic, clay, and sand that came from disintegrated rocks; chemical (rock salt and gypsum), formed by evaporation of aqueous solutions; and biogenic (coal), formed from animal or plant remnants.

> **Review Video: Igneous, Sedimentary, and Metamorphic Rocks**
> Visit mometrix.com/academy and enter code: 689294

GLACIERS

Glaciers start high in the mountains, where snow and ice accumulate inside a cirque (a small semicircular depression). The snow becomes firmly packed into masses of coarse-grained ice that are slowly pulled down a slope by gravity. Glaciers grow with large amounts of snowfall and retreat (diminish) if warm weather melts more ice than can be replaced. Glaciers once covered large areas of both the northern and southern hemispheres with mile-thick ice that carved out valleys, fjords, and other land formations. They also moved plants, animals, and rocks from one area to another. There were two types of glaciers: **valley**, which produced U-shaped erosion and sharp-peaked mountains; and **continental**, which moved over and rounded mountain tops and ridges. These glaciers existed during the ice ages, the last of which occurred from 2.5 million years ago to 12,000 years ago.

Earth Science and Weather

LAYERS ABOVE THE SURFACE OF EARTH

The **ozone layer**, although contained within the stratosphere, is determined by ozone (O_3) concentrations. It absorbs the majority of ultraviolet light from the Sun. The ionosphere is part of both the exosphere and the thermosphere. It is characterized by the fact that it is a plasma, a partially ionized gas in which free electrons and positive ions are attracted to each other, but are too energetic to remain fixed as a molecule. It starts at about 50 km above Earth's surface and goes to 1,000 km. It affects radio wave transmission and auroras. The ionosphere pushes against the inner edge of the Earth's magnetosphere, which is the highly magnetized, non-spherical region around the Earth. The homosphere encompasses the troposphere, stratosphere, and mesosphere. Gases in the homosphere are considered well mixed. In the heterosphere, the distance that particles can move without colliding is large. As a result, gases are stratified according to their molecular weights. Heavier gases such as oxygen and nitrogen occur near the bottom of the heterosphere, while hydrogen, the lightest element, is found at the top.

> **Review Video: Earth's Atmosphere**
> Visit mometrix.com/academy and enter code: 417614

TROPOSPHERIC CIRCULATION

Most weather takes place in the **troposphere**. Air circulates in the atmosphere by convection and in various types of "cells." Air near the equator is warmed by the Sun and rises. Cool air rushes under it, and the higher, warmer air flows toward Earth's poles. At the poles, it cools and descends to the surface. It is now under the hot air, and flows back to the equator. Air currents coupled with ocean currents move heat around the planet, creating winds, weather, and climate. Winds can change direction with the seasons. For example, in Southeast Asia and India, summer monsoons are caused by air being heated by the Sun. This air rises, draws moisture from the ocean, and causes daily rains. In winter, the air cools, sinks, pushes the moist air away, and creates dry weather.

COMMON WEATHER PHENOMENA AND EQUIPMENT TO MEASURE THEM

Common **atmospheric conditions** that are frequently measured are temperature, precipitation, wind, and humidity. These weather conditions are often measured at permanently fixed **weather stations** so weather data can be collected and compared over time and by region. Measurements may also be taken by ships, buoys, and underwater instruments. Measurements may also be taken under special circumstances. The measurements taken include temperature, barometric pressure, humidity, wind speed, wind direction, and precipitation. Usually, the following instruments are used: A *thermometer* is used for measuring temperature; a *barometer* is used for measuring barometric/air pressure; a *hygrometer* is used for measuring humidity; an *anemometer* is used for measuring wind speed; a *weather vane* is used for measuring wind direction; and a *rain gauge* is used for measuring precipitation.

WEATHER, CLIMATE, AND METEOROLOGY

Meteorology is the study of the atmosphere, particularly as it pertains to forecasting the weather and understanding its processes. **Weather** is the condition of the atmosphere at any given moment. Most weather occurs in the troposphere and includes changing events such as clouds, storms, and temperature, as well as more extreme events such as tornadoes, hurricanes, and blizzards. **Climate** refers to the average weather for a particular area over time, typically at least 30 years. Latitude is an indicator of climate. Changes in climate occur over long time periods.

Winds and Global Wind Belts

Winds are the result of air moving by convection. Masses of warm air rise, and cold air sweeps into their place. The warm air also moves, cools, and sinks. The term "prevailing wind" refers to the wind that usually blows in an area in a single direction. *Dominant winds* are the winds with the highest speeds. Belts or bands that run latitudinally and blow in a specific direction are associated with *convection cells*. *Hadley cells* are formed directly north and south of the equator. The *Farrell cells* occur at about 30° to 60°. The jet stream runs between the Farrell cells and the polar cells. At the higher and lower latitudes, the direction is easterly. At mid latitudes, the direction is westerly. From the North Pole to the south, the surface winds are Polar High Easterlies, Subpolar Low Westerlies, Subtropical High or Horse Latitudes, North-East Trade winds, Equatorial Low or Doldrums, South-East Trades, Subtropical High or Horse Latitudes, Subpolar Low Easterlies, and Polar High.

> **Review Video: Where Does Wind Come From?**
> Visit mometrix.com/academy and enter code: 451712

Relative Humidity, Absolute Humidity, and Dew Point Temperature

Humidity refers to water vapor contained in the air. The amount of moisture contained in air depends upon its temperature. The higher the air temperature, the more moisture it can hold. These higher levels of moisture are associated with higher humidity. **Absolute humidity** refers to the total amount of moisture air is capable of holding at a certain temperature. **Relative humidity** is the ratio of water vapor in the air compared to the amount the air is capable of holding at its current temperature. As temperature decreases, absolute humidity stays the same and relative humidity increases. A hygrometer is a device used to measure humidity. The **dew point** is the temperature at which water vapor condenses into water at a particular humidity.

Precipitation

After clouds reach the dew point, **precipitation** occurs. Precipitation can take the form of a liquid or a solid. It is known by many names, including rain, snow, ice, dew, and frost. **Liquid** forms of precipitation include rain and drizzle. Rain or drizzle that freezes on contact is known as freezing rain or freezing drizzle. **Solid or frozen** forms of precipitation include snow, ice needles or diamond dust, sleet or ice pellets, hail, and graupel or snow pellets. Virga is a form of precipitation that evaporates before reaching the ground. It usually looks like sheets or shafts falling from a cloud. The amount of rainfall is measured with a rain gauge. Intensity can be measured according to how fast precipitation is falling or by how severely it limits visibility. Precipitation plays a major role in the water cycle since it is responsible for depositing much of the Earth's fresh water.

Clouds

Clouds form when air cools and warm air is forced to give up some of its water vapor because it can no longer hold it. This vapor condenses and forms tiny droplets of water or ice crystals called clouds. Particles, or aerosols, are needed for water vapor to form water droplets. These are called **condensation nuclei**. Clouds are created by surface heating, mountains and terrain, rising air masses, and weather fronts. Clouds precipitate, returning the water they contain to Earth. Clouds can also create atmospheric optics. They can scatter light, creating colorful phenomena such as rainbows, colorful sunsets, and the green flash phenomenon.

> **Review Video: Clouds**
> Visit mometrix.com/academy and enter code: 803166

High, Middle, and Low Cloud Types

Most clouds can be classified according to the altitude of their base above Earth's surface. **High clouds** occur at altitudes between 5,000 and 13,000 meters. **Middle clouds** occur at altitudes between 2,000 and 7,000 meters. **Low clouds** occur from the Earth's surface to altitudes of 2,000 meters. Types of high clouds include cirrus (Ci), thin wispy mare's tails that consist of ice; cirrocumulus (Cc), small, pillow-like puffs that often appear in rows; and cirrostratus (Cs), thin, sheet-like clouds that often cover the entire sky. Types of middle clouds include altocumulus (Ac), gray-white clouds that consist of liquid water; and altostratus (As), grayish or blue-gray clouds that span the sky. Types of low clouds include stratus (St), gray and fog-like clouds consisting of water droplets that take up the whole sky; stratocumulus (Sc), low-lying, lumpy gray clouds; and nimbostratus (Ns), dark gray clouds with uneven bases that indicate rain or snow. Two types of clouds, cumulus (Cu) and cumulonimbus (Cb), are capable of great vertical growth. They can start at a wide range of altitudes, from the Earth's surface to altitudes of 13,000 meters.

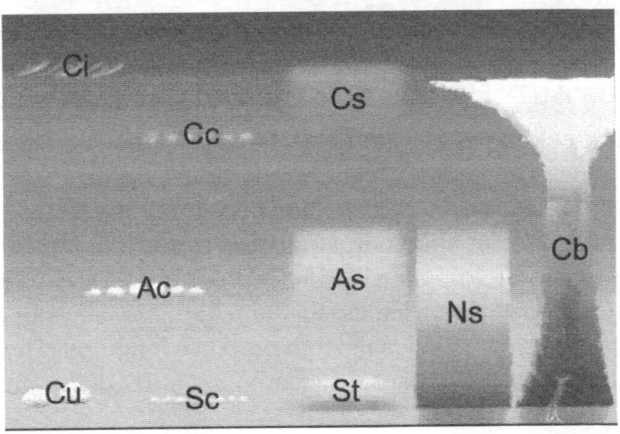

Air Masses

Air masses are large volumes of air in the troposphere of the Earth. They are categorized by their temperature and by the amount of water vapor they contain. *Arctic* and *Antarctic* air masses are cold, polar air masses are cool, and tropical and equatorial air masses are hot. Other types of air masses include *maritime* and *monsoon*, both of which are moist and unstable. There are also *continental* and *superior* air masses, which are dry. A **weather front** separates two masses of air of different densities. It is the principal cause of meteorological phenomena. Air masses are quickly and easily affected by the land they are above. They can have certain characteristics, and then develop new ones when they get blown over a different area.

Weather Fronts and Weather Maps

A **weather front** is the area between two differing masses of air that affects weather. Frontal movements are influenced by the jet stream and other high winds. Movements are determined by the type of front. Cold fronts move up to twice as fast as warm ones. It is in the turbulent frontal area that commonplace and dramatic weather events take place. This area also creates temperature changes. Weather phenomena include rain, thunderstorms, high winds, tornadoes, cloudiness, clear skies, and hurricanes. Different fronts can be plotted on weather maps using a set of designated symbols. Surface weather maps can also include symbols representing clouds, rain, temperature, air pressure, and fair weather.

Space Science

ASTRONOMY

Astronomy is the scientific study of celestial objects and their positions, movements, and structures. *Celestial* does not refer to the Earth by itself, but does include its movement through space. Other celestial objects include the Sun, the Moon, planets, satellites, asteroids, meteors, comets, stars, galaxies, the universe, and other space phenomena. The term astronomy has its roots in the Greek words "astro" and "nomos," which means "laws of the stars."

> **Review Video: Astronomy**
> Visit mometrix.com/academy and enter code: 640556

UNIVERSE

ORIGIN

The **universe** can be said to consist of everything and nothing. The universe contains all of space, matter, energy, and time. There are likely still phenomena that have yet to be discovered. The universe can also be thought of as nothing, since a vast portion of the known universe is empty space. It is believed that the universe is expanding. The *Big Bang theory*, which is widely accepted among astronomers, was developed to explain the origin of the universe. There are other theories regarding the origin of the universe, such as the *Steady-State theory* and the *Creationist theory*. The Big Bang theory states that all the matter in the universe was once in one place. This matter underwent a huge explosion that spread it into space. Galaxies formed from this material and the universe is still expanding.

STRUCTURE

What can be seen of the universe is believed to be at least 93 billion light years across. To put this into perspective, the Milky Way galaxy is about 100,000 light years across. Our view of matter in the universe is that it forms into clumps which become stars, galaxies, clusters of galaxies, superclusters, and the Great Wall of galaxies. **Galaxies** consist of stars, some with planetary systems. Some estimates state that the universe is about 13 billion years old. It is not considered dense and is believed to consist of 73% dark energy, 23% cold dark matter, and 4% regular matter. Cosmology is the study of the universe. Interstellar medium (ISM) is the gas and dust in the interstellar space between a galaxy's stars.

GALAXIES

Galaxies consist of stars, stellar remnants, and dark matter. **Dwarf galaxies** contain as few as 10 million stars, while giant galaxies contain as many as 1 trillion stars. Galaxies are gravitationally bound, meaning that stars, star systems, other gases, and dust orbit the galaxy's center. The Earth exists in the **Milky Way galaxy** and the nearest galaxy to ours is the **Andromeda galaxy**. Galaxies can be classified by their visual shape into elliptical, spiral, irregular, and starburst galaxies. It is estimated that there are more than 100 billion galaxies in the universe ranging from 1,000 to 100,000 parsecs in diameter. Galaxies can be megaparsecs apart. Intergalactic space consists of a gas with an average density of less than one atom per cubic meter. Galaxies are organized into clusters which form superclusters. Dark matter may account for up to 90% of the mass of galaxies. Dark matter is still not well understood.

PLANETS

In order of their distance from the sun (closest to furthest away), the **planets** are: Mercury, Venus, Earth, Mars, Jupiter, Saturn, Uranus, and Neptune (Pluto is now considered to be a dwarf planet). All the planets revolve around the sun, which is an average-sized star in the spiral Milky Way galaxy. They revolve in the same direction in nearly circular orbits. If the planets were viewed by looking down from the sun, they would rotate in a counter-clockwise direction. All the planets are in, or near, the same plane, called the ecliptic, and their axis of rotation is nearly perpendicular to the ecliptic. The only exception is Uranus, which is tipped on its side.

TERRESTRIAL PLANETS, JOVIAN PLANETS, AND MASS OF PLANETS

The **Terrestrial Planets** are: Mercury, Venus, Earth, and Mars. These are the four planets closest to the sun. They are called terrestrial because they all have a compact, rocky surface similar to the Earth's. Venus, Earth, and Mars have significant atmospheres, but Mercury has almost no atmosphere.

The **Jovian Planets** are: Jupiter (the largest planet), Saturn, Uranus, and Neptune. They are called Jovian (Jupiter-like) because of their huge sizes in relation to that of the Earth, and because they all have a gaseous nature like Jupiter. Although gas giants, some or all of the Jovian Planets may have small, solid cores.

The sun represents 99.85% of all the matter in our solar system. Combined, the planets make up only 0.135% of the mass of the solar system, with Jupiter having twice the mass of all the other planets combined. The remaining 0.015% of the mass comes from comets, planetary satellites, asteroids, meteoroids, and interplanetary medium.

DEFINITION OF PLANET

On August 24, 2006, the International Astronomical Union redefined the criteria a body must meet to be classified as a planet, stating that the following conditions must be met:

- "A planet orbits around a star and is neither a star nor a moon."
- "Its shape is spherical due to its gravity."
- "It has 'cleared' the space of its orbit."

A **dwarf planet** such as Pluto does not meet the third condition. Small solar system bodies such as asteroids and comets meet only the first condition.

SOLAR SYSTEM

The **solar system** developed about 4.6 billion years ago out of an enormous cloud of dust and gas circling around the sun. Four rocky planets orbit relatively close to the sun. Their inside orbits are separated from the outside orbits of the four, larger gaseous planets by an asteroid belt. Pluto, some comets, and several small objects circle in the Kuiper belt outside Neptune's orbit. The Oort cloud, composed of icy space objects, encloses the planetary system like a shell.

> **Review Video: Solar System**
> Visit mometrix.com/academy and enter code: 273231

EARTH'S MOON

Earth's **moon** is the closest celestial body to earth. Its proximity has allowed it to be studied since the invention of the telescope. As a result, its landforms have been named after astronomers, philosophers, and other scholars. Its surface has many craters created by asteroids since it has no protective atmosphere. These dark lowlands looked like seas to early astronomers, but there is virtually no water on the moon except possibly in its polar regions. These impact craters and depressions actually contain solidified lava flows. The bright highlands were thought to be continents, and were named terrae. The rocks of the moon have been pounded by asteroids so often that there is a layer of rubble and dust called the regolith. Also, because there is no protective atmosphere, temperatures on the moon vary widely, from 265°F to -255°F.

EARTH'S SUN AND OTHER STARS

A **star** begins as a cloud of hydrogen and some heavier elements drawn together by their own mass. This matter then begins to rotate. The core heats up to several million degrees Fahrenheit, which causes the hydrogen atoms to lose their shells and their nuclei to fuse. This releases enormous amounts of energy. The star then becomes stable during a stage called the **main sequence**. This is the stage our sun is in, and it will remain in this stage until its supply of hydrogen fuel runs out. Stars are not always alone like our sun, and may exist in pairs or groups. The hottest stars shine blue-white; medium-hot stars like our sun glow yellow; and cooler stars appear orange. The earth's sun is an **average star** in terms of mass, light production, and size. All stars, including our sun, have a **core** where fusion happens; a **photosphere** (surface) that produces sunspots (cool, dark areas); a red **chromosphere** that emits solar (bright) flares and shooting gases; and a **corona**, the transparent area only seen during an eclipse.

> **Review Video: The Sun**
> Visit mometrix.com/academy and enter code: 699233

COMETS, ASTEROIDS, AND METEOROIDS

Comets are celestial bodies composed of dust, rock, frozen gases, and ice. Invisible until they near the sun, comets emit volatile components in jets of gas and dust when exposed to the sun's heat. The **coma** is the comet's fog-like envelope that glows as it reflects sunlight and releases radiation. **Solar winds** blow a comet away from the sun and give it a tail of dust or electrically charged molecules. Each orbit of a comet causes it to lose matter until it breaks up or vaporizes into the sun.

Asteroids are irregularly-shaped boulders, usually less than 60 miles in diameter, that orbit the sun. Most are made of graphite; about 25% are silicates, or iron and nickel. Collisions or gravitational forces can cause them to fly off and possibly hit a planet.

Meteoroids are fragments of asteroids of various sizes. If they come through earth's atmosphere, they are called meteors or shooting stars. If they land on earth, they are called meteorites, and create craters on impact (the Barringer Crater in Arizona).

Safety and Equipment

LABORATORY ACCIDENTS

Any spills or accidents should be **reported** to the teacher so that the teacher can determine the safest clean-up method. The student should start to wash off a **chemical** spilled on the skin while reporting the incident. Some spills may require removal of contaminated clothing and use of the **safety shower**. Broken glass should be disposed of in a designated container. If someone's clothing catches fire they should walk to the safety shower and use it to extinguish the flames. A fire blanket may be used to smother a **lab fire**. A fire extinguisher, phone, spill neutralizers, and a first aid box are other types of **safety equipment** found in the lab. Students should be familiar with **routes** out of the room and the building in case of fire. Students should use the **eye wash station** if a chemical gets in the eyes.

SAFETY PROCEDURES

Students should wear a **lab apron** and **safety goggles**. Loose or dangling clothing and jewelry, necklaces, and earrings should not be worn. Those with long hair should tie it back. Care should always be taken not to splash chemicals. Open-toed shoes such as sandals and flip-flops should not be worn, nor should wrist watches. Glasses are preferable to contact lenses since the latter carries a risk of chemicals getting caught between the lens and the eye. Students should always be supervised. The area where the experiment is taking place and the surrounding floor should be free of clutter. Only the lab book and the items necessary for the experiment should be present. Smoking, eating, and chewing gum are not permitted in the lab. Cords should not be allowed to dangle from work stations. There should be no rough-housing in the lab. Hands should be washed after the lab is complete.

FUME HOODS

Because of the potential safety hazards associated with chemistry lab experiments, such as fire from vapors and the inhalation of toxic fumes, a **fume hood** should be used in many instances. A fume hood carries away vapors from reagents or reactions. Equipment or reactions are placed as far back in the hood as practical to help enhance the collection of the fumes. The **glass safety shield** automatically closes to the appropriate height, and should be low enough to protect the face and body. The safety shield should only be raised to move equipment in and out of the hood. One should not climb inside a hood or stick one's head inside. All spills should be wiped up immediately and the glass should be cleaned if a splash occurs.

COMMON SAFETY HAZARDS

Some specific safety hazards possible in a chemistry lab include:

- **Fire**: Fire can be caused by volatile solvents such as ether, acetone, and benzene being kept in an open beaker or Erlenmeyer flask. Vapors can creep along the table and ignite if they reach a flame or spark. Solvents should be heated in a hood with a steam bath, not on a hot plate.
- **Explosion**: Heating or creating a reaction in a closed system can cause an explosion, resulting in flying glass and chemical splashes. The system should be vented to prevent this.
- **Chemical and thermal burns**: Many chemicals are corrosive to the skin and eyes.
- **Inhalation of toxic fumes**: Some compounds severely irritate membranes in the eyes, nose, throat, and lungs.

- **Absorption** of toxic chemicals such as dimethyl sulfoxide (DMSO) and nitrobenzene through the skin.
- **Ingestion** of toxic chemicals.

SAFETY GLOVES

There are many types of **gloves** available to help protect the skin from cuts, burns, and chemical splashes. There are many considerations to take into account when choosing a glove. For example, gloves that are highly protective may limit dexterity. Some gloves may not offer appropriate protection against a specific chemical. Other considerations include degradation rating, which indicates how effective a glove is when exposed to chemicals; breakthrough time, which indicates how quickly a chemical can break through the surface of the glove; and permeation rate, which indicates how quickly chemicals seep through after the initial breakthrough. Disposable latex, vinyl, or nitrile gloves are usually appropriate for most circumstances, and offer protection from incidental splashes and contact. Other types of gloves include butyl, neoprene, PVC, PVA, viton, silver shield, and natural rubber. Each offers its own type of protection, but may have drawbacks as well. **Double-gloving** can improve resistance or dexterity in some instances.

PROPER HANDLING AND STORAGE OF CHEMICALS

Students should take care when **carrying chemicals** from one place to another. Chemicals should never be taken from the room, tasted, or touched with bare hands. **Safety gloves** should be worn when appropriate and glove/chemical interactions and glove deterioration should be considered. Hands should always be **washed** thoroughly after a lab. Potentially hazardous materials intended for use in chemistry, biology, or other science labs should be secured in a safe area where relevant **Safety Data Sheets (SDS)** can be accessed. Chemicals and solutions should be used as directed and labels should be read before handling solutions and chemicals. Extra chemicals should not be returned to their original containers, but should be disposed of as directed by the school district's rules or local ordinances. Local municipalities often have hazardous waste disposal programs. Acids should be stored separately from other chemicals. Flammable liquids should be stored away from acids, bases, and oxidizers.

BUNSEN BURNERS

When using a **Bunsen burner**, loose clothing should be tucked in, long hair should be tied back, and safety goggles and aprons should be worn. Students should know what to do in case of a fire or accident. When lighting the burner, strikers should always be used instead of matches. Do not touch the hot barrel. Tongs (never fingers) should be used to hold the material in the flame. To heat liquid, a flask may be set upon wire gauze on a tripod and secured with an iron ring or clamp on a stand. The flame is extinguished by turning off the gas at the source.

SAFETY PROCEDURES RELATED TO ANIMALS

Animals to be used for **dissections** should be obtained from a company that provides animals for this purpose. Road kill or decaying animals that a student brings in should not be used. It is possible that such an animal may have a pathogen or a virus, such as rabies, which can be transmitted via the saliva of even a dead animal. Students should use gloves and should not participate if they have open sores or moral objections to dissections. It is generally accepted that biological experiments may be performed on lower-order life forms and invertebrates, but not on mammalian vertebrates and birds. No animals should be harmed physiologically. Experimental animals should be kept, cared for, and handled in a safe manner and with compassion. Pathogenic (anything able to cause a disease) substances should not be used in lab experiments.

LAB NOTEBOOKS

A **lab notebook** is a record of all pre-lab work and lab work. It differs from a lab report, which is prepared after lab work is completed. A lab notebook is a formal record of lab preparations and what was done. **Observational recordings** should not be altered, erased, or whited-out to make corrections. Drawing a single line through an entry is sufficient to make changes. Pages should be numbered and should not be torn out. Entries should be made neatly, but don't necessarily have to be complete sentences. **Entries** should provide detailed information and be recorded in such a way that another person could use them to replicate the experiment. **Quantitative data** may be recorded in tabular form, and may include calculations made during an experiment. Lab book entries can also include references and research performed before the experiment. Entries may also consist of information about a lab experiment, including the objective or purpose, the procedures, data collected, and the results.

LAB REPORTS

A **lab report** is an item developed after an experiment that is intended to present the results of a lab experiment. Generally, it should be prepared using a word processor, not hand-written or recorded in a notebook. A lab report should be formally presented. It is intended to persuade others to accept or reject a hypothesis. It should include a brief but descriptive **title** and an **abstract**. The abstract is a summary of the report. It should include a purpose that states the problem that was explored or the question that was answered. It should also include a **hypothesis** that describes the anticipated results of the experiment. The experiment should include a **control** and one **variable** to ensure that the results can be interpreted correctly. Observations and results can be presented using written narratives, tables, graphs, and illustrations. The report should also include a **summation** or **conclusion** explaining whether the results supported the hypothesis.

TYPES OF LABORATORY GLASSWARE

Two types of flasks are Erlenmeyer flasks and volumetric flasks. **Volumetric flasks** are used to accurately prepare a specific volume and concentration of solution. **Erlenmeyer flasks** can be used for mixing, transporting, and reacting, but are not appropriate for accurate measurements.

A **pipette** can be used to accurately measure small amounts of liquid. Liquid is drawn into the pipette through a bulb. The liquid measurement is read at the **meniscus**. There are also plastic disposable pipettes. A **repipette** is a hand-operated pump that dispenses solutions.

Beakers can be used to measure mass or dissolve a solvent into a solute. They do not measure volume as accurately as a volumetric flask, pipette, graduated cylinder, or burette.

Graduated cylinders are used for precise measurements and are considered more accurate than Erlenmeyer flasks or beakers. To read a graduated cylinder, it should be placed on a flat surface and read at eye level. The surface of a liquid in a graduated cylinder forms a lens-shaped curve. The measurement should be taken from the bottom of the curve. A ring may be placed at the top of tall, narrow cylinders to help avoid breakage if they are tipped over.

A **burette**, or buret, is a piece of lab glassware used to accurately dispense liquid. It looks similar to a narrow graduated cylinder, but includes a stopcock and tip. It may be filled with a funnel or pipette.

MICROSCOPES

There are different kinds of microscopes, but **optical** or **light microscopes** are the most commonly used in lab settings. Light and lenses are used to magnify and view samples. A specimen or sample is placed on a slide and the slide is placed on a stage with a hole in it. Light passes through the hole and illuminates the sample. The sample is magnified by lenses and viewed through the eyepiece. A simple microscope has one lens, while a typical compound microscope has three lenses. The light source can be room light redirected by a mirror or the microscope can have its own independent light source that passes through a condenser. In this case, there are diaphragms and filters to allow light intensity to be controlled. Optical microscopes also have coarse and fine adjustment knobs.

Other types of microscopes include **digital microscopes**, which use a camera and a monitor to allow viewing of the sample. **Scanning electron microscopes (SEMs)** provide greater detail of a sample in terms of the surface topography and can produce magnifications much greater than those possible with optical microscopes. The technology of an SEM is quite different from an optical microscope in that it does not rely on lenses to magnify objects, but uses samples placed in a chamber. In one type of SEM, a beam of electrons from an electron gun scans and actually interacts with the sample to produce an image.

Wet mount slides designed for use with a light microscope typically require a thin portion of the specimen to be placed on a standard glass slide. A drop of water is added and a cover slip or cover glass is placed on top. Air bubbles and fingerprints can make viewing difficult. Placing the cover slip at a 45-degree angle and allowing it to drop into place can help avoid the problem of air bubbles. A **cover slip** should always be used when viewing wet mount slides. The viewer should start with the objective in its lowest position and then fine focus. The microscope should be carried with two hands and stored with the low-power objective in the down position. **Lenses** should be cleaned with lens paper only. A **graticule slide** is marked with a grid line, and is useful for counting or estimating a quantity.

BALANCES

Balances such as triple-beam balances, spring balances, and electronic balances measure mass and force. An **electronic balance** is the most accurate, followed by a **triple-beam balance** and then a **spring balance**. One part of a **triple-beam balance** is the plate, which is where the item to be weighed is placed. There are also three beams that have hatch marks indicating amounts and hold the weights that rest in the notches. The front beam measures weights between 0 and 10 grams, the middle beam measures weights in 100 gram increments, and the far beam measures weights in 10 gram increments. The sum of the weight of each beam is the total weight of the object. A triple beam balance also includes a set screw to calibrate the equipment and a mark indicating the object and counterweights are in balance.

CHROMATOGRAPHY

Chromatography refers to a set of laboratory techniques used to separate or analyze **mixtures**. Mixtures are dissolved in their mobile phases. In the stationary or bonded phase, the desired component is separated from other molecules in the mixture. In chromatography, the analyte is the substance to be separated. **Preparative chromatography** refers to the type of chromatography that involves purifying a substance for further use rather than further analysis. **Analytical chromatography** involves analyzing the isolated substance. Other types of chromatography include column, planar, paper, thin layer, displacement, supercritical fluid, affinity, ion exchange, and size exclusion chromatography. Reversed phase, two-dimensional, simulated moving bed, pyrolysis, fast protein, counter current, and chiral are also types of chromatography. **Gas**

chromatography refers to the separation technique in which the mobile phase of a substance is in gas form.

> **Review Video: Paper Chromatography**
> Visit mometrix.com/academy and enter code: 543963

REAGENTS AND REACTANTS

A **reagent** or **reactant** is a chemical agent for use in chemical reactions. When preparing for a lab, it should be confirmed that glassware and other equipment has been cleaned and/or sterilized. There should be enough materials, reagents, or other solutions needed for the lab for every group of students completing the experiment. Distilled water should be used instead of tap water when performing lab experiments because distilled water has most of its impurities removed. Other needed apparatus such as funnels, filter paper, balances, Bunsen burners, ring stands, and/or microscopes should also be set up. After the lab, it should be confirmed that sinks, workstations, and any equipment used have been cleaned. If chemicals or specimens need to be kept at a certain temperature by refrigerating them or using another storage method, the temperature should be checked periodically to ensure the sample does not spoil.

DILUTING ACIDS

When preparing a solution of **dilute acid**, always add the concentrated acid solution to water, not water to concentrated acid. Start by adding approximately $\frac{2}{3}$ of the total volume of water to the graduated cylinder or volumetric flask. Next, add the concentrated acid to the water. Add additional water to the diluted acid to bring the solution to the final desired volume.

CLEANING AFTER ACID SPILLS

In the event of an **acid spill**, any clothes that have come into contact with the acid should be removed and any skin contacted with acid must be rinsed with clean water. To the extent a window can be opened or a fume hood can be turned on, do so. Do not try force circulation, such as by adding a fan, as acid fumes can be harmful if spread.

Next, pour one of the following over the spill area: sodium bicarbonate, baking soda, soda ash, or cat litter. Start from the outside of the spill and then move towards the center, in order to prevent splashing. When the clumps have thoroughly dried, sweep up the clumps and dispose of them as chemical waste.

CENTRIFUGES

A **centrifuge** is used to separate the components of a heterogeneous mixture (consisting of two or more compounds) by spinning it. The solid precipitate settles in the bottom of the container and the liquid component of the solution, called the **centrifugate**, is at the top. A well-known application of this process is using a centrifuge to separate blood cells and plasma. The heavier cells settle on the bottom of the test tube and the lighter plasma stays on top. Another example is using a salad spinner to help dry lettuce.

Electrophoresis, Calorimetry, and Titration

- **Electrophoresis** is the separation of molecules based on electrical charge. This is possible because particles disbursed in a fluid usually carry electric charges on their surfaces. Molecules are pulled through the fluid toward the positive end if the molecules have a negative charge and are pulled through the fluid toward the negative end if the molecules have a positive charge.
- **Calorimetry** is used to determine the heat released or absorbed in a chemical reaction.
- **Titration** helps determine the precise endpoint of a reaction. With this information, the precise quantity of reactant in the titration flask can be determined. A burette is used to deliver the second reactant to the flask and an indicator or pH meter is used to detect the endpoint of the reaction.

Field Studies and Research Projects

Field studies may facilitate scientific inquiry in a manner similar to indoor lab experiments. Field studies can be interdisciplinary in nature and can help students learn and apply scientific concepts and processes. **Research projects** can be conducted in any number of locations, including school campuses, local parks, national parks, beaches, or mountains. Students can practice the general techniques of observation, data collection, collaborative planning, and analysis of experiments. Field studies give students the chance to learn through hands-on applications of scientific processes, such as map making in geography, observation of stratification in geology, observation of life cycles of plants and animals, and analysis of water quality.

Students should watch out for obvious outdoor **hazards**. These include poisonous flora and fauna such as poison ivy, poison oak, and sumac. Depending on the region of the United States in which the field study is being conducted, hazards may also include rattlesnakes and black widow or brown recluse spiders. Students should also be made aware of potentially hazardous situations specific to **geographic locales** and the possibility of coming into contact with **pathogens**.

Field studies allow for great flexibility in the use of traditional and technological methods for **making observations** and **collecting data**. For example, a nature study could consist of a simple survey of bird species within a given area. Information could be recorded using still photography or a video camera. This type of activity gives students the chance to use technologies other than computers. Computers could still be used to create a slide show of transferred images or a digital lab report. If a quantitative study of birds was being performed, the simple technique of using a pencil and paper to tabulate the number of birds counted in the field could also be used. Other techniques used during field studies could include collecting specimens for lab study, observing coastal ecosystems and tides, and collecting weather data such as temperature, precipitation amounts, and air pressure in a particular locale.

Scientific Inquiry and Reasoning

SCIENTIFIC INQUIRY

Teaching with the concept of **scientific inquiry** in mind encourages students to think like scientists rather than merely practice the rote memorization of facts and history. This belief in scientific inquiry puts the burden of learning on students, which is a much different approach than expecting them to simply accept and memorize what they are taught. Standards for science as inquiry are intended to be comprehensive, encompassing a student's K-12 education, and helping to develop independent and integrated thought toward scientific concepts, rather than teaching individual concepts in isolation. For instance, teaching students to solve physics problems through engineering a real solution, rather than memorizing textbook concepts alone. The following five skills are generally recognized as necessary for students to be engaged in scientific thinking.

- Understand scientific concepts.
- Appreciate "how we know" what we know in science.
- Understand the nature of science.
- Develop the skills necessary to become independent inquirers about the natural world.
- Develop the skills necessary to use the skills, abilities, and attitudes associated with science.

SCIENTIFIC KNOWLEDGE

Science as a whole and its unifying concepts and processes are a way of thought that is taught throughout a student's K-12 education. There are eight areas of content, and all the concepts, procedures, and underlying principles contained within make up the body of **scientific knowledge**. The areas of content are: unifying concepts and processes in science, science as inquiry, physical science, life science, earth and space science, science and technology, science in personal and social perspectives, and history and nature of science. Specific unifying concepts and processes included in the standards and repeated throughout the content areas are: systems, order, and organization; evidence, models, and explanation; change, constancy, and measurement; evolution and equilibrium; and form and function.

> **Review Video: Science Process Skills**
> Visit mometrix.com/academy and enter code: 601624

HISTORY OF SCIENTIFIC KNOWLEDGE

When one examines the history of **scientific knowledge**, it is clear that it is constantly **evolving**. The body of facts, models, theories, and laws grows and changes over time. In other words, one scientific discovery leads to the next. Some advances in science and technology have important and long-lasting effects on science and society. Some discoveries were so alien to the accepted beliefs of the time that not only were they rejected as wrong, but were also considered outright blasphemy. Today, however, many beliefs once considered incorrect have become an ingrained part of scientific knowledge, and have also been the basis of new advances. Examples of advances include: Copernicus's heliocentric view of the universe, Newton's laws of motion and planetary orbits, relativity, geologic time scale, plate tectonics, atomic theory, nuclear physics, biological evolution, germ theory, industrial revolution, molecular biology, information and communication, quantum theory, galactic universe, and medical and health technology.

IMPORTANT TERMINOLOGY

- A **scientific fact** is considered an objective and verifiable observation.
- A **scientific theory** is a greater body of accepted knowledge, principles, or relationships that might explain why something happens.
- A **hypothesis** is an educated guess that is not yet proven. It is used to predict the outcome of an experiment in an attempt to solve a problem or answer a question.
- A **law** is an explanation of events that always leads to the same outcome. It is a fact that an object falls. The law of gravity explains why an object falls. The theory of relativity, although generally accepted, has been neither proven nor disproved.
- A **model** is used to explain something on a smaller scale or in simpler terms to provide an example. It is a representation of an idea that can be used to explain events or applied to new situations to predict outcomes or determine results.

SCIENTIFIC INQUIRY AND SCIENTIFIC METHOD

Scientists use a number of generally accepted techniques collectively known as the **scientific method**. The scientific method generally involves carrying out the following steps:

- Identifying a problem or posing a question
- Formulating a hypothesis or an educated guess
- Conducting experiments or tests that will provide a basis to solve the problem or answer the question
- Observing the results of the test
- Drawing conclusions

An important part of the scientific method is using acceptable experimental techniques. Objectivity is also important if valid results are to be obtained. Another important part of the scientific method is peer review. It is essential that experiments be performed and data be recorded in such a way that experiments can be reproduced to verify results. Historically, the scientific method has been taught with a more linear approach, but it is important to recognize that the scientific method should be a cyclical or **recursive process**. This means that as hypotheses are tested and more is learned, the questions should continue to change to reflect the changing body of knowledge. One cycle of experimentation is not enough.

> **Review Video: The Scientific Method**
> Visit mometrix.com/academy and enter code: 191386

METRIC AND INTERNATIONAL SYSTEM OF UNITS

The **metric system** is the accepted standard of measurement in the scientific community. The **International System of Units (SI)** is a set of measurements (including the metric system) that is almost globally accepted. The United States, Liberia, and Myanmar have not accepted this system. **Standardization** is important because it allows the results of experiments to be compared and reproduced without the need to laboriously convert measurements. The SI is based partially on the **meter-kilogram-second (MKS) system** rather than the **centimeter-gram-second (CGS) system**. The MKS system considers meters, kilograms, and seconds to be the basic units of measurement, while the CGS system considers centimeters, grams, and seconds to be the basic units of measurement. Under the MKS system, the length of an object would be expressed as 1 meter instead of 100 centimeters, which is how it would be described under the CGS system.

> **Review Video: Metric System Conversions**
> Visit mometrix.com/academy and enter code: 163709

BASIC UNITS OF MEASUREMENT

Using the **metric system** is generally accepted as the preferred method for taking measurements. Having a **universal standard** allows individuals to interpret measurements more easily, regardless of where they are located. The basic units of measurement are: the **meter**, which measures length; the **liter**, which measures volume; and the **gram**, which measures mass. The metric system starts with a base unit and increases or decreases in units of 10. The prefix and the base unit combined are used to indicate an amount. For example, deka- is 10 times the base unit. A dekameter is 10 meters; a dekaliter is 10 liters; and a dekagram is 10 grams. The prefix hecto- refers to 100 times the base amount; kilo- is 1,000 times the base amount. The prefixes that indicate a fraction of the base unit are deci-, which is $\frac{1}{10}$ of the base unit; centi-, which is $\frac{1}{100}$ of the base unit; and milli-, which is $\frac{1}{1,000}$ of the base unit.

COMMON PREFIXES

The prefixes for multiples are as follows:

Deka	(da)	10^1 (deka is the American spelling, but deca is also used)
Hecto	(h)	10^2
Kilo	(k)	10^3
Mega	(M)	10^6
Giga	(G)	10^9
Tera	(T)	10^{12}

The prefixes for subdivisions are as follows:

Deci	(d)	10^{-1}
Centi	(c)	10^{-2}
Milli	(m)	10^{-3}
Micro	(μ)	10^{-6}
Nano	(n)	10^{-9}
Pico	(p)	10^{-12}

The rule of thumb is that prefixes greater than 10^3 are capitalized when abbreviating. Abbreviations do not need a period after them. A decimeter (dm) is a tenth of a meter, a deciliter (dL) is a tenth of a liter, and a decigram (dg) is a tenth of a gram. Pluralization is understood. For example, when referring to 5 mL of water, no "s" needs to be added to the abbreviation.

BASIC SI UNITS OF MEASUREMENT

SI uses **second(s)** to measure time. Fractions of seconds are usually measured in metric terms using prefixes such as millisecond ($\frac{1}{1,000}$ of a second) or nanosecond ($\frac{1}{1,000,000,000}$ of a second).

Increments of time larger than a second are measured in **minutes** and **hours**, which are multiples of 60 and 24. An example of this is a swimmer's time in the 800-meter freestyle being described as

7:32.67, meaning 7 minutes, 32 seconds, and 67 one-hundredths of a second. One second is equal to $\frac{1}{60}$ of a minute, $\frac{1}{3,600}$ of an hour, and $\frac{1}{86,400}$ of a day. Other SI base units are the **ampere** (A) (used to measure electric current), the **kelvin** (K) (used to measure thermodynamic temperature), the **candela** (cd) (used to measure luminous intensity), and the **mole** (mol) (used to measure the amount of a substance at a molecular level). **Meter** (m) is used to measure length and **kilogram** (kg) is used to measure mass.

SIGNIFICANT FIGURES

The mathematical concept of **significant figures** or **significant digits** is often used to determine the accuracy of measurements or the level of confidence one has in a specific measurement. The significant figures of a measurement include all the digits known with certainty plus one estimated or uncertain digit. There are a number of rules for determining which digits are considered "important" or "interesting." They are: all non-zero digits are *significant*, zeros between digits are *significant*, and leading and trailing zeros are *not significant* unless they appear to the right of the non-zero digits in a decimal. For example, in 0.01230 the significant digits are 1230, and this number would be said to be accurate to the hundred-thousandths place. The zero indicates that the amount has actually been measured as 0. Other zeros are considered place holders, and are not important. A decimal point may be placed after zeros to indicate their importance (in 100. for example). **Estimating**, on the other hand, involves approximating a value rather than calculating the exact number. This may be used to quickly determine a value that is close to the actual number when complete accuracy does not matter or is not possible. In science, estimation may be used when it is impossible to measure or calculate an exact amount, or to quickly approximate an answer when true calculations would be time consuming.

GRAPHS AND CHARTS

Graphs and charts are effective ways to present scientific data such as observations, statistical analyses, and comparisons between dependent variables and independent variables. On a line chart, the **independent variable** (the one that is being manipulated for the experiment) is represented on the horizontal axis (the x-axis). Any **dependent variables** (the ones that may change as the independent variable changes) are represented on the y-axis. An **XY** or **scatter plot** is often used to plot many points. A "best fit" line is drawn, which allows outliers to be identified more easily. Charts and their axes should have titles. The x and y interval units should be evenly spaced and labeled. Other types of charts are **bar charts** and **histograms**, which can be used to compare differences between the data collected for two variables. A **pie chart** can graphically show the relation of parts to a whole.

> **Review Video: Identifying Variables**
> Visit mometrix.com/academy and enter code: 627181
>
> **Review Video: Data Interpretation of Graphs**
> Visit mometrix.com/academy and enter code: 200439

DATA PRESENTATION

Data collected during a science lab can be organized and **presented** in any number of ways. While **straight narrative** is a suitable method for presenting some lab results, it is not a suitable way to present numbers and quantitative measurements. These types of observations can often be better presented with **tables** and **graphs**. Data that is presented in tables and organized in rows and columns may also be used to make graphs quite easily. Other methods of presenting data include illustrations, photographs, video, and even audio formats. In a **formal report**, tables and figures are labeled and referred to by their labels. For example, a picture of a bubbly solution might be labeled Figure 1, Bubbly Solution. It would be referred to in the text in the following way: "The reaction created bubbles 10 mm in size, as shown in Figure 1, Bubbly Solution." Graphs are also labeled as figures. Tables are labeled in a different way. Examples include: Table 1, Results of Statistical Analysis, or Table 2, Data from Lab 2.

> **Review Video: Understanding Charts and Tables**
> Visit mometrix.com/academy and enter code: 882112

STATISTICAL PRECISION AND ERRORS

Errors that occur during an experiment can be classified into two categories: random errors and systematic errors. **Random errors** can result in collected data that is wildly different from the rest of the data, or they may result in data that is indistinguishable from the rest. Random errors are not consistent across the data set. In large data sets, random errors may contribute to the variability of data, but they will not affect the average. Random errors are sometimes referred to as noise. They may be caused by a student's inability to take the same measurement in exactly the same way or by outside factors that are not considered variables, but influence the data. A **systematic error** will show up consistently across a sample or data set, and may be the result of a flaw in the experimental design. This type of error affects the average, and is also known as bias.

SCIENTIFIC NOTATION

Scientific notation is used because values in science can be very large or very small, which makes them unwieldy. A number in **decimal notation** is 93,000,000. In **scientific notation**, it is 9.3×10^7. The first number, 9.3, is the **coefficient**. It is always greater than or equal to 1 and less than 10. This number is followed by a multiplication sign. The base is always 10 in scientific notation. If the number is greater than ten, the exponent is positive. If the number is between zero and one, the exponent is negative. The first digit of the number is followed by a decimal point and then the rest of the number. In this case, the number is 9.3, and the decimal point was moved seven places to the right from the end of the number to get 93,000,000. The number of places moved, seven, is the exponent.

STATISTICAL TERMINOLOGY

Mean - The average, found by taking the sum of a set of numbers and dividing by the number of numbers in the set.

Median - The middle number in a set of numbers sorted from least to greatest. If the set has an even number of entries, the median is the average of the two in the middle.

Mode - The value that appears most frequently in a data set. There may be more than one mode. If no value appears more than once, there is no mode.

Range - The difference between the highest and lowest numbers in a data set.

Standard deviation - Measures the dispersion of a data set or how far from the mean a single data point is likely to be.

Regression analysis - A method of analyzing sets of data and sets of variables that involves studying how the typical value of the dependent variable changes when any one of the independent variables is varied and the other independent variables remain fixed.

> **Review Video: Mean, Median, and Mode**
> Visit mometrix.com/academy and enter code: 286207
>
> **Review Video: Standard Deviation**
> Visit mometrix.com/academy and enter code: 419469

History and Impact of Science

GREENHOUSE EFFECT

The **greenhouse effect** refers to a naturally occurring and necessary process. **Greenhouse gases**, which are ozone, carbon dioxide, water vapor, and methane, trap infrared radiation that is reflected toward the atmosphere. Without the greenhouse effect, it is estimated that the temperature on Earth would be 30 degrees less on average. The problem occurs because human activity generates more greenhouse gases than necessary. Practices that increase the amount of greenhouse gases include the burning of natural gas and oil, farming practices that result in the release of methane and nitrous oxide, factory operations that produce gases, and deforestation practices that decrease the amount of oxygen available to offset greenhouse gases. Population growth also increases the volume of gases released. Excess greenhouse gases cause more infrared radiation to become trapped, which increases the temperature at the Earth's surface.

OZONE DEPLETION

Ultraviolet light breaks O_2 into two very reactive oxygen atoms with unpaired electrons, which are known as **free radicals**. A free radical of oxygen pairs with another oxygen molecule to form **ozone** (O_3). Ultraviolet light also breaks ozone (O_3) into O_2 and a free radical of oxygen. This process usually acts as an ultraviolet light filter for the planet. Other free radical catalysts are produced by natural phenomena such as volcanic eruptions and by human activities. When these enter the atmosphere, they disrupt the normal cycle by breaking down ozone so it cannot absorb more ultraviolet radiation. One such catalyst is the chlorine in chlorofluorocarbons (CFCs). CFCs were used as aerosols and refrigerants. When a CFC like CF_2Cl_2 is broken down in the atmosphere, chlorine free radicals are produced. These act as catalysts to break down ozone. Whether a chlorine free radical reacts with an ozone or oxygen molecule, it is able to react again.

HUMAN IMPACTS ON ECOSYSTEMS

Human impacts on **ecosystems** take many forms and have many causes. They include widespread disruptions and specific niche disturbances. Humans practice many forms of **environmental manipulation** that affect plants and animals in many biomes and ecosystems. Many human practices involve the consumption of natural resources for food and energy production, the changing of the environment to produce food and energy, and the intrusion on ecosystems to provide shelter. These general behaviors include a multitude of specific behaviors, including the use and overuse of pesticides, the encroachment upon habitat, over hunting and over fishing, the introduction of plant and animal species into non-native ecosystems, and the introduction of hazardous wastes and chemical byproducts into the environment. These behaviors have led to a number of consequences, such as acid rain, ozone depletion, deforestation, urbanization, accelerated species loss, genetic abnormalities, endocrine disruption in populations, and harm to individual animals.

GLOBAL WARMING

Global warming may cause the permanent loss of glaciers and permafrost. There might also be increases in air pollution and acid rain. Rising temperatures may lead to an increase in sea levels as polar ice melts, lower amounts of available fresh water as coastal areas flood, species extinction because of changes in habitat, increases in certain diseases, and a decreased standard of living for humans. Less fresh water and losses of habitat for humans and other species can also lead to decreased agricultural production and food supply shortages. Increased desertification leads to habitat loss for humans and other species. There may be more moisture in the atmosphere due to evaporation.

ACID RAIN AND EUTROPHICATION

Acid rain is made up water droplets for which the pH has been lowered due atmospheric pollution. The common sources of this pollution are **sulfur** and **nitrogen** that have been released through the burning of fossil fuels. This can lead to a lowering of the pH of lakes and ponds, thereby destroying aquatic life, or damaging the leaves and bark of trees. It can also destroy buildings, monuments, and statues made of rock.

Eutrophication is the depletion of oxygen in a body of water. It may be caused by an increase in the amount of nutrients, particularly **phosphates**, which leads to an increase in plant and algae life that use up the oxygen. The result is a decrease in water quality and death of aquatic life. Sources of excess phosphates may be detergents, industrial run-off, or fertilizers that are washed into lakes or streams.

WASTE DISPOSAL METHODS

- Landfills – **Methane** (CH_4) is a greenhouse gas emitted from landfills. Some is used to generate electricity and some gets into the atmosphere. CO_2 is also emitted, and landfill gas can contain nitrogen, oxygen, water vapor, sulfur, mercury, and radioactive contaminants such as tritium. **Landfill leachate** contains acids from car batteries, solvents, heavy metals, pesticides, motor oil, paint, household cleaning supplies, plastics, and many other potentially harmful substances. Some of these are dangerous when they get into the ecosystem.
- Incinerators – These contribute to air pollution in that they can release nitric and sulfuric oxides, which cause **acid rain**.
- Sewage – When dumped in raw form into oceans, sewage can introduce **fecal contaminants** and **pathogenic organisms**, which can harm ocean life and cause disease in humans.

EFFECTS OF CONSUMERISM

Economic growth and quality of living are associated with a wasteful cycle of production. Goods are produced as cheaply as possible with little or no regard for the **ecological effects**. The ultimate goal is profitability. The production process is wasteful, and often introduces **hazardous byproducts** into the environment. Furthermore, byproducts may be dumped into a landfill instead of recycled. When consumer products get dumped in landfills, they can leach **contamination** into groundwater. Landfills can also leach gases. These are or have been dumping grounds for illegal substances, business and government waste, construction industry waste, and medical waste. These items also get dumped at illegal dump sites in urban and remote areas.

ETHICAL AND MORAL CONCERNS

Ethical and moral concerns related to genetic engineering arise in the scientific community and in smaller communities within society. Religious and moral beliefs can conflict with the economic interests of businesses, and with research methods used by the scientific community. For example, the United States government allows genes to be patented. A company has patented the gene for breast and ovarian cancer and will only make it available to researchers for a fee. This leads to a decrease in research, a decrease in medical solutions, and possibly an increase in the occurrence of breast and ovarian cancers. The possibility of lateral or incidental discoveries as a result of research is also limited. For example, a researcher working on a genetic solution to treat breast cancer might accidentally discover a cure for prostate cancer. This, however, would not occur if the researcher could not use the patented gene in the first place.

ENERGY PRODUCTION

- **Coal-fired power plants**: These generate electricity fairly cheaply, but are the largest source of **greenhouse gases**.
- **Gasoline**: Gasoline is cheap, generates less CO_2 than coal, and requires less water than coal. But it nevertheless releases a substantial amount of CO_2 in the aggregate and is a limited resource. The burning of gas and other fossil fuels releases carbon dioxide (a greenhouse gas) into the atmosphere.
- **Nuclear power plants**: A small nuclear power plant can cheaply produce a large amount of electricity. But the waste is potentially harmful and a substantial amount of **water** is required to generate electricity. The cost of storing and transporting the **radioactive waste** is also very large.
- **Hydropower**: Hydropower is sustainable and environmentally benign once established. A disadvantage is that the building of a dam and the re-routing of a river can be very **environmentally disruptive**.
- **Wind power**: Wind power is sustainable, non-polluting, and requires little to no cooling water. But it will not produce power in the absence of **wind** and requires a large area over which the turbines can be laid out.
- **Solar power**: Solar power is sustainable, can be used for a single house or building, and generates peak energy during times of peak usage. But production is limited to when the sun is shining, the panels themselves are expensive to make, and making the panels generates harmful **toxins**.
- **Geothermal power:** Geothermal power is sustainable, relatively cheap, and non-polluting. Disadvantages are that it can only be utilized in areas with specific **volcanic activity**.

REMOTE SENSING

Remote sensing refers to the gathering of data about an object or phenomenon without physical or intimate contact with the object being studied. The data can be viewed or recorded and stored in many forms (visually with a camera, audibly, or in the form of data). Gathering weather data from a ship, satellite, or buoy might be thought of as remote sensing. The monitoring of a fetus through the use of ultrasound technology provides a remote image. Listening to the heartbeat of a fetus is another example of remote sensing. Methods for remote sensing can be grouped as radiometric, geodetic, or acoustic. Examples of **radiometric remote sensing** include radar, laser altimeters, light detection and ranging (LIDAR) used to determine the concentration of chemicals in the air, and radiometers used to detect various frequencies of radiation. **Geodetic remote sensing** involves measuring the small fluctuations in Earth's gravitational field. Examples of **acoustic remote sensing** include underwater sonar and seismographs.

CELL PHONES AND GPS

A **cell phone** uses **radio waves** to communicate information. When speaking into a cell phone, the user's voice is converted into an electrical signal which is transmitted via radio waves to a cell tower, then to a satellite, then to a cell tower near the recipient, and then to the recipient's cell phone. The recipient's cell phone converts the digital signal back into an electrical signal.

A similar process occurs when data is transmitted over the **Internet** via a wireless network. The cell phone will convert any outgoing communication into a radio wave that will be sent to a wireless router. The router is "wireless" in the sense that the router is not wired to the phone. But the router is connected to the Internet via a cable. The router converts the radio signal into digital form and sends the communication through the Internet. The same basic process also occurs when a cell phone receives information from the Internet.

Wireless networks use radio frequencies of 2.4 GHz or 5 GHz.

Global Positioning System (GPS) is a system of **satellites** that orbit the Earth and communicate with mobile devices to pinpoint the mobile device's **position**. This is accomplished by determining the distance between the mobile device and at least three satellites. A mobile device might calculate a distance of 400 miles between it and the first satellite. The possible locations that are 400 miles from the first satellite and the mobile device will fall along a circle. The possible locations on Earth relative to the other two satellites will fall somewhere along different circles. The point on Earth at which these three circles intersect is the location of the mobile device. The process of determining position based on distance measurements from three satellites is called **trilateration**.

Social Studies Skills

COLLECTING INFORMATION AND ORGANIZING AND REPORTING RESULTS

The first step of compiling data for useful implementation requires narrowing down on a **topic**. The student should first read background information to identify areas that are interesting or need further study and that the student does not have a strong opinion about. The research question should be identified, and the student should refer to general sources that can point to more specific information. When he or she begins to take notes, his or her information must be **organized** with a clear system to identify the source. Any information from outside sources must be acknowledged with **footnotes** or a **bibliography**. To gain more specific information about his or her topic, the student can then research bibliographies from general sources to narrow down on information pertinent to the topic at hand. He or she should draft a thesis statement that summarizes the main point of the research. This should lead to a working **outline** that incorporates all the ideas needed to support the main point in a logical order. A rough draft should incorporate the results of the research in the outlined order, with all citations clearly inserted. The paper should then be edited for clarity, style, flow, and content.

FORMULATING RESEARCH QUESTIONS OR HYPOTHESES

Formulating research questions or hypotheses is the process of finding questions to answer that have not yet been asked. The first step in the process is reading **background information**. Knowing about a general topic and reading about how other people have addressed it helps identify areas that are well understood. Areas that are not as well understood may either be lightly addressed in the available literature or distinctly identified as a topic that is not well understood and deserves further study. Research questions or hypotheses may address such an unknown aspect, or they may focus on drawing parallels between similar, well-researched topics that have not been connected before. Students usually need practice in developing research questions that are of the appropriate scope so that they will find enough information to answer the question, yet not so much that they become overwhelmed. Hypotheses tend to be more specific than research questions.

IDENTIFYING MAIN IDEAS IN A DOCUMENT

Main ideas in a paragraph are often found in the **topic sentence**, which is usually the first or second sentence in the paragraph. Every following sentence in the paragraph should relate to that initial information. Sometimes, the first or second sentence doesn't obviously set up the main idea. When that happens, each sentence in the paragraph should be read carefully to find the **common theme** between them all. This common theme is the main idea of the paragraph. Main ideas in an entire document can be found by analyzing the structure of the document. Frequently, the document begins with an introductory paragraph or abstract that will summarize the main ideas. Each paragraph often discusses one of the main ideas and contributes to the overall goal of the document. Some documents are divided up into chapters or sections, each of which discusses a main idea. The way that main ideas are described in a document (either in sentences, paragraphs, or chapters) depends on the length of the document.

USING ELECTRONIC RESOURCES AND PERIODICALS FOR REFERENCE

Electronic resources are often the quickest, most convenient way to get background information on a topic. One of the particular strengths of **electronic resources** is that they can also provide primary-source multimedia video, audio, or other visual information on a topic that would not be accessible in print. Information available on the internet is not often carefully screened for accuracy or for bias, so choosing the **source** of electronic information is often very important. Electronic encyclopedias can provide excellent overview information, but publicly edited resources like

Wikipedia are open to error, rapid change, incompleteness, or bias. Students should be made aware of the different types and reliabilities of electronic resources, and they should be taught how to distinguish between them. Electronic resources can often be too detailed and overwhelm students with irrelevant information. **Periodicals** provide current information on social science events, but they too must be screened for bias. Some amount of identifiable bias can actually be an important source of information, because it indicates prevailing culture and standards. Periodicals generally have tighter editorial standards than electronic resources, so completeness and overt errors are not usually as problematic. Periodicals can also provide primary-source information with interviews and photographs.

USING ENCYCLOPEDIAS, BIBLIOGRAPHIES, OR ALMANACS FOR SOCIAL SCIENCE RESEARCH

Encyclopedias are ideal for getting background information on a topic. They provide an overview of the topic and link it to other concepts that can provide additional keywords, information, or subjects. They can help students narrow their topic by showing the subtopics within the overall topic and by relating it to other topics. **Encyclopedias** may sometimes prove to be more useful than the internet because they provide a clearly organized, concise overview of material. **Bibliographies** are bound collections of references to periodicals and books, organized by topic. Students can begin researching more efficiently after they identify a topic, look it up in a bibliography, and look up the references listed there. This provides a branching network of information a student can follow. A pitfall of bibliographies is that when in textbooks or other journal articles, the references in them are chosen to support the author's point of view and so may be limited in scope. **Almanacs** are volumes of facts published annually. They provide numerical information on just about every topic, and are organized by subject or geographic region. They are often helpful for supporting arguments made using other resources and do not provide any interpretation of their own.

PRIMARY AND SECONDARY RESOURCES

Primary resources provide information about an event from the perspective of people who were present at the event. They might be letters, autobiographies, interviews, speeches, artworks, or anything created by people with first-hand experience. **Primary resources** are valuable because they provide not only facts about the event but also information about the surrounding circumstances; for example, a letter might provide commentary about how a political speech was received. The internet is a source of primary information, but care must be taken to evaluate the perspective of the website providing that information. Websites hosted by individuals or special-interest organizations are more likely to be biased than those hosted by public organizations, governments, educational institutions, or news associations. **Secondary resources** provide information about an event but were not written at the time the event occurred. They draw information from primary sources. Because secondary sources were written later, they have the added advantage of historical perspective, multiple points of view, or resultant outcomes. Newsmagazines that write about an event even a week after it occurred count as secondary sources. Secondary sources tend to analyze events more effectively or thoroughly than primary sources.

> **Review Video: What are Primary and Secondary Resources?**
> Visit mometrix.com/academy and enter code: 383328

ORGANIZING INFORMATION CHRONOLOGICALLY AND ANALYZING THE SEQUENCE OF EVENTS

To organize information chronologically, each piece of information must be associated with a time or a date. Events are ordered according to the time or date at which they happened. In social sciences, chronological organization is the most straightforward way to arrange information, because it relies on a uniform, fixed scale—the passage of time. Information can also be organized based on any of the "who, what, when, where, why?" principles.

Analyzing the sequence of chronological events involves not only examining the event itself but the preceding and following events. This can put the event in question into perspective, showing how a certain thing might have happened based on preceding history. One large disadvantage of chronological organization is that it may not highlight important events clearly relative to less important events. Determining the relative importance of events depends more strongly on interpreting their relationships to neighboring events.

RECOGNIZING CAUSE-AND-EFFECT RELATIONSHIPS AND COMPARING SIMILARITIES AND DIFFERENCES

Cause-and-effect relationships are simply linkages between an event that happened (the **effect**) because of some other event (the **cause**). Effects are always chronologically ordered after causes. Effects can be found by asking why something happened or looking for information following words like *so, consequently, since, because, therefore, this led to, as a result*, and *thus*. Causes can also be found by asking what happened. **Comparing similarities and differences** involves mentally setting two concepts next to each other and then listing the ways they are the same and the ways they are different. The level of comparison varies by student level; for example, younger students may compare the physical characteristics of two animals while older students compare the themes of a book. Similarity/difference comparisons can be made by listing written descriptions in a point-by-point approach, or they can be done in several graphic ways. Venn diagrams are commonly used to organize information, showing non-overlapping clouds filled with information about the different characteristics of A and B, and the overlapping area shows ways in which A and B are the same. Idea maps using arrows and bubbles can also be developed to show these differences.

DISTINGUISHING BETWEEN FACT AND OPINION

Students easily recognize that **facts** are true statements that everyone agrees on, such as an object's name or a statement about a historical event. Students also recognize that **opinions** vary about matters of taste, such as preferences in food or music, that rely on people's interpretation of facts. Simple examples are easy to spot. **Fact-based passages** include certainty-grounded words like *is, did,* or *saw*. On the other hand, **passages containing opinions** often include words that indicate possibility rather than certainty, such as *would, should,* or *believe*. First-person verbs also indicate opinions, showing that one person is talking about his or her experience. Less clear are examples found in higher-level texts. For example, primary-source accounts of a Civil War battle might include facts ("*x* battle was fought today") and also opinions ("Union soldiers are not as brave as Confederate soldiers") that are not clearly written as such ("I believe Union soldiers..."). At the same time that students learn to interpret sources critically (Was the battle account written by a Southerner?), they should practice sifting fact from these types of opinion. Other examples where fact and opinion blend together are self-authored internet websites.

> **Review Video: Fact or Opinion**
> Visit mometrix.com/academy and enter code: 870899

DETERMINING THE ADEQUACY, RELEVANCE, AND CONSISTENCY OF INFORMATION

Before information is sought, a list of **guiding questions** should be developed to help determine whether information found is adequate, relevant, and consistent. These questions should be based on the **research goals**, which should be laid out in an outline or concept map. For example, a student writing a report on Navajo social structure might begin with questions concerning the general lifestyle and location of Navajos and follow with questions about how Navajo society was organized. While researching his questions, he or she will come up with pieces of information. This information can be compared to his or her research questions to determine whether it is **relevant** to his or her report. Information from several sources should be compared to determine whether the information is **consistent**. Information that is **adequate** helps answer specific questions that are part of the research goals. Inadequate information for this particular student might be a statement such as "Navajos had a strong societal structure," because the student is probably seeking more specific information.

Drawing Conclusions and Making Generalizations About a Topic

Students reading about a topic will encounter different facts and opinions that contribute to their overall impression of the material. The student can critically examine the material by thinking about what facts have been included, how they have been presented, what they show, what they relate to outside the written material, and what the author's conclusion is. Students may agree or disagree with the author's conclusion, based on the student's interpretation of the facts the author presented. When working on a research project, a student's research questions will help him or her gather details that will enable him or her to **draw a conclusion** about the research material.

Generalizations are blanket statements that apply to a wide number of examples. They are similar to conclusions but do not have to summarize the information as completely as conclusions. Generalizations in reading material may be flagged by words such as *all*, *most*, *none*, *many*, *several*, *sometimes*, *often*, *never*, *overall*, or *in general*. Generalizations are often followed by supporting information consisting of a list of facts. Generalizations can refer to facts or the author's opinions, and they provide a valuable summary of the text overall.

Evaluating and Interpreting Maps

The **map legend** is an area that provides interpretation information such as the key, the scale, and how to interpret the map. The **key** is the area that defines symbols, abbreviations, and color schemes used on the map. Any feature identified on the map should be defined in the key. The **scale** is a feature of the map legend that tells how distance on the map relates to distance on the ground. It can either be presented mathematically in a ratio or visually with a line segment. For example, it could say that one inch on the map equals one foot on the ground, or it could show a line segment and tell how much distance on the map the line symbolizes. **Latitude** and **longitude** are often shown on maps to relate their area to the world. Latitude shows how far a location is north or south from Earth's equator, and longitude shows how far a location is east or west from Earth's prime meridian. Latitude runs from 90°N (North Pole) to 0° (equator) to 90°S (South Pole), and longitude runs 180°E (International Date Line) to 0° (prime meridian) to 180°W (International Date Line).

> **Review Video: 5 Elements of any Map**
> Visit mometrix.com/academy and enter code: 437727

Popular Map Projections

- **Globe**: Earth's features are shown on a sphere. No distortion of distances, directions, or areas occurs.
- **Mercator**: Earth's features are projected onto a cylinder wrapped around a globe. This generates a rectangular map that is not distorted at the equator but is greatly distorted near the poles. Lines of latitude and longitude form a square grid.
- **Robinson**: Earth's features are projected onto an oval-looking map. Areas near the poles are truer to size than in the Mercator. Some distortion affects every point.

- **Orthographic**: Earth's features are shown on a circle, which is tangent to the globe at any point chosen by the mapmaker. This generates a circular, 3D-appearing map similar to how Earth is seen from space.
- **Conic maps**: This family of maps is drawn by projecting the globe's features onto a cone set onto the globe. Some distortion affects most points.
- **Polar maps**: The land around the poles has been projected onto a circle. This provides much less distortion of Antarctica and the land around the North Pole than other map types.

CARTOGRAPHIC DISTORTION AND ITS INFLUENCE ON MAP PROJECTIONS

Cartographic distortion is the distortion caused by projecting a three-dimensional structure, in this case, Earth's surface, onto the two-dimensional surface of a map. Numerous map projections have been developed to minimize distortion, but the only way to eliminate distortion completely is to render Earth in three dimensions. Most map projections have minimal distortion in some location, usually the center, and the distortion becomes greater close to the edges of the map. Some map projections try to compromise and distribute the distortion more evenly across the map. Different categories of maps preserve, or do not distort, different features. Maps that preserve directions accurately are **azimuthal**, and maps that preserve shapes properly are **conformal**. Area-preserving maps are called **equal-area maps**, and maps that preserve distance are called **distance-preserving**. Maps that preserve the shortest routes are **gnomonic projections**.

> **Review Video: Map Projections**
> Visit mometrix.com/academy and enter code: 327303

COMPARING MAPS OF THE SAME PLACE FROM DIFFERENT TIME PERIODS

Maps of the same place from different time periods can often be initially aligned by **geographic features**. Political and land-use boundaries are most likely to change between time periods, whereas locations of waterways and geologic features such as mountains are relatively constant. Once geographic features have been used to align maps, they can be compared side-by-side to examine the changing locations of human settlement, smaller waterways, etc. This kind of map interpretation, at the smallest scale, provides information about how small groups of humans **interact with their environment**. For example, such analysis might show that major cities began around ports and then moved inland as modes of transportation, like railroads and cars, became more common. Lands that were initially used for agriculture might become incorporated into a nearby city as the population grows. This kind of map analysis can also show the evolution of the **socio-economics** of an area, providing information about the relative importance of economic activities (manufacturing, agriculture, or trade) and even the commuting behavior of workers.

NATURAL, POLITICAL, AND CULTURAL FEATURES ON MAPS

Map legends will provide information about the types of natural, political, or cultural features on a map. Some maps show only one of these three features. **Natural features** such as waterways, wetlands, beaches, deserts, mountains, highlands, and plains can be compared between regions by type, number, distribution, or any other physical characteristic. **Political features** such as state and county divisions or roads and railroads can be compared numerically, but examining their geographic distribution may be more informative. This provides information on settlement density and population. In addition, road and railroad density may show regions of intense urbanization, agricultural regions, or industrial centers. **Cultural features** may include roads and railroads, but might also include historic areas, museums, archaeological digs, early settlements, and even campgrounds. Comparing and contrasting the number, distribution, and types of these features may provide information on the history of an area, the duration of settlement of an area, or the current use of the area (for example, many museums are found in current-day cultural centers).

COMPARING MAPS WITH DATASETS OR TEXTS

Maps can provide a great deal of information about an area by showing specific locations where certain types of settlement, land use, or population growth occurred. **Datasets** and **texts** can provide more specific information about events that might only otherwise be hypothesized from maps. This specific information may provide dates of significant events (for example, the date of a fire that gutted a downtown region, forcing suburban development) or important numerical data (e.g., population growth by year). Written datasets and texts enable map interpretation to become concrete and allow observed trends to be linked with specific causes ("Real estate prices rose in 2004, causing middle-class citizens to move northwest of the city"). Without specific information from additional sources, inferences drawn from maps cannot be put in **context** and interpreted in more than a vague way.

EVALUATING AND INTERPRETING OTHER GRAPHIC FORMATS

The type of information being conveyed guides the choice of **format**. Textual information and numeric information must be displayed with different techniques. Text-only information may be most easily summarized in a diagram or a timeline. If the text includes numeric information, it may be converted into a chart that shows the size of groups, connects ideas in a table or graphic, or shows information in a hybridized format. Numeric information is often most helpfully presented in tables or graphs. When information will be referred to and looked up again and again, tables are often most helpful for the reader. When the trends in the numeric information are more important than the numbers themselves, graphs are often the best choice. Information that is linked to the land and has a spatial component is best conveyed using maps.

INTERPRETING CHARTS AND TABLES

Charts used in social science are a visual representation of data. They combine graphic and textual elements to convey information in a concise format. Often, **charts** divide the space up in blocks, which are filled with text and/or pictures to convey a point. Charts are often organized in tabular form, where blocks below a heading all have information in common. Charts also divide information into conceptual, non-numeric groups (for example, "favorite color"), which are then plotted against a numerical axis (e.g., "number of students"). Charts should be labeled in such a way that a reader can locate a point on the chart and then consult the surrounding axes or table headings to understand how it compares to other points. **Tables** are a type of chart that divides textual information into rows and columns. Each row and column represent a characteristic of the information. For example, a table might be used to convey demographic information. The first column would provide "year," and the second would provide "population." Reading across the rows, one could see that in the year 1966, the population of Middletown was 53,847. Tracking the columns would show how frequently the population was counted.

INTERPRET GRAPHS AND DIAGRAMS

Graphs are similar to charts, except that they graphically show numeric information on both axes. For example, a **graph** might show population through the years, with years on the x axis and population on the y axis. One advantage of graphs is that the population during the time in between censuses can be estimated by locating that point on the graph. Each axis should be labeled to allow the information to be interpreted correctly, and the graph should have an informative title.

Diagrams are usually drawings that show the progression of events. The drawings can be fairly schematic, as in a flow chart, or they can be quite detailed, as in a depiction of scenes from a battle. Diagrams usually have arrows connecting the events or boxes shown. Each event or box should be labeled to show what it represents. Diagrams are interpreted by following the progression along the arrows through all events.

> **Review Video: Understanding Charts and Tables**
> Visit mometrix.com/academy and enter code: 882112

USING TIMELINES IN SOCIAL SCIENCE

Timelines are used to show the relationships between people, places, and events. They are ordered chronologically and usually are shown left-to-right or top-to-bottom. Each event on the **timeline** is associated with a date, which determines its location on the timeline. On electronic resources, timelines often contain hyperlinks associated with each event. Clicking on the event's hyperlink will open a page with more information about the event. **Cause-and-effect relationships** can be observed on timelines, which often show a key event and then resulting events following in close succession. These can be helpful for showing the order of events in time or the relationships between similar events. They help make the passage of time a concrete concept and show that large periods pass between some events, while other events cluster very closely.

USING POLITICAL CARTOONS IN SOCIAL SCIENCE STUDIES

Political cartoons are drawings that memorably convey an opinion. These opinions may be supportive or critical and may summarize a series of events or pose a fictional situation that summarizes an attitude. **Political cartoons** are, therefore, secondary sources of information that provide social and cultural context about events. Political cartoons may have captions that help describe the action or put it in context. They may also have dialogue, labels, or other recognizable cultural symbols. For example, Uncle Sam frequently appears in political cartoons to represent the United States government. Political cartoons frequently employ caricatures to call attention to a situation or a person. The nature of the caricature helps show the cartoonist's attitude toward the issue being portrayed. Every element of the cartoon is included to support the artist's point and should be considered in the cartoon's interpretation. When interpreting political cartoons, students should examine what issue is being discussed, what elements the artist chose to support his or her point, and what the message is. Considering who might agree or disagree with the cartoon is also helpful in determining the message of the cartoon.

ANALYZING ARTIFACTS

Artifacts, or everyday objects used by previous cultures, are useful for understanding life in those cultures. Students should first discover, or be provided with, a **description** of the item. This description should depict what time period the **artifact** was used in and what culture used it. From that description and/or from examination of the artifact, students should be able to discuss what the artifact is, what it is made of, its potential uses, and the people who likely used it. They should then be able to draw **conclusions** from all these pieces of evidence about life in that culture. For example, analysis of coins from an early American archaeological site might show that settlers brought coins with them, or that some classes of residents were wealthy, or that trade occurred with many different nations. The interpretation will vary depending on the circumstances surrounding the artifact. Students should consider these circumstances when drawing conclusions.

Social and Behavioral Sciences

U.S. History

COLONIAL PERIOD (1607-1765)

The **colonial period** describes a time in which several European countries attempted to settle and colonize the Americas to expand their territories. The earliest attempts to colonize were by Spain and France, who conquered and settled much of what are now the southern and central parts of the United States of America. In the process of colonizing the Americas, many Native American groups were displaced or killed by disease and territorial expansion. The main focus of the colonial period in what is now the United States is often placed on the **thirteen English colonies**, which were located on the east coast. The primary reasons for the English colonization in the Americas were in response to England's policy of mercantilism and colonists' desire to be free from **religious persecution**. **Mercantilism** in England required the colonies to provide raw materials to England to continue to grow and support the mother country while also limiting trade with other nations. The other primary motivation for settlement included escape from persecution by the Church of England toward Catholic and other religious groups.

THE 13 COLONIES

The **thirteen colonies** were a group of English colonies that were overtly similar in their political and religious beliefs. The thirteen colonies were comprised of:

NEW ENGLAND COLONIES:
- New Hampshire
- Massachusetts
- Rhode Island
- Connecticut

CHESAPEAKE BAY COLONIES:
- Virginia
- Maryland

> **Review Video: The English Colony of Virginia**
> Visit mometrix.com/academy and enter code: 537399

MIDDLE COLONIES:
- New York
- Pennsylvania
- New Jersey
- Delaware

SOUTHERN COLONIES:
- North Carolina
- South Carolina
- Georgia

> **Review Video: Southern Colonies**
> Visit mometrix.com/academy and enter code: 703830

FRENCH AND INDIAN WAR

The **French and Indian War** was essentially a war over territory between the English colonies and the French colonies. Rising competition between the English and French empires brought more British military support into the colonies, which created a stronger feeling of unity between the colonies and England than ever before. In 1763, the **Treaty of Paris** brought an end to the war, as France relinquished some of its Eastern territory to England, including the territory east of modern-day Louisiana all the way to the Great Lakes. In the aftermath of the war, **tensions** rose between the colonies and England because of unequal investment in the war. British taxpayers had supplied the majority of funding for the war, while the colonists were forced to fight in a war that served the monarchy's interests rather than their own interests. These tensions, along with continued British occupation, were the foundation for the coming revolution.

AMERICAN REVOLUTION (1765-1783)
THE INTOLERABLE ACTS

Following the French and Indian War, Britain increased taxes and continued to impose quartering on the colonies. The most famous of these included the Stamp Acts, the Tea Acts, and the Quartering Acts. The purpose of these laws was to force the colonies to be dependent on Britain, and to help restore the British economy following the wars of the previous years. These laws were known to the British as the **Coercive Acts**. In America, they were called the **Intolerable Acts,** due to the offensive nature of England's attempt to control and stifle the colonies. As tensions rose, members of the colonies began organizing rebellious protests, such as the Boston Tea Party, in response to particular tax laws that were passed. These inciting reasons and protests led up to the official start of the **American Revolution.**

IMPORTANT EVENTS AND GROUPS LEADING UP TO AMERICAN REVOLUTION

Over several years, various events and groups contributed to the rebellion that became a revolution:

- **Sons of Liberty** – This was the protest group headed by Samuel Adams that incited the Revolution.
- **Boston Massacre** – On March 5, 1770, British soldiers fired on a crowd and killed five people.
- **Committees of Correspondence** – These were set up throughout the colonies to transmit revolutionary ideas and create a unified response.
- **The Boston Tea Party** – On December 6, 1773, the Sons of Liberty, dressed as Mohawks, dumped tea into the harbor from a British ship to protest the tea tax. The harsh British response further aggravated the situation.
- **First Continental Congress** – This was held in 1774 to list grievances and develop a response, including boycotts. It was attended by all the colonies with the exception of Georgia.
- **The Shot Heard Round the World** – In April, 1775, English soldiers on their way to confiscate arms in Concord passed through Lexington, Massachusetts and met the colonial militia called the Minutemen. A fight ensued. In Concord, a larger group of Minutemen forced the British to retreat.

> **Review Video: The First and Second Continental Congress**
> Visit mometrix.com/academy and enter code: 835211

ORIGINAL 13 COLONIES AND MAJOR TURNING POINTS OF THE REVOLUTION

The original **13 colonies** were: Connecticut, Delaware, Georgia, Maryland, Massachusetts, New Hampshire, New Jersey, New York, North Carolina, Pennsylvania, Rhode Island, South Carolina, and Virginia. Delaware was the first state to ratify the **constitution**.

The major turning points of the American Revolution were:

- The actions of the **Second Continental Congress** – This body established the Continental Army and chose George Washington as its commanding general. They allowed printing of money and created government offices.
- **"Common Sense"** – Published in 1776 by Thomas Paine, this pamphlet calling for independence was widely distributed.
- The **Declaration of Independence** – Written by Thomas Jefferson, it was ratified on July 4, 1776 by the Continental Congress assembled in Philadelphia.
- **Alliance with France** – Benjamin Franklin negotiated an agreement with France to fight with the Americans in 1778.
- **Treaty of Paris** – Signaled the official end of the war in 1782, granted independence to the colonies, and gave them generous territorial rights.

> **Review Video: Declaration of Independence**
> Visit mometrix.com/academy and enter code: 256838
>
> **Review Video: Colonization of the Americas**
> Visit mometrix.com/academy and enter code: 438412

FOUNDING OF A NATION

Each of the colonies overthrew the British representation within their own colonies and established their own state constitutions. The newly formed 13 states, with the guidance and primary authorship of Thomas Jefferson, unanimously adopted the **Declaration of Independence,** which officially separated the colonies from British rule. Shortly thereafter, the **Second Continental Congress**, made up of state representatives, met together to ratify the **Articles of Confederation**, which was the original constitution for the United States of America, outlining how sovereignty would be shared among the states in the new country. With the assistance of the French, the Americans were able to fend off a large scale naval and military invasion from the British and secure their revolution.

> **Review Video: Who are the Founding Fathers?**
> Visit mometrix.com/academy and enter code: 704562

CONFEDERATION PERIOD

The **Confederation Period** (1783-1788) was the period in U.S. history directly following the American Revolution. The Articles of Confederation held the states loosely, and the states were largely self-governing and did not have much political unity. In this format, the federal government was very weak, with no chief executive or judicial system. The weak federal government was bound to continue degrading in unity and would eventually fail if left without reform. In 1787, political leaders met to write a new constitution with more thoroughly written policies that would establish federal powers, while still sharing power with the state governments. This new constitution ended the confederation period and led the way into the Federalist Era.

FEDERALIST ERA (1788-1801)

The 1787 convention that wrote the new **Constitution of the United States of America** established three government branches, the **legislative** (making laws) the **executive** (enforcing laws), and the **judicial** (interpreting and judging laws). Having three branches with separate powers helped to provide what is known as **checks and balances** in government, so that no one branch will have too much power. This was meant to maintain liberty and state powers, while giving the federal government enough power to effectively govern the new country. The new constitution also established voting practices on the individual and state level, including the controversial topic of slavery and voting practices for states that did not abolish slavery. At this point, some northern states had made slavery illegal, but the constitution of the time allowed for the states to determine their own laws on the matter. The Federalist Era placed more power in the hands of the federal government, but also established a place for political parties to advocate for the rights of the people.

BILL OF RIGHTS AND AMENDMENTS

Over the next few years, the need for revision to the constitution was made clear. In 1789, congress adopted several **amendments** to the constitution, mostly dealing with individual rights, such as the right to freedom of speech, the right to bear arms, and several others. The first ten amendments are called "**The Bill of Rights**." In the process of instituting these amendments, it was also laid out that any declarations (such as rights or laws) not specifically granted in the constitution or amendments to the constitution are reserved for the states or lower jurisdictions to establish.

JEFFERSONIAN ERA (1801-1817)

The **Jeffersonian Era** is defined by the influences of Thomas Jefferson and his political activism. In the Federalist Era, many of the political voices advocated for power going to those with wealth and property, rather than the equal rights of all people. Jefferson's political outlook was called **American Republicanism** (now the Democratic-Republican Party), which opposed aristocracy, elitism, and corruption in government. During Jefferson's presidency, he made significant strides toward a more inclusive voting system. He also managed to purchase Louisiana from France at an extremely reasonable price, thus roughly doubling the size of the United States at the time. From 1812-1815, a war ensued between the United Kingdom and the United States due to the British cutting off trade routes and fostering hostility between the Native Americans and the United States. The war concluded with no changes to boundaries, leading to the beginning of the **Era of Good Feelings**.

ERA OF GOOD FEELINGS AND THE JACKSONIAN ERA

The **Era of Good Feelings** (1817-1825) followed the Jeffersonian Era, and was marked by the collapse of the Federalist system. President James Monroe attempted to deter the partisan political system and prevent political parties from driving national politics. During the Era of Good Feelings, there was a **temporary sense of national security** and a **desire for unity** in America following the war of previous years. Following Monroe's presidency, votes were largely split between the two major parties of the time, the **Whigs** and the **Democrats**.

During the **Jacksonian Era** (1825-1849), **voting rights** were extended to most white men over 21 years old and revised other federal policies. The policy favored the idea of election by the "common man," which expanded voting rights, while continuing to deny rights to women, Native Americans and African Americans. This period also saw an increase in **expansionism**, encouraging territorial expansion to the west in the name of manifest destiny. During this period, issues of slavery were largely avoided at first, though they grew over the coming years, leading into the Civil War Era.

Civil War Era (1850-1865)

The **Civil War Era** began with continued push from the northern states to expand democratic rights to Black people. The constitution of the time allowed for slavery to be a state's right to determine and enforce. Eleven states (with two to join later) determined to secede from the United States of America and become their own nation. In these eleven states, slavery was a major mode and means for the economy, and despite the overt ethical issues with slavery, these southern states were adamant about maintaining their way of life. The official Confederacy was formed in 1861 and continued until the end of the civil war in 1865.

Reconstruction Era (1865-1877)

Reconstruction and 13th, 14th, and 15th Amendments

Reconstruction was the period from 1865 to 1877, during which the South was under strict control of the U.S. government. In March, 1867, all state governments of the former Confederacy were terminated, and **military occupation** began. Military commanders called for constitutional conventions to reconstruct the state governments, to which delegates were to be elected by universal male suffrage. After a state government was in operation and the state had **ratified the 14th Amendment**, its representatives were admitted to Congress. Three constitutional amendments from 1865 to 1870, which tried to rectify the problems caused by slavery, became part of the Reconstruction effort. The **13th Amendment** declared slavery illegal. The **14th Amendment** made all persons born or naturalized in the country U.S. citizens, and forbade any state to interfere with their fundamental civil rights. The **15th Amendment** made it illegal to deny individuals the right to vote on the grounds of race. In his 1876 election campaign, President **Rutherford B. Hayes** promised to withdraw troops from the South, and did so in 1877.

Major Changes in Industry in the Late 1800s

Important events during this time of enormous business growth and large-scale exploitation of natural resources include:

- **Industrialization** – Like the rest of the world, the United States' entry into the Industrial Age was marked by many new inventions and the mechanization of factories.
- **Railroad expansion** – The Transcontinental Railroad was built from 1865 to 1969. Railroad tracks stretched over 35,000 miles in 1865, but that distance reached 240,000 miles by 1910. The raw materials and manufactured goods needed for the railroads kept mines and factories very busy.
- **Gold and silver mining** – Mines brought many prospectors to the West from 1850 to about 1875, but mining corporations soon took over.
- **Cattle ranching** – This was a large-scale enterprise beginning in the late 1860s, but by the 1880s open ranges were being fenced and plowed for farming and pastures. Millions of farmers moved into the high plains, establishing the "Bread Basket," which was the major wheat growing area of the country.

Gilded Age (1877-1895)

The **Gilded Age**, from the 1870s to 1890, was so named because of the enormous wealth and grossly opulent lifestyle enjoyed by a handful of powerful families. This was the time when huge mansions were built as summer "cottages" in Newport, Rhode Island, and great lodges were built in mountain areas for the pleasure of families such as the Vanderbilts, Ascots, and Rockefellers.

Control of the major industries was held largely by the following men:

- Jay Gould—railroads
- Andrew Carnegie—steel
- John D. Rockefeller Sr.—oil
- Philip Danforth Armour—meatpacking
- J. P. Morgan—banking
- John Jacob Astor—fur pelts
- Cornelius Vanderbilt—steamboat shipping

These men were were known as **Robber Barons** for their ruthless business practices and exploitation of workers. Of course, all of these heads of industry diversified and became involved in multiple business ventures. To curb cutthroat competition, particularly among the railroads, and to prohibit restrained trade, Congress created the **Interstate Commerce Commission** and the **Sherman Anti-Trust Act**. Neither of these, however, was enforced.

> **Review Video: The Gilded Age: An Overview**
> Visit mometrix.com/academy and enter code: 684770
>
> **Review Video: The Gilded Age: Chinese Immigration**
> Visit mometrix.com/academy and enter code: 624166

IMMIGRATION TRENDS IN LATE 1800S

The population of the United States doubled between 1860 and 1890, with the arrival of 10 million immigrants. Most lived in the north. Cities and their **slums** grew tremendously because of immigration and industrialization. While previous immigrants had come from Germany, Scandinavia, and Ireland, the 1880s saw a new wave of immigrants from Italy, Poland, Hungary, Bohemia, and Greece, as well as Jewish groups from central and eastern Europe, especially Russia. The Roman Catholic population grew from 1.6 million in 1850 to 12 million in 1900, a growth that ignited an anti-Catholic backlash from the anti-Catholic Know-Nothing Party of the 1880s and the Ku Klux Klan. Exploited immigrant workers started **labor protests** in the 1870s, and the **Knights of Labor** was formed in 1878, calling for sweeping social and economic reform. Its membership reached 700,000 by 1886. Eventually, this organization was replaced by the **American Federation of Labor**, headed by Samuel Gompers.

PROGRESSIVE ERA (1896–1916)

The **Progressive Era**, which was the time period from the 1890s to the 1920s, got its name from progressive, reform-minded political leaders who wanted to export a just and rational social order to the rest of the world while increasing trade with foreign markets. Consequently, the United States interfered in a dispute between Venezuela and Britain. America invoked the **Monroe Doctrine** and sided with Cuba in its struggle for independence from Spain. The latter resulted in the **Spanish-American Wars** in 1898 that ended with Cuba, Puerto Rico, the Philippines, and Guam becoming American protectorates at the same time the United States annexed Hawaii. In 1900, America declared an **Open Door policy** with China to support its independence and open markets. In 1903, Theodore Roosevelt helped Panama become independent of Colombia, and then secured the right to build the **Panama Canal**. Roosevelt also negotiated the peace treaty to end the Russo-Japanese War, which earned him the Nobel Peace prize. He then sent the American fleet on a world cruise to display his country's power.

> **Review Video: The Progressive Era**
> Visit mometrix.com/academy and enter code: 722394

DOMESTIC ACCOMPLISHMENTS OF THE PROGRESSIVE ERA

To the Progressives, promoting law and order meant cleaning up city governments to make them honest and efficient, bringing more democracy and humanity to state governments, and establishing a core of social workers to improve slum housing, health, and education. Also during the **Progressive Era**, the national government strengthened or created the following regulatory agencies, services, and acts to oversee business enterprises:

- Passed in 1906, the **Hepburn Act** reinforced the Interstate Commerce Commission. In 1902, Roosevelt used the Justice Department and lawsuits to try to break monopolies and enforce the **Sherman Anti-Trust Act**. The **Clayton Anti-Trust Act** was added in 1914.
- From 1898 to 1910, the **Forest Service** guided lumber companies in the conservation and more efficient use of woodland resources under the direction of Gifford Pinchot.
- In 1906, the **Pure Food and Drug Act** was passed to protect consumers from fraudulent labeling and adulteration of products.
- In 1913, the **Federal Reserve System** was established to supervise banking and commerce. In 1914, the **Fair Trade Commission** was established to ensure fair competition.

WORLD WAR I (1917–1919)

When World War I broke out in 1914, America declared **neutrality**. The huge demand for war goods by the Allies broke a seven-year industrial stagnation and gave American factories full-time work. The country's sympathies lay mostly with the Allies, and before long American business and banking were heavily invested in an Allied victory. In 1916, **Woodrow Wilson** campaigned on the slogan "He kept us out of war." However, when the British ship the *Lusitania* was torpedoed in 1915 by a German submarine and many Americans were killed, the United States broke its neutrality and directly entered the war. Eventually, when it was proven that Germany was trying to incite Mexico and Japan into attacking the United States, Wilson declared war in 1917, even though America was unprepared. Nonetheless, America quickly armed and transferred sufficient troops to Europe, bringing the **Allies** to victory in 1918.

> **Review Video: WWI Overview**
> Visit mometrix.com/academy and enter code: 659767

ROARING TWENTIES AND THE GREAT DEPRESSION

The **Roaring Twenties** (1920–1929) refers to the economically successful period of time following World War I. New technologies such as automobiles, new forms of media such as films, and new communication technology became widely available. In the wake of industrial growth and revolution, culture shifted toward more modern sentiments, and moved toward a more **practical** approach to life. New forms of art and music were born and thrived during this period, and during this timeframe civil rights were expanded to allow **women to vote**. In 1929, the stock market crashed and caused the end of the Roaring Twenties and the beginning of the **Great Depression**, which lasted from 1930 until 1941. The Great Depression was characterized by high unemployment rates and a slow-moving market with little profit to be made. Many banks failed during this time, and there was no governmental protection against bank failures. As a result, many depositors withdrew their money from banks to protect themselves, removing much of the money from the economy in an effect called economic contraction.

WORLD WAR II (1939–1945)

World War II began in 1939. As with World War I, the United States tried to stay out of World War II, even though the **Lend-Lease program** transferred munitions to Great Britain. However, on

December 7, 1941, Japan attacked **Pearl Harbor** in Hawaii. Since Japan was an ally of Germany, the United States declared war on all the Axis powers. Although there was fighting in both Europe and the Pacific, the decision was made to concentrate on defeating Hitler first. Since it did not have combat within its borders, the United States became the great manufacturer of goods and munitions for the war effort. Women went to work in the factories, while the men entered the military. All facets of American life were centered on the war effort, including rationing, metal collections, and buying war bonds. The benefit of this production was an **end to the economic depression**. The influx of American personnel and supplies eventually brought victory in Europe in April of 1945, and in Asia the following August.

> **Review Video: World War II**
> Visit mometrix.com/academy and enter code: 759402

MAJOR PROGRAMS AND EVENTS RESULTING FROM THE COLD WAR

After World War II, the Soviet Union kept control of Eastern Europe, including half of Germany. **Communism** spread around the world. Resulting fears led to:

- The **Truman Doctrine** (1947) – This was a policy designed to protect free peoples everywhere against oppression.
- The **Marshall Plan** (1948) – This devoted $12 billion to rebuild Western Europe and strengthen its defenses.
- The **Organization of American States** (1948) – This was established to bolster democratic relations in the Americas.
- The **Berlin Blockade** (1948-49) – The Soviets tried to starve out West Berlin, so the United States provided massive supply drops by air.
- The **North Atlantic Treaty Organization** (1949) – This was formed to militarily link the United States and western Europe so that an attack on one was an attack on both.
- The **Korean War** (1950-53) – This divided the country into the communist North and the democratic South.
- The **McCarthy era** (1950-54) – Senator Joseph McCarthy of Wisconsin held hearings on supposed Communist conspiracies that ruined innocent reputations and led to the blacklisting of suspected sympathizers in the government, Hollywood, and the media.

MAJOR EVENTS OF THE 1960S

The 1960s were a tumultuous time for the United States. Major events included:

- The **Cuban Missile Crisis** (1961) – This was a stand-off between the United States and the Soviet Union over a build-up of missiles in Cuba. Eventually, the Soviets stopped their shipments and a nuclear war was averted.
- The **assassinations** of President Kennedy (1963), Senator Robert Kennedy (1968), and Dr. Martin Luther King, Jr. (1968).
- The **Civil Rights Movement** – Protest marches were held across the nation to draw attention to the plight of Black citizens. From 1964 to 1968, race riots exploded in more than 100 cities.
- The **Vietnam War** (1964-73) – This resulted in a military draft. There was heavy involvement of American personnel and money. There were also protest demonstrations, particularly on college campuses. At Kent State, several students died after being shot by National Guardsmen.

- **Major legislation** – Legislation passed during this decade included the Civil Rights Act, the Clean Air Act, and the Water Quality Act. This decade also saw the creation of the Peace Corps, Medicare, and the War on Poverty, in which billions were appropriated for education, urban redevelopment, and public housing.

PRESIDENTS AND VICE PRESIDENTS FROM 1972 TO 1974

In a two-year time span, the United States had two presidents and two vice presidents. This situation resulted first from the resignation of Vice President **Spiro T. Agnew** in October of 1973 because of alleged kickbacks. President **Richard M. Nixon** then appointed House Minority Leader **Gerald R. Ford** to be vice president. This was accomplished through Senate ratification, a process that had been devised after Harry Truman succeeded to the presidency upon the death of Franklin Roosevelt and went through nearly four years of his presidency without a vice president. Nixon resigned the presidency in August of 1974 because some Republican party members broke into Democratic headquarters at the **Watergate** building in Washington, DC, and the president participated in covering up the crime. Ford succeeded Nixon, and had to appoint another vice president. He chose **Nelson Rockefeller**, former governor of New York.

POST-WAR ERA AND THE CIVIL RIGHTS ERA

The **Post-War Era** (1945-1964) was a time of **economic recovery** and general growth in America. The wars of the past several decades inspired a more active foreign policy to deter such violent wars from occurring again. This largely focused on the Soviet Union and the expansion of Communism around the world. Several countries at this time participated in both a space race and an **arms race**, a rush to develop and accumulate more powerful weapons, particularly nuclear weapons, to become the world's strongest military power. The political differences and concerns over powerful armaments eventually led to the Cold War, Vietnam War, and Korean War. The 60s were also a major pivot-point for civil rights, leading into the **Civil Rights Era** (1965-1980). Due to the protesting and activism of several groups, including **Dr. Martin Luther King Jr.** and the **NAACP**, civil rights landmarks were made regarding racial equality, including laws dealing with **segregation**, **employment opportunity**, and **voting** rights.

REAGAN ERA (1981–1991)

The **Reagan Era** is an era largely describing the foreign policy of the United States during the 1980s and sometimes viewed as extending through the 1990s or early-2000s. During this period, conservative reforms worked to **increase military spending** while also **cutting taxes** and reducing or restricting the involvement of the national government. Ronald Reagan's financial policy revolved around the idea that if the government stepped back, the economy could grow, which would in turn help to reduce national debt.

1990S AND EARLY-2000S

The 1990s and early-2000s were characterized largely by new economic developments surrounding the availability of computers and the development of the internet, allowing new technology to drive the economy in new ways. The economy boomed in the late 1990s leading into the early 2000s. Amid all of the economic success, the United States faced attacks by terrorist groups such as al-Qaeda, which caused alarm and greater restriction to national security and border control. The most influential of these terror attacks was the September 11, 2001 airliner hijacking, where al-Qaeda members took over four airplanes and used them as weapons to crash into key governmental and trade buildings. These attacks triggered a focus of American attention on terrorist groups, and led to several wars in Afghanistan and Iraq.

2008 TO PRESENT

Following the economic success of the 1990s and 2000s, the housing industry collapsed, leading to what is known as the **Great Recession** in 2008. In 2008, President Barack Obama was elected as the country's first African-American president. The war on terror continued until 2011, when Obama announced the death of Osama bin Laden, the al-Qaeda leader of the time. Obama's primary focus during his presidency included large stimulus packages and reforms to health insurance programs, an attempt to make healthcare affordable and available to all Americans. In 2016, President Donald Trump took office. His campaigns centered around immigration laws and tax reforms. Other major trends within this time period include a new wave of social equality issues surrounding same-sex rights and racial tension issues within America.

World History

PRE-HISTORICAL AND PRE-MODERN PERIODS

The earliest history of the human race is known as **pre-historical** due to the lack of record keeping. The earliest writing did not appear until the Sumerian civilization in Mesopotamia. In addition to the overt lack of writing from early civilizations, historical records were much more localized than more modern historical records. Ancient history can be broken down many ways, but a common distinction is the **pre-modern period**, including early civilizations such as Egypt, Babylon, and the Greek and Roman Empires. These early civilizations saw invention of technologies such as wood and early metalwork and the domestication of animals. Early civilizations were heavily dependent on agriculture and usually needed access to rivers for a consistent water source. The pre-modern period is viewed as ending with the connection of mainland Europe and some of Africa and Asia by the Greek and Roman Empires. The growth of these empires during this period also saw the worldwide spread of religions such as Judaism and Christianity.

IMPORTANT CONTRIBUTIONS OF THE ANCIENT CIVILIZATIONS OF SUMER, EGYPT, AND INDUS VALLEY

These three ancient civilizations are distinguished by their unique contributions to the development of world civilization:

- **Sumer** used the first known writing system, which enabled the Sumerians to leave a sizeable written record of their myths and religion, advanced the development of the wheel and irrigation, and urbanized their culture.
- **Egypt** was united by the Nile River. Egyptians originally settled in villages on its banks, had a national religion that held their pharaohs as gods, had a central government that controlled civil and artistic affairs, and had writing and libraries.
- The **Indus Valley** was also called Harappan after the city of Harappa. This civilization started in the 3rd and 4th centuries BC and was widely dispersed over 400,000 square miles. It had a unified culture of luxury and refinement, no known national government, an advanced civic system, and prosperous trade routes.

> **Review Video: The Sumerians**
> Visit mometrix.com/academy and enter code: 939880
>
> **Review Video: Ancient Egypt**
> Visit mometrix.com/academy and enter code: 398041

COMMON TRAITS AND CULTURAL IDENTIFIERS OF THE EARLY EMPIRES OF MESOPOTAMIA, EGYPT, GREECE, AND ROME

These empires all had: a strong military; a centralized government; control and standardization of commerce, money, and taxes; a weight system; and an official language.

- **Mesopotamia** had a series of short-term empires that failed because of their oppression of subject peoples.
- **Egypt** also had a series of governments after extending its territory beyond the Nile area. Compared to Mesopotamia, these were more stable and long-lived because they blended different peoples to create a single national identity.

- **Greece** started as a group of city-states that were united by Alexander the Great and joined to create an empire that stretched from the Indus River to Egypt and the Mediterranean coast. Greece blended Greek values with those of the local cultures, which collectively became known as Hellenistic society.
- **Rome** was an Italian city-state that grew into an empire extending from the British Isles across Europe to the Middle East. It lasted for 1,000 years and became the foundation of the Western world's culture, language, and laws.

> **Review Video: Ancient Greece**
> Visit mometrix.com/academy and enter code: 800829

CHARACTERISTICS OF CHINESE AND INDIAN EMPIRES

While the Chinese had the world's longest lasting and continuous empires, the Indians had more of a cohesive culture than an empire system. Their distinct characteristics are as follows:

- **China** – Since the end of the Warring States period in 221 BC, China has functioned as an empire. Although the dynasties changed several times, the basic governmental structure remained the same into the 20th century. The Chinese also have an extensive written record of their culture which heavily emphasizes history, philosophy, and a common religion.
- **India** – The subcontinent was seldom unified in terms of government until the British empire controlled the area in the 19th and 20th centuries. In terms of culture, India has had persistent institutions and religions that have loosely united the people, such as the caste system and guilds. These have regulated daily life more than any government.

MIDDLE AGES IN EUROPEAN HISTORY

The **Middle Ages**, or Medieval times, was a period that ran from approximately 500-1500 AD. The fall of the Greek and Roman civilizations marks the beginning of this period, allowing for the rise of new independent countries, largely relying on the feudal system of government, with kings who allotted power and territory to governors. During this time, the centers of European civilization moved from the Mediterranean countries to France, Germany, and England, where strong national governments were developing. Key events of this time include:

- **Roman Catholicism** was the cultural and religious center of medieval life, extending into politics and economics.
- **Knights**, with their systems of honor, combat, and chivalry, were loyal to their king.
- **Peasants**, or serfs, served a particular lord and his lands.
- Many **universities** were established that still function in modern times.
- The **Crusades**, the recurring wars between European Christians and Middle East Muslims, raged over the Holy Lands.
- Charles the Great, or **Charlemagne**, created an empire across France and Germany around 800 AD.
- The **Black Death plague** swept across Europe from 1347-1350, leaving between one third and one half of the population dead.

> **Review Video: The Middle Ages**
> Visit mometrix.com/academy and enter code: 413133
>
> **Review Video: Trade in the Middle Ages**
> Visit mometrix.com/academy and enter code: 650839

PROTESTANT REFORMATION

The dominance of the **Catholic Church** during the Middle Ages in Europe gave it immense power, which encouraged corrupt practices such as the selling of indulgences and clerical positions. The **Protestant Reformation** began as an attempt to reform the Catholic Church, but eventually led to separation from it. In 1517, Martin Luther posted his *Ninety-Five Theses* on the door of a church in Saxony, which criticized unethical practices, various doctrines, and the authority of the pope. Other reformers such as John Calvin and John Wesley soon followed, but disagreed among themselves and divided along doctrinal lines. Consequently, the Lutheran, Reformed, Calvinist, and Presbyterian churches were founded, among others. In England, King Henry VIII was denied a divorce by the pope, so he broke away and established the **Anglican Church**. The Protestant reformation caused the Catholic Church to finally reform itself, but the Protestant movement continued, resulting in a proliferation of new denominations.

RENAISSANCE

Renaissance is the French word for rebirth, and is used to describe the renewal of interest in ancient Greek and Latin art, literature, and philosophy that occurred in Europe, especially Italy, from the 14th through the 16th centuries. Historically, it was also a time of great scientific inquiry, the rise of individualism, extensive geographical exploration, and the rise of secular values.

Notable figures of the Renaissance include:

- **Petrarch** – An Italian scholar, writer, and key figure in northern Italy, which is where the Renaissance started and where chief patrons came from the merchant class
- **Leonardo da Vinci** – Artist and inventor
- **Michelangelo** and **Raphael** – Artists
- **Desiderius Erasmus** – Applied historical scholarship to the New Testament and laid the seeds for the Protestant Reformation
- **Sir Thomas More** – A lawyer and author who wrote *Utopia*
- **Niccolò Machiavelli** – Author of *The Prince* and *Discourses*, which proposed a science of human nature and civil life
- **William Shakespeare** – A renowned playwright and poet

> **Review Video: Renaissance**
> Visit mometrix.com/academy and enter code: 123100

AGE OF DISCOVERY AND COLONIALISM

Throughout world history, there have been several waves of so-called **new imperialism**, in which established countries attempted to **colonize** territories that had not been explored by European nations. This was called the **Age of Discovery** largely because of the overseas exploration, "discovering" new lands, even though many of the explored lands were already populated. This colonialism was largely driven by the desire for increased wealth and resources, though many participants also sought after religious freedoms. Some of the earliest colonization attempts came from Spain and Portugal, who launched expeditions into Africa and Asia. These early colonial missions established the slave trade throughout Europe and for future colonial expansions. Later waves of colonialism included exploration of the **Americas** by Britain, France, and Spain. Other countries, such as China, Japan, and Russia, practiced imperialism in Asia. The process of colonizing many of these territories led to great injustices, such as the slave trade, and the horrific spread of disease and massacres of people groups such as the Aztecs in central Mexico and many Native American tribes in North America.

Decolonization

Following the powerful race for colonization throughout the world, many of the territories secured by European imperialism fought for their own **freedoms** and **independence**. Supporting these colonial missions was extremely costly and oftentimes, the colonials and the people from the ruling countries had very different priorities, which led to many disagreements. This was the case in the British colonies. Britain enacted many invasive and overcontrolling policies on the 13 established colonies. Tensions grew until the colonials revolted and declared their independence beginning the American Revolutionary War, which would solidify the United States of America as an independent nation. Several other countries worldwide followed suit and eventually secured their own independence. Decolonization largely began in the Americas and ended as late as 1960 in many African countries.

Worldwide Abolition of Slavery

Slavery has been accepted in various forms throughout most of known history. Contemporary to the decolonization period, the issue of slavery started to gain attention as an ethical matter worldwide. The movement to end slavery worldwide is known as **abolitionism** and roughly began in the late 1700s, however, anti-slavery sentiment was a slow-moving cause. The profitability of the slave trade and the use of slaves as the primary workforce for much of agriculture and shipping was a huge deterrent to change. In America, slavery was largely left as a states' right until tensions grew, leading into the American Civil War. Slavery was abolished progressively throughout the world, though at varying rates. Eventually, the United Nations adopted a firm doctrine on slavery, known as the Universal Declaration of Human Rights in 1948, which abolished slavery internationally.

Industrial Revolution

The **Industrial Revolution** started in England with the construction of the first **cotton mill** in 1733. Other inventions and factories followed in rapid succession. The **steel industry** grew exponentially when manufacturers realized that cheap, abundant English coal could be used instead of wood for melting metals. The **steam engine**, which revolutionized transportation and work power, came next. Around 1830, a factory-based, **technological era** was ushered into the rest of Europe. Society changed from agrarian to urban. A need for cheap, unskilled labor resulted in the extensive employment and abuse of women and children, who worked up to 14 hours a day, six days a week in deplorable conditions. Expanding populations brought crowded, unsanitary conditions to the cities, and the factories created air and water pollution. Societies had to deal with these new situations by enacting **child labor laws** and creating **labor unions** to protect the safety of workers.

> **Review Video: The Industrial Revolution**
> Visit mometrix.com/academy and enter code: 372796

Participants of World War I and World War II

World War I, which began in 1914, was fought by the **Allies** including Britain, France, Russia, Greece, Italy, Romania, and Serbia. They fought against the **Central Powers** of Germany, Austria-Hungary, Bulgaria, and Turkey. In 1917, the United States joined the Allies, and Russia withdrew to pursue its own revolution. World War I ended in 1918.

World War II was truly a world war, with fighting occurring on nearly every continent. Germany occupied most of Europe and Northern Africa. It was opposed by the countries of the British Empire, free France and its colonies, Russia, and various national resistance forces. Japan, an **Axis** ally of Germany, had been forcefully expanding its territories in Korea, China, Indonesia, the Philippines, and the South Pacific for many years. When Japan attacked Pearl Harbor in 1941, the

United States joined the **Allied** effort. Italy changed from the Axis to the Allied side mid-war after deposing its own dictator. The war ended in Europe in April 1945, and in Japan in August 1945.

IMPORTANCE OF CROSS-CULTURAL COMPARISONS IN WORLD HISTORY INSTRUCTION

It is important to make **cross-cultural comparisons** when studying world history so that the subject is **holistic** and not oriented to just Western civilization. Not only are the contributions of civilizations around the world important, but they are also interesting and more representative of the mix of cultures present in the United States. It is also critical to the understanding of world relations to study the involvement of European countries and the United States in international commerce, colonization, and development. **Trade routes** from ancient times linked Africa, Asia, and Europe, resulting in exchanges and migrations of people, philosophies, and religions, as well as goods. While many civilizations in the Americas thrived, and some became very sophisticated, many were eventually overcome or even erased by **European expansion**. The historic isolation of China and the modern industrialization of Japan have had huge impacts on their relations with the rest of the world. The more students understand this history and its effects on the modern world, the better they will able to function in their own spheres.

U.S. Government and Citizenship

PRINCIPLES OF THE CONSTITUTION

The six basic principles of the Constitution are:

1. **Popular Sovereignty** – The people establish government and give power to it; the government can function only with the consent of the people.
2. **Limited Government** – The Constitution specifies limits on government authority, and no official or entity is above the law.
3. **Separation of Powers** – Power is divided among three government branches: the legislative (Congress), the executive (President), and the judicial (federal courts).
4. **Checks and Balances** – This is a system that enforces the separation of powers and ensures that each branch has the authority and ability to restrain the powers of the other two branches, thus preventing tyranny.
5. **Judicial Review** – Judges in the federal courts ensure that no act of government is in violation of the Constitution. If an act is unconstitutional, the judicial branch has the power to nullify it.
6. **Federalism** – This is the division of power between the central government and local governments, which limits the power of the federal government and allows states to deal with local problems.

CLASSIC FORMS OF GOVERNMENT

Forms of government that have appeared throughout history include:

- **Feudalism** – This is based on the rule of local lords who are loyal to the king and control the lives and production of those who work on their land.
- **Classical republic** – This form is a representative democracy. Small groups of elected leaders represent the interests of the electorate.
- **Absolute monarchy** – A king or queen has complete control of the military and government.
- **Authoritarianism** – An individual or group has unlimited authority. There is no system in place to restrain the power of the government.
- **Dictatorship** – Those in power are not held responsible to the people.
- **Autocracy** – This is rule by one person (despot), not necessarily a monarch, who uses power tyrannically.
- **Oligarchy** – A small, usually self-appointed elite rules a region.
- **Liberal democracy** – This is a government based on the consent of the people that protects individual rights and freedoms from any intolerance by the majority.
- **Totalitarianism** – All facets of the citizens' lives are controlled by the government.

INFLUENCES OF PHILOSOPHERS ON POLITICAL STUDY

Ancient Greek philosophers **Aristotle** and **Plato** believed political science would lead to order in political matters, and that this scientifically organized order would create stable, just societies.

Thomas Aquinas adapted the ideas of Aristotle to a Christian perspective. His ideas stated that individuals have certain rights, but also certain duties, and that these rights and duties should determine the type and extent of government rule. In stating that laws should limit the role of government, he laid the groundwork for ideas that would eventually become modern constitutionalism.

Niccolò Machiavelli, author of *The Prince*, was a proponent of politics based solely on power.

PARLIAMENTARY AND DEMOCRATIC SYSTEMS OF GOVERNMENT

In a **parliamentary system**, government involves a legislature and a variety of political parties. The head of government, usually a Prime Minister, is typically the head of the dominant party. A head of state can be elected, or this position can be taken by a monarch, such as in Great Britain's constitutional monarchy system.

In a **democratic system** of government, the people elect their government representatives. The term democracy is a Greek term that means "for the rule of the people." There are two forms of democracy—direct and indirect. In a direct democracy, each issue or election is decided by a vote where each individual is counted separately. An indirect democracy employs a legislature that votes on issues that affect large number of people whom the legislative members represent. Democracy can exist as a Parliamentary system or a Presidential system. The US is a presidential, indirect democracy.

BILL OF RIGHTS

The **United States Bill of Rights** was based on principles established by the **Magna Carta** in 1215, the 1688 **English Bill of Rights**, and the 1776 **Virginia Bill of Rights**. In 1791, the federal government added 10 amendments to the United States Constitution that provided the following **protections**:

- Freedom of speech, religion, peaceful assembly, petition of the government, and petition of the press
- The right to keep and bear arms
- No quartering of soldiers on private property without the consent of the owner
- Regulations on government search and seizure
- Provisions concerning prosecution
- The right to a speedy, public trial and the calling of witnesses
- The right to trial by jury
- Freedom from excessive bail or cruel punishment
- These rights are not necessarily the only rights
- Powers not prohibited by the Constitution are reserved to the states

> **Review Video: Bill of Rights**
> Visit mometrix.com/academy and enter code: 585149

MAKING A FORMAL AMENDMENT TO THE CONSTITUTION

So far, there have been only **27 amendments** to the federal Constitution. There are four different ways to change the constitution: two methods for proposal and two methods for ratification:

1. An amendment is proposed by a two-thirds vote in each house of Congress and ratified by three-fourths of the state legislatures.
2. An amendment is proposed by a two-thirds vote in each house of Congress and ratified by three-fourths of the states in special conventions called for that purpose.
3. An amendment is proposed by a national convention that is called by Congress at the request of two-thirds of the state legislatures and ratified by three-fourths of the state legislatures.

4. An amendment is proposed by a national convention that is called by Congress at the request of two-thirds of the state legislatures and ratified by three-fourths of the states in special conventions called for that purpose.

DIVISION OF POWERS

The **division of powers** in the federal government system is as follows:

- **National** – This level can coin money, regulate interstate and foreign trade, raise and maintain armed forces, declare war, govern United States territories and admit new states, and conduct foreign relations.
- **Concurrent** – This level can levy and collect taxes, borrow money, establish courts, define crimes and set punishments, and claim private property for public use.
- **State** – This level can regulate trade and business within the state, establish public schools, pass license requirements for professionals, regulate alcoholic beverages, conduct elections, and establish local governments.

There are three types of **delegated powers** granted by the Constitution:

1. **Expressed or enumerated powers** – These are specifically spelled out in the Constitution.
2. **Implied** – These are not expressly stated, but are reasonably suggested by the expressed powers.
3. **Inherent** – These are powers not expressed by the Constitution but ones that national governments have historically possessed, such as granting diplomatic recognition.

Powers can also be classified as reserved or exclusive. **Reserved powers** are not granted to the national government, but not denied to the states. **Exclusive powers** are those reserved to the national government, including concurrent powers.

STAGES OF EXTENDING SUFFRAGE IN THE U.S.

Originally, the Constitution of 1789 provided the right to vote only to white male property owners. Through the years, suffrage was extended through the following five stages.

1. In the early 1800s, states began to eliminate **property ownership** and **tax payment qualifications**.
2. By 1810, there were no more **religious tests** for voting. In the late 1800s, the 15th Amendment protected citizens from being denied the right to vote because of **race or color**.
3. In 1920, the 19th Amendment prohibited the denial of the right to vote because of **gender**, and women were given the right to vote.
4. Passed in 1961 and ratified in 1964, the 23rd Amendment added the voters of the **District of Columbia** to the presidential electorate and eliminated the poll tax as a condition for voting in federal elections. The **Voting Rights Act of 1965** prohibited disenfranchisement through literacy tests and various other means of discrimination.
5. In 1971, the 26th Amendment set the minimum voting age at **18 years of age**.

MAJOR SUPREME COURT CASES

Out of the many Supreme Court rulings, several have had critical historical importance. These include:

- **Marbury v. Madison** (1803) – This ruling established judicial review as a power of the Supreme Court.
- **Dred Scott v. Sandford** (1857) – This decision upheld property rights over human rights in the case of a slave who had been transported to a free state by his master, but was still considered a slave.
- **Brown v. Board of Education** (1954) – The Court ruled that segregation was a violation of the Equal Protection Clause and that the "separate but equal" practice in education was unconstitutional. This decision overturned the 1896 Plessy v. Ferguson ruling that permitted segregation if facilities were equal.
- **Miranda v. Arizona** (1966) – This ruling compelled the reading of Miranda rights to those arrested for crimes the law. It ensured that confessions could not be illegally obtained and that citizen rights to fair trials and protection under the law would be upheld.

> **Review Video: Marbury v. Madison**
> Visit mometrix.com/academy and enter code: 573964
>
> **Review Video: What was the Dred Scott Decision?**
> Visit mometrix.com/academy and enter code: 364838

FAMOUS SPEECHES IN U.S. HISTORY THAT DEFINED GOVERNMENT POLICY, FOREIGN RELATIONS, AND AMERICAN SPIRIT

Among the best-known speeches and famous lines known to modern Americans are the following:

- The **Gettysburg Address** – Made by Abraham Lincoln on November 19, 1863, it dedicated the Gettysburg battleground's cemetery.
- The **Fourteen Points** – Made by Woodrow Wilson on January 18, 1918, this outlined Wilson's plans for peace and the League of Nations.
- **Address to Congress** – Made by Franklin Roosevelt on December 8, 1941, it declared war on Japan and described the attack on Pearl Harbor as "a day which will live in infamy."
- **Inaugural Address** – Made by John F. Kennedy on January 20, 1961, it contained the famous line: "Ask not what your country can do for you, ask what you can do for your country."
- **Berlin Address** – Made by John F. Kennedy on June 26, 1963, it contained the famous line "Ich bin ein Berliner," which expressed empathy for West Berliners in their conflict with the Soviet Union.
- **"I Have a Dream"** and **"I See the Promised Land"** – Made by Martin Luther King, Jr. on August 28, 1963 and April 3, 1968, respectively, these speeches were hallmarks of the Civil Rights Movement.
- **Brandenburg Gate speech** – Made by Ronald Reagan on June 12, 1987, this speech was about the Berlin Wall and the end of the Cold War. It contained the famous line "Tear down this wall."

CLOSED AND OPEN PRIMARIES IN A DIRECT PRIMARY SYSTEM

The **direct primary system** is a means for members of a political party to participate in the selection of a candidate from their party to compete against the other party's candidate in a general election. A **closed primary** is a party nominating election in which only declared party members can vote. Party membership is usually established by registration. Currently, 26 states and the District of Columbia use this system. An **open primary** is a party nominating election in which any qualified voter can take part. The voter makes a public choice at the polling place about which primary to participate in, and the choice does not depend on any registration or previous choices. A **blanket primary**, which allowed voters to vote in the primaries of both parties, was used at various times by three states. The Supreme Court ruled against this practice in 2000.

IMPORTANT DOCUMENTS IN UNITED STATES HISTORY AND GOVERNMENT

The following are among the greatest **American documents** because of their impact on foreign and domestic policy:

- Declaration of Independence (1776)
- The Articles of Confederation (1777)
- The Constitution (1787) and the Bill of Rights (1791)
- The Northwest Ordinance (1787)
- The Federalist Papers (1787-88)
- George Washington's Inaugural Address (1789) and Farewell Address (1796)
- The Alien and Sedition Act (1798)
- The Louisiana Purchase Treaty (1803)
- The Monroe Doctrine (1823); The Missouri Compromise (1830)
- The Compromise of 1850
- The Kansas-Nebraska Act (1854)
- The Homestead Act (1862)
- The Emancipation Proclamation (1863)
- The agreement to purchase Alaska (1866)
- The Sherman Anti-Trust Act (1890)
- Theodore Roosevelt's Corollary to the Monroe Doctrine (1905)
- The Social Security Act (1935) and other acts of the New Deal in the 1930s; The Truman Doctrine (1947); The Marshall Plan (1948)
- The Civil Rights Act (1964)

FEDERAL TAXES

The four types of **federal taxes** are:

- **Income taxes on individuals** – This is a complex system because of demands for various exemptions and rates. Further, the schedule of rates can be lowered or raised according to economic conditions in order to stimulate or restrain economic activity. For example, a tax cut can provide an economic stimulus, while a tax increase can slow down the rate of inflation. Personal income tax generates about five times as much as corporate taxes. Rates are based on an individual's income, and range from 10 to 35 percent.
- **Income taxes on corporations** – The same complexity of exemptions and rates exists for corporations as individuals. Taxes can be raised or lowered according to the need to stimulate or restrain the economy.
- **Excise taxes** – These are taxes on specific goods such as tobacco, liquor, automobiles, gasoline, air travel, and luxury items, or on activities such as highway usage by trucks.
- **Customs duties** – These are taxes imposed on imported goods. They serve to regulate trade between the United States and other countries.

UNITED STATES CURRENCY SYSTEM

The Constitution of 1787 gave the United States Congress the central authority to **print or coin money** and to **regulate its value**. Before this time, states were permitted to maintain separate currencies. The currency system is based on a **modified gold standard**. There is an enormous store of gold to back up United States currency housed at Fort Knox, Kentucky. Paper money is actually **Federal Reserve notes** and coins. It is the job of the Bureau of Engraving and Printing in the Treasury Department to design plates, special types of paper, and other security measures for bills and bonds. This money is put into general circulation by the Treasury and Federal Reserve Banks, and is taken out of circulation when worn out. Coins are made at the Bureau of the Mint in Philadelphia, Denver, and San Francisco.

EMPLOYMENT ACT OF 1946

The **Employment Act of 1946** established the following entities to combat unemployment:

- The **Council of Economic Advisers** (CEA) – Composed of a chair and two other members appointed by the President and approved by the Senate, this council assists the President with the development and implementation of U.S. economic policy. The Council members and their staff, located in the Executive Office, are professionals in economics and statistics who forecast economic trends and provide analysis based on evidence-based research.
- The **Economic Report of the President** – This is presented every January by the President to Congress. Based on the work of the Council, the report recommends a program for maximizing employment, and may also recommend legislation.
- **Joint Economic Committee** (JEC) – This is a committee composed of 10 members of the House and 10 members of the Senate that makes a report early each year on its continuous study of the economy. Study is conducted through hearings and research, and the report is made in response to the president's recommendations.

QUALIFICATIONS OF A U.S. CITIZEN

Anyone born in the US, born abroad to a US citizen, or who has gone through a process of **naturalization** to become a citizen, is considered a **citizen** of the United States. It is possible to lose US citizenship as a result of conviction of certain crimes such as treason. Citizenship may also be lost if a citizen pledges an oath to another country or serves in the military of a country engaged in hostilities with the US. A US citizen can also choose to hold dual citizenship, work as an expatriate in another country without losing US citizenship, or even renounce citizenship if he or she so chooses.

RIGHTS, DUTIES, AND RESPONSIBILITIES GRANTED TO OR EXPECTED FROM US CITIZENS

Citizens are granted certain rights under the US government. The most important of these are defined in the **Bill of Rights**, and include freedom of speech, religion, assembly, and a variety of other rights the government is not allowed to remove.

Duties of a U.S. citizen include:

- Paying taxes
- Loyalty to the government, though the US does not prosecute those who criticize or seek to change the government
- Support and defend the Constitution
- Serve in the Armed Forces as required by law
- Obeying laws as set forth by the various levels of government.

Responsibilities of a U.S. citizen include:

- Voting in elections
- Respecting one another's rights and not infringing upon them
- Staying informed about various political and national issues
- Respecting one another's beliefs

United States Political Systems

REPRESENTATIVE DEMOCRACY

In a system of government characterized as a representative democracy, voters elect **representatives** to act in their interests. Typically, a representative is elected by and responsible to a specific subset of the total population of eligible voters; this subset of the electorate is referred to as a representative's constituency. A **representative democracy** may foster a more powerful legislature than other forms of government systems; to compensate for a strong legislature, most constitutions stipulate that measures must be taken to balance the powers within government, such as the creation of a separate judicial branch. Representative democracy became popular in post-industrial nations where increasing numbers of people expressed an interest in politics, but where technology and census counts remained incompatible with systems of direct democracy. Today, the majority of the world's population resides in representative democracies, including constitutional monarchies that possess a strong representative branch.

DEMOCRACY

Democracy, or rule by the people, is a form of government in which power is vested in the people and in which policy decisions are made by the majority in a decision-making process such as an election that is open to all or most citizens. Definitions of democracy have become more generalized and include aspects of society and political culture in democratic societies that do not necessarily represent a form of government. What defines a democracy varies, but some of the characteristics of a democracy could include the presence of a middle class, the presence of a civil society, a free market, political pluralism, universal suffrage, and specific rights and freedoms. In practice however, democracies do have limits on specific freedoms, which are justified as being necessary to maintain democracy and ensure democratic freedoms. For example, freedom of association is limited in democracies for individuals and groups that pose a threat to government or to society.

PRESIDENTIAL/CONGRESSIONAL SYSTEM

In a **presidential system**, also referred to as a **congressional system**, the legislative branch and the executive branches are elected separately from one another. The features of a presidential system include a *president* who serves as both the head of state and the head of the government, who has no formal relationship with the legislative branch, who is not a voting member, who cannot introduce bills, and who has a fixed term of office. *Elections* are held at scheduled times. The president's *cabinet* carries out the policies of the executive branch and the legislative branch.

POLITICAL PARTIES

A **political party** is an organization that advocates a particular ideology and seeks to gain power within government. The tendency of members of political parties to support their party's policies and interests relative to those of other parties is referred to as partisanship. Often, a political party is comprised of members whose positions, interests and perspectives on policies vary, despite having shared interests in the general ideology of the party. As such, many political parties will have divisions within them that have differing opinions on policy. Political parties are often placed on a political spectrum, with one end of the spectrum representing conservative, traditional values and policies and the other end of the spectrum representing radical, progressive value and policies.

TYPES OF PARTY SYSTEMS

There is a variety of **party systems**, including single-party systems, dominant-party systems, and dual-party systems. In a **single-party system**, only one political party may hold power. In this type of system, minor parties may be permitted, but they must accept the leadership of the dominant party. **Dominant-party systems** allow for multiple parties in opposition of one another, however the dominant party is the only party considered to have power. A **two-party system**, such as in the United States, is one in which there are two dominant political parties. In such a system, it is very difficult for any other parties to win an election. In most two-party systems, there is typically one right wing party and one left wing party.

DEMOCRATIC PARTY

The **Democratic Party** was founded in 1792. In the United States, it is one of the two dominant political parties, along with the Republican Party. The Democratic Party is to the left of the Republican Party. The Democratic Party began as a conservative party in the mid-1800s, shifting to the left during the 1900s. There are many factions within the Democratic Party in the United States. The **Democratic National Committee (DNC)** is the official organization of the Democratic Party, and it develops and promotes the party's platform and coordinates fundraising and election strategies. There are Democratic committees in every U.S. state and most U.S. counties. The official symbol of the Democratic Party is the donkey.

REPUBLICAN PARTY

The **Republican Party** is often referred to as the **GOP**, which stands for *Grand Old Party*. The Republican Party is considered socially conservative and economically neoliberal relative to the Democratic Party. Like the Democratic Party, there are factions within the Republic Party that agree with the party's overall ideology, but disagree with the party's positions on specific issues. The official symbol of the Republican Party is the elephant. The **Republican National Committee (RNC)** is the official organization of the Republican Party, and it develops and promotes the party's platform and coordinates fundraising and election strategies. There are Republican committees in every U.S. state and most U.S. counties.

POLITICAL CAMPAIGNS

A **political campaign** is an organized attempt to influence the decisions of a particular group of people. Examples of campaigns could include elections or efforts to influence policy changes. One of the first steps in a campaign is to develop a **campaign message**. The message must then be delivered to the individuals and groups that the campaign is trying to reach and influence through a campaign plan. There are various ways for a campaign to communicate its message to the intended audience, including public media; paid media such as television, radio and newspaper ads, billboards and the internet; public events such as protests and rallies; meetings with speakers; mailings; canvassing; fliers; and websites. Through these efforts, the campaign attempts to attract additional support and, ultimately, to reach the goal of the campaign.

> **Review Video: Political Campaigns**
> Visit mometrix.com/academy and enter code: 838608

VOTING

Voting is a method of decision making that allows people to express their opinion or preference for a candidate or for a proposed resolution of an issue. In a democratic system, voting typically takes place as part of an **election**. An individual participates in the voting process by casting a vote, or a **ballot**; ballots are produced by states A *secret ballot* can be used at polls to protect voters' privacy. Individuals can also vote via *absentee ballot*. In some states voters can write-in a name to cast a vote for a candidate that is not on the ballot. Some states also use *straight ticket voting*, allowing the voter to vote for one party for all the elected positions on the ballot.

U.S. ELECTIONS

In the United States, **officials** are elected at the federal, state and local levels. The first two articles of the Constitution, as well as various amendments, establish how **federal elections** are to be held. The **President** is elected indirectly, by electors of an electoral college. Members of the electoral college nearly always vote along the lines of the popular vote of their respective states. Members of **Congress** are directly elected. At the state level, state law establishes most aspects of how elections are held. There are many elected offices at the state level, including a governor and state legislature. There are also elected offices at the local level.

VOTER ELIGIBILITY

The United States Constitution establishes that individual people are permitted to **vote** in elections if they are citizens of the United States and are at least eighteen years old. The **fifteenth** and **nineteenth amendments** of the United States Constitution stipulate that the right to vote cannot be denied to any United States citizen based on race or sex, respectively. States regulate voter eligibility beyond the minimum qualifications stipulated by the United States Constitution. Depending on the regulations of individual states, individuals may be denied the right to vote if they are convicted criminals.

ADVANTAGES AND DISADVANTAGES TO TWO-PARTY SYSTEM

Advocates of the **two-party system** argue that its advantages are that they are stable because they enable policies and government to change slowly rather than rapidly due to the relative lack of influence from small parties representing unconventional ideologies. In addition, they seem to drive voters toward a middle ground and are less susceptible to revolutions, coups, or civil wars. Among the critiques of the two-party system is the claim that stability in and of itself is not necessarily desirable, as it often comes at the expense of democracy. Critics also argue that the two-party system promotes negative political campaigns, in which candidates and their respective parties only take positions on issues that will differentiate themselves from their opponents, rather than focusing on policy issues that are of significance to citizens. Another concern is that if one of the two major parties becomes weak, a dominant-party system may develop.

CAMPAIGN MESSAGE

Political campaigns consist of three main elements, which are the campaign message, the money that is necessary to run the campaign, and the "machine," or the capital that is necessary to run the campaign. A campaign message is a succinct statement expressing why voters should support the campaign and the individual or policy associated with that campaign. The message is one of the most significant aspects of a political campaign, and a considerable amount of time, money and effort is invested in devising a successful campaign message, as it will be repeated throughout the campaign and will be one of the most identifying factors of the campaign.

MODERN ELECTION CAMPAIGNS IN THE U.S.

Political campaigns in the U.S. have changed and continue to change as advances in technology permit varied campaign methods. Campaigns represent a civic practice, and today they are a high profit industry. The U.S. has an abundance of professional political consultants that employ highly sophisticated campaign management strategies and tools. The election process varies widely between the federal, state and local levels. Campaigns are typically controlled by individual candidates, rather than by the parties that they are associated with. Larger campaigns utilize a vast array of media to reach their targeted audiences, while smaller campaigns are typically limited to direct contact with voters, direct mailings and other forms of low-cost advertising to reach their audiences. In addition to fundraising and spending done by individual candidates, party committees and political action committees also raise money and spend it in ways that will advance the cause of the particular campaign they are associated with.

VOTER REGISTRATION

Individuals have the responsibility of **registering to vote**. Every state except North Dakota requires citizens to register to vote. In an effort to increase voter turnout, Congress passed the **National Voter Registration Act** in 1993. This Act is also known as "Motor Voter," because it required states to make the voter registration process easier by providing registration services through drivers' license registration centers, as well as through disability centers, schools, libraries, and mail-in registration. Some states are exempt because they permit same-day voter registration, which enables voters to register to vote on the day of the election.

PRESIDENTIAL ELECTIONS

The President of the United States is elected **indirectly**, by members of an **electoral college**. Members of the electoral college nearly always vote along the lines of the popular vote of their respective states. The winner of a presidential election is the candidate with at least 270 electoral college votes. It is possible for a candidate to win the electoral vote, and lose the popular vote. Incumbent Presidents and challengers typically prefer a balanced ticket, where the President and Vice President are elected together and generally balance one another with regard to geography, ideology, or experience working in government. The nominated Vice Presidential candidate is referred to as the President's *running mate*.

ELECTORAL COLLEGE

Electoral college votes are cast by state by a group of electors; each elector casts one electoral college vote. State law regulates how states cast their electoral college votes. In all states except Maine and Nebraska, the candidate winning the most votes receives all the state's electoral college votes. In Maine and Nebraska two electoral votes are awarded based on the winner of the statewide election, and the rest go to the highest vote-winner in each of the state's congressional districts. Critics of the electoral college argue that it is undemocratic because the President is elected indirectly as opposed to directly, and that it creates inequality between voters in different states because candidates focus attention on voters in swing states who could influence election results. Critics argue that the electoral college provides more representation for voters in small states than large states, where more voters are represented by a single electoral than in small states and discriminates against candidates that do not have support concentrated in a given state.

CONGRESSIONAL ELECTIONS

Congressional elections are every two years. Members of the **House of Representatives** are elected for a two year term and elections occur every two years on the first Tuesday after November 1st in even years. A Representative is elected from each of the 435 House districts in the U.S. House elections usually occur in the same year as Presidential elections. Members of the **Senate** are elected to six year terms; one-third of the Senate is elected every two years. Per the Seventeenth Amendment to the Constitution, which was passed in 1913, Senators are elected by the electorate of states. The country is divided into **Congressional districts**. Critics argue that this division eliminates voter choice, sometimes creating areas in which Congressional races are uncontested. Every ten years **redistricting** of Congressional districts occurs. However, redistricting is often partisan and therefore reduces the number of competitive districts. The division of voting districts resulting in an unfair advantage to one party in elections is known as gerrymandering. Gerrymandering has been criticized as being undemocratic.

State and Local Elections

State elections are regulated by state laws and constitutions. In keeping with the ideal of separation of powers, the legislature and the executive are elected separately at the state level, as they are at the federal level. In each state, a **Governor** and a **Lieutenant Governor** are elected. In some states, the Governor and Lieutenant Governor are elected on a joint ticket, while in other states they are elected separately from one another. In some states, executive positions such as Attorney General and Secretary of State are also elected offices. All members of state legislatures are elected, including state senators and state representatives. Depending on the state, members of the state supreme court and other members of the state judiciary may be chosen in elections. Local government can include the governments of counties and cities. At this level, nearly all government offices are filled through an election process. Elected local offices may include sheriffs, county school boards, and city mayors.

Campaign Finance and Independent Expenditures

An individual or group is legally permitted to make unlimited **independent expenditures** in association with federal elections. An independent expenditure is an expenditure that is made to pay for a form of communication that supports the election or defeat of a candidate; the expenditure must be made independently from the candidate's own campaign. To be considered independent, the communication may not be made with the cooperation or consultation with, or at the request or suggestion of, any candidate, any committees or political party associated with the candidate, or any agent that acts on behalf of the candidate. There are no restrictions on the amount that anyone may spend on an independent expenditure, however, any individual making an independent expenditure must report it and disclose the source of the funds they used.

Campaign Finance and Activities of Political Parties

Political parties participate in federal elections at the local, state and national levels. Most **party committees** must register with the **Federal Election Committee** and file reports disclosing federal campaign activities. While party committees may contribute funds directly to federal candidates, the amounts that they contribute are restricted by the campaign finance contribution limits. National and state party committees are permitted to make additional **coordinated expenditures**, within limits, to assist their nominees in general elections. However, national party committees are not permitted to make unlimited **independent expenditures**, also known as soft money, to support or oppose federal candidates. State and local party committees are also not permitted to use soft money for the purpose of supporting or opposing federal candidates, but they are allowed to spend soft money, up to a limit of $10,000 per source, on voter registration and on efforts aimed at increasing voter participation. All party committees are required to register themselves and file disclosure reports with the Federal Election Committee once their federal election activities exceed specified monetary limits.

Public Opinion

Public opinion represents the collective attitudes of individual members of the adult population in the United States of America. There are many varied forces that may influence public opinion. These forces include *public relations efforts* on the part of political campaigns and political parties. Another force affecting political opinion is the *political media* and the *mass media*. Public opinion is very important during elections, particularly Presidential elections, as it is an indicator of how candidates are perceived by the public and of how well candidates are doing during their election campaigns. Public opinion is often measured and evaluated using survey sampling.

Mass Media and Public Opinion

The **mass media** is critical in developing public opinion. In the short term people generally evaluate information they receive relative to their own beliefs; in the long term the media may have a considerable impact on people's beliefs. Due to the impact of the media on an individual's beliefs, some experts consider the effects of the media on an individual's independence and autonomy to be negative. Others view the impact of the media on individuals as a positive one, because the media provides information that expands worldviews and enriches lives, and fosters the development of opinions that are informed by many sources of information. A critical aspect of the relationship between the media and public opinion is who is in control of the knowledge and information that is disseminated through the media. Whoever controls the media can propagate their own agenda. The extent to which an individual interprets and evaluates information received through the media can influence behaviors such as voting patterns, consumer behavior, and social attitudes.

Economics

EFFECTS ECONOMY CAN HAVE ON PURCHASING DECISIONS OF CONSUMERS

The **economy** plays an important role in how careful consumers are when using their resources. It also affects what they perceive as needs as opposed to what they perceive as wants. When the economy is doing well, unemployment figures are low, which means that people can easily attain their basic necessities. As a result, consumers are typically more willing to spend their financial resources. Consumers will also be more willing to spend their resources on products and services that are not necessary to their survival, but are instead products and services that they enjoy having and believe increase their quality of life. On the other hand, when the economy is in a slump, consumers are much more likely to cut back on their spending because they perceive a significantly higher risk of being unable to acquire basic necessities due to a lack of financial resources.

COMMON TERMINOLOGY IN ECONOMICS

- **Supply** is the amount of a product or service available to consumers.
- **Demand** is how much consumers are willing to pay for the product or service. These two facets of the market determine the price of goods and services. The higher the demand, the higher the price the supplier will charge; the lower the demand, the lower the price.
- **Scarcity** is a measure of supply. Demand is high when there is a scarcity, or low supply, of an item.
- **Choice** is related to scarcity and demand in that when an item in demand is scarce, consumers have to make difficult choices. They can pay more for an item, go without it, or go elsewhere for the item.
- **Money** is the cash or currency available for payment.
- **Resources** are the items one can barter in exchange for goods. Money is the cash reserves of a nation, while resources are the minerals, labor force, armaments, and other raw materials or assets a nation has available for trade.
- **Taxes** are legally required payments to the government for income, goods bought, or property owned. Taxes are categorized as direct or indirect.
- **Tariffs** are taxes specifically imposed on imports from another country.

EFFECTS OF ECONOMIC DOWNTURN OR RECESSION

When a **recession** happens, people at all levels of society feel the economic effects. For example:

- High **unemployment** results because businesses have to cut back to keep costs low, and may no longer have the work for the labor force they once did.
- **Mortgage rates** go up on variable-rate loans as banks try to increase their revenues, but the higher rates cause some people who cannot afford increased housing costs to sell or suffer foreclosure.
- **Credit** becomes less available as banks try to lessen their risk. This decreased lending affects business operations, home and auto loans, etc.
- **Stock market prices** drop, and the lower dividends paid to stockholders reduce their income. This is especially hard on retired people who rely on stock dividends.
- **Psychological depression and trauma** may occur in those who suffer bankruptcy, unemployment, or foreclosure during a depression.

Economic Effects of Abundant Natural Resources

The **positive economic aspects** of abundant natural resources are an increase in **revenue and new jobs** where those resources have not been previously accessed. For example, the growing demand for oil, gas, and minerals has led companies to venture into new regions.

The **negative economic aspects** of abundant natural resources are:

- **Environmental degradation**, if sufficient regulations are not in place to counter strip mining, deforestation, and contamination.
- **Corruption**, if sufficient regulations are not in place to counter bribery, political favoritism, and exploitation of workers as greedy companies try to maximize their profits.
- **Social tension**, if the resources are privately owned such that the rich become richer and the poor do not reap the benefits of their national resources. Class divisions become wider, resulting in social unrest.
- **Dependence**, if income from the natural resources is not used to develop other industries as well. In this situation, the economy becomes dependent on one source, and faces potential crises if natural disasters or depletion take away that income source.

Economics and Kinds of Economies

Economics is the study of the buying choices that people make, the production of goods and services, and how our market system works. The two kinds of economies are command and market. In a **command economy**, the government controls what and how much is produced, the methods used for production, and the distribution of goods and services. In a **market economy**, producers make decisions about methods and distribution on their own. These choices are based on what will sell and bring a profit in the marketplace. In a market economy, consumers ultimately affect these decisions by choosing whether or not to buy certain goods and services. The United States has a market economy.

Market Economy

The five characteristics of a **market economy** are:

- **Economic freedom** – There is freedom of choice with respect to jobs, salaries, production, and price.
- **Economic incentives** – A positive incentive is to make a profit. However, if the producer tries to make too high a profit, the consequences might be that no one will purchase the item at that price. A negative incentive would be a drop in profits, causing the producer to decrease or discontinue production. A boycott, which might cause the producer to change business practices or policies, is also a negative economic incentive.
- **Competition** – There is more than one producer for any given product. Consumers thereby have choices about what to buy, which are usually made based on quality and price. Competition is an incentive for a producer to make the best product at the best price. Otherwise, producers will lose business to the competition.
- **Private ownership** – Production and profits belong to an individual or to a private company, not to the government.
- **Limited government** – Government plays no role in the economic decisions of its individual citizens.

Factors of Production and Types of Markets That Create Economic Flow

The factors of **production** are:

- **Land** – This includes not only actual land, but also forests, minerals, water, etc.
- **Labor** – This is the work force required to produce goods and services, including factors such as talent, skills, and physical labor.
- **Capital** – This is the cash and material equipment needed to produce goods and services, including buildings, property, tools, office equipment, roads, etc.
- **Entrepreneurship** – Persons with initiative can capitalize on the free market system by producing goods and services.

The two types of markets are factor and product markets. The **factor market** consists of the people who exchange their services for wages. The people are sellers and companies are buyers. The **product market** is the selling of products to the people who want to buy them. The people are the buyers and the companies are the sellers. This exchange creates a circular economic flow in which money goes from the producers to workers as wages, and then flows back to producers in the form of payment for products.

Economic Impact of Technology

At the start of the 21st century, the role of **information and communications technologies** (ICT) grew rapidly as the economy shifted to a knowledge-based one. Output is increasing in areas where ICT is used intensively, which are service areas and knowledge-intensive industries such as finance; insurance; real estate; business services; health care; environmental goods and services; and community, social, and personal services. Meanwhile, the economic share for manufacturers is declining in medium- and low-technology industries such as chemicals, food products, textiles, gas, water, electricity, construction, and transport and communication services. Industries that have traditionally been high-tech, such as aerospace, computers, electronics, and pharmaceuticals are remaining steady in terms of their economic share. Technology has become the strongest factor in determining **per capita income** for many countries. The ease of technology investments as compared to industries that involve factories and large labor forces has resulted in more foreign investments in countries that do not have natural resources to call upon.

Geography

GEOGRAPHY

Geography involves learning about the world's primary **physical and cultural patterns** to help understand how the world functions as an interconnected and dynamic system. Combining information from different sources, geography teaches the basic patterns of climate, geology, vegetation, human settlement, migration, and commerce. Thus, geography is an **interdisciplinary** study of history, anthropology, and sociology. **History** incorporates geography in discussions of battle strategies, slavery (trade routes), ecological disasters (the Dust Bowl of the 1930s), and mass migrations. Geographic principles are useful when reading **literature** to help identify and visualize the setting, and also when studying **earth science**, **mathematics** (latitude, longitude, sun angle, and population statistics), and **fine arts** (song, art, and dance often reflect different cultures). Consequently, a good background in geography can help students succeed in other subjects as well.

THEMES OF GEOGRAPHY

The five themes of geography are:

- **Location** – This includes relative location (described in terms of surrounding geography such as a river, sea coast, or mountain) and absolute location (the specific point of latitude and longitude).
- **Place** – This includes physical characteristics (deserts, plains, mountains, and waterways) and human characteristics (features created by humans, such as architecture, roads, religion, industries, and food and folk practices).
- **Human-environmental interaction** – This includes human adaptation to the environment (using an umbrella when it rains), human modification of the environment (building terraces to prevent soil erosion), and human dependence on the environment for food, water, and natural resources.
- **Movement** – Interaction through trade, migration, communications, political boundaries, ideas, and fashions.
- **Regions** – This includes formal regions (a city, state, country, or other geographical organization as defined by political boundaries), functional regions (defined by a common function or connection, such as a school district), and vernacular regions (informal divisions determined by perceptions or one's mental image, such as the "Far East").

> **Review Video: Regional Geography**
> Visit mometrix.com/academy and enter code: 350378

AREAS COVERED BY GEOGRAPHY

Geography is connected to many issues and provides answers to many everyday questions. Some of the areas covered by geography include:

- Geography investigates global climates, landforms, economies, political systems, human cultures, and migration patterns.
- Geography answers questions not only about where something is located, but also why it is there, how it got there, and how it is related to other things around it.
- Geography explains why people move to certain regions (climate, availability of natural resources, arable land, etc.).
- Geography explains world trade routes and modes of transportation.
- Geography identifies where various animals live and where various crops and forests grow.

- Geography identifies and locates populations that follow certain religions.
- Geography provides statistics on population numbers and growth, which aids in economic and infrastructure planning for cities and countries.

PHYSICAL AND CULTURAL GEOGRAPHY AND PHYSICAL AND POLITICAL LOCATIONS

- **Physical geography** is the study of climate, water, and land and their relationships with each other and humans. Physical geography locates and identifies the earth's surface features and explores how humans thrive in various locations according to crop and goods production.
- **Cultural geography** is the study of the influence of the environment on human behaviors as well as the effect of human activities such as farming, building settlements, and grazing livestock on the environment. Cultural geography also identifies and compares the features of different cultures and how they influence interactions with other cultures and the earth.
- **Physical location** refers to the placement of the hemispheres and the continents.
- **Political location** refers to the divisions within continents that designate various countries. These divisions are made with borders, which are set according to boundary lines arrived at by legal agreements.

Both physical and political locations can be precisely determined by geographical surveys and by latitude and longitude.

SPATIAL ORGANIZATION

Spatial organization in geography refers to how things or people are grouped in a given space anywhere on earth. Spatial organization applies to the **placement of settlements**, whether hamlets, towns, or cities. These settlements are located to make the distribution of goods and services convenient. For example, in farm communities, people come to town to get groceries, to attend church and school, and to access medical services. It is more practical to provide these things to groups than to individuals. These settlements, historically, have been built close to water sources and agricultural areas. Lands that are topographically difficult, have few resources, or experience extreme temperatures do not have as many people as temperate zones and flat plains, where it is easier to live. Within settlements, a town or city will be organized into commercial and residential neighborhoods, with hospitals, fire stations, and shopping centers centrally located. All of these organizational considerations are spatial in nature.

IMPORTANT TERMS RELATED TO MAPS

The most important terms used when describing items on a map or globe are:

- **Latitude and longitude** – Latitude and longitude are the imaginary lines (horizontal and vertical, respectively) that divide the globe into a grid. Both are measured using the 360 degrees of a circle.
- **Coordinates** – These are the latitude and longitude measures for a place.
- **Absolute location** – This is the exact spot where coordinates meet. The grid system allows the location of every place on the planet to be identified.
- **Equator** – This is the line at 0° latitude that divides the earth into two equal halves called hemispheres.
- **Parallels** – This is another name for lines of latitude because they circle the earth in parallel lines that never meet.

- **Meridians** – This is another name for lines of longitude. The Prime Meridian is located at 0° longitude, and is the starting point for measuring distance (both east and west) around the globe. Meridians circle the earth and connect at the Poles.

> **Review Video: 5 Elements of any Map**
> Visit mometrix.com/academy and enter code: 437727

TYPES OF MAPS
- A **physical map** is one that shows natural features such as mountains, rivers, lakes, deserts, and plains. Color is used to designate the different features.
- A **topographic map** is a type of physical map that shows the relief and configuration of a landscape, such as hills, valleys, fields, forest, roads, and settlements. It includes natural and human-made features.
- A **topological map** is one on which lines are stretched or straightened for the sake of clarity, but retain their essential geometric relationship. This type of map is used, for example, to show the routes of a subway system.
- A **political map** uses lines for state, county, and country boundaries; points or dots for cities and towns; and various other symbols for features such as airports and roads.

MAP STYLES
There are three basic styles of maps:

- **Base maps** – Created from aerial and field surveys, base maps serve as the starting point for topographic and thematic maps.
- **Topographic maps** – These show the natural and human-made surface features of the earth, including mountain elevations, river courses, roads, names of lakes and towns, and county and state lines.
- **Thematic maps** – These use a base or topographic map as the foundation for showing data based on a theme, such as population density, wildlife distribution, hill-slope stability, economic trends, etc.

Scale is the size of a map expressed as a ratio of the actual size of the land (for example, 1 inch on a map represents 1 mile on land). In other words, it is the proportion between a distance on the map and its corresponding distance on earth. The scale determines the level of detail on a map. **Small-scale maps** depict larger areas, but include fewer details. **Large-scale maps** depict smaller areas, but include more details.

TIME ZONES
Time is linked to **longitude** in that a complete rotation of the Earth, or 360° of longitude, occurs every 24 hours. Each hour of time is therefore equivalent to 15° of longitude, or 4 minutes for each 1° turn. By the agreement of 27 nations at the 1884 International Meridian Conference, the time zone system consists of **24 time zones** corresponding to the 24 hours in a day. Although high noon technically occurs when the sun is directly above a meridian, calculating time that way would result in 360 different times for the 360 meridians. Using the 24-hour system, the time is the same for all locations in a 15° zone. The 1884 conference established the meridian passing through Greenwich, England, as the zero point, or **prime meridian**. The halfway point is found at the 180th meridian, a half day from Greenwich. It is called the **International Date Line**, and serves as the place where each day begins and ends on earth.

CARTOGRAPHY

Cartography is the art and science of **mapmaking**. Maps of local areas were drawn by the Egyptians as early as 1300 BC, and the Greeks began making maps of the known world in the 6th century BC. Cartography eventually grew into the field of geography. The first step in modern mapmaking is a **survey**. This involves designating a few key sites of known elevation as benchmarks to allow for measurement of other sites. **Aerial photography** is then used to chart the area by taking photos in sequence. Overlapping photos show the same area from different positions along the flight line. When paired and examined through a stereoscope, the cartographer gets a three-dimensional view that can be made into a **topographical map**. In addition, a field survey (on the ground) is made to determine municipal borders and place names. The second step is to compile the information and **computer-draft** a map based on the collected data. The map is then reproduced or printed.

GLOBE AND MAP PROJECTIONS

A **globe** is the only accurate representation of the earth's size, shape, distance, and direction since it, like the earth, is **spherical**. The flat surface of a map distorts these elements. To counter this problem, mapmakers use a variety of "**map projections**," a system for representing the earth's curvatures on a flat surface through the use of a grid that corresponds to lines of latitude and longitude. Some distortions are still inevitable, though, so mapmakers make choices based on the map scale, the size of the area to be mapped, and what they want the map to show. Some projections can represent a true shape or area, while others may be based on the equator and therefore become less accurate as they near the poles. In summary, all maps have some distortion in terms of the shape or size of features of the spherical earth.

TYPES OF MAP PROJECTIONS

There are three main types of map projections:

- **Conical** – This type of projection superimposes a cone over the sphere of the earth, with two reference parallels secant to the globe and intersecting it. There is no distortion along the standard parallels, but distortion increases further from the chosen parallels. A Bonne projection is an example of a conical projection, in which the areas are accurately represented but the meridians are not on a true scale.
- **Cylindrical** – This is any projection in which meridians are mapped using equally spaced vertical lines and circles of latitude (parallels) are mapped using horizontal lines. A Mercator's projection is a modified cylindrical projection that is helpful to navigators because it allows them to maintain a constant compass direction between two points. However, it exaggerates areas in high latitudes.
- **Azimuthal** – This is a stereographic projection onto a plane centered so that a straight line from the center to any other point represents the shortest distance. This distance can be measured to scale.

> **Review Video: Map Projections**
> Visit mometrix.com/academy and enter code: 327303

HEMISPHERES AND PARALLELS ON THE WORLD MAP

The definitions for these terms are as follows:

- **Northern Hemisphere** – This is the area above, or north, of the equator.
- **Southern Hemisphere** – This is the area below, or south, of the equator.

- **Western Hemisphere** – This is the area between the North and South Poles. It extends west from the Prime Meridian to the International Date Line.
- **Eastern Hemisphere** – This is the area between the North and South Poles. It extends east from the Prime Meridian to the International Date Line.
- **North and South Poles** – Latitude is measured in terms of the number of degrees north and south from the equator. The North Pole is located at 90°N latitude, while the South Pole is located at 90°S latitude.
- **Tropic of Cancer** – This is the parallel, or latitude, 23½° north of the equator.
- **Tropic of Capricorn** – This is the parallel, or latitude, 23½° south of the equator. The region between these two parallels is the tropics. The subtropics is the area located between 23½° and 40° north and south of the equator.
- **Arctic Circle** – This is the parallel, or latitude, 66½° north of the equator.
- **Antarctic Circle** – This is the parallel, or latitude, 66½° south of the equator.

> **Review Video: Geographical Features**
> Visit mometrix.com/academy and enter code: 773539

GPS

Global Positioning System (GPS) is a system of satellites that orbit the Earth and communicate with mobile devices to pinpoint the mobile device's position. This is accomplished by determining the distance between the mobile device and at least three satellites. A mobile device might calculate a distance of 400 miles between it and the first satellite. The possible locations that are 400 miles from the first satellite and the mobile device will fall along a circle. The possible locations on Earth relative to the other two satellites will fall somewhere along different circles. The point on Earth at which these three circles intersect is the location of the mobile device. The process of determining position based on distance measurements from three satellites is called **trilateration**.

Physical and Cultural Features of Geographic Locations and Countries

Physical Features

- **Vegetation zones, or biomes** – Forests, grasslands, deserts, and tundra are the four main types of vegetation zones.
- **Climate zones** – Tropical, dry, temperate, continental, and polar are the five different types of climate zones. Climate is the long-term average weather conditions of a place.

Cultural Features

- **Population density** – This is the number of people living in each square mile or kilometer of a place. It is calculated by dividing population by area.
- **Religion** – This is the identification of the dominant religions of a place, whether Christianity, Hinduism, Judaism, Buddhism, Islam, Shinto, Taoism, or Confucianism. All of these originated in Asia.
- **Languages** – This is the identification of the dominant or official language of a place. There are 12 major language families. The Indo-European family (which includes English, Russian, German, French, and Spanish) is spoken over the widest geographic area, but Mandarin Chinese is spoken by the most people.

Geomorphology

The study of landforms is call **geomorphology** or physiography, a science that considers the relationships between *geological structures* and *surface landscape features*. It is also concerned with the processes that change these features, such as erosion, deposition, and plate tectonics. Biological factors can also affect landforms. Examples are when corals build a coral reef or when plants contribute to the development of a salt marsh or a sand dune. Rivers, coastlines, rock types, slope formation, ice, erosion, and weathering are all part of geomorphology. A **landform** is a landscape feature or geomorphological unit. These include hills, plateaus, mountains, deserts, deltas, canyons, mesas, marshes, swamps, and valleys. These units are categorized according to elevation, slope, orientation, stratification, rock exposure, and soil type. Landform elements include pits, peaks, channels, ridges, passes, pools, and plains. The highest order landforms are continents and oceans. Elementary landforms such as segments, facets, and relief units are the smallest homogenous divisions of a land surface at a given scale or resolution.

OCEANS, SEAS, LAKES, RIVERS, AND CANALS

- **Oceans** are the largest bodies of water on earth and cover nearly 71% of the earth's surface. There are five major oceans: Atlantic, Pacific (largest and deepest), Indian, Arctic, and Southern (surrounds Antarctica).
- **Seas** are smaller than oceans and are somewhat surrounded by land like a lake, but lakes are fresh water and seas are salt water. Seas include the Mediterranean, Baltic, Caspian, Caribbean, and Coral.
- **Lakes** are bodies of water in a depression on the earth's surface. Examples of lakes are the Great Lakes and Lake Victoria.
- **Rivers** are a channeled flow of water that start out as a spring or stream formed by runoff from rain or snow. Rivers flow from higher to lower ground, and usually empty into a sea or ocean. Great rivers of the world include the Amazon, Nile, Rhine, Mississippi, Ganges, Mekong, and Yangtze.
- **Canals** are artificial waterways constructed by humans to connect two larger water bodies. Examples of canals are the Panama and the Suez.

MOUNTAINS, HILLS, FOOTHILLS, VALLEYS, PLATEAUS, AND MESAS

The definitions for these geographical features are as follows:

- **Mountains** are elevated landforms that rise fairly steeply from the earth's surface to a summit of at least 1,000-2,000 feet (definitions vary) above sea level.
- **Hills** are elevated landforms that rise 500-2,000 feet above sea level.
- **Foothills** are a low series of hills found between a plain and a mountain range.
- **Valleys** are a long depression located between hills or mountains. They are usually products of river erosion. Valleys can vary in terms of width and depth, ranging from a few feet to thousands of feet.
- **Plateaus** are elevated landforms that are fairly flat on top. They may be as high as 10,000 feet above sea level and are usually next to mountains.
- **Mesas** are flat areas of upland. Their name is derived from the Spanish word for table. They are smaller than plateaus and often found in arid or semi-arid areas.

FORMATION OF MOUNTAINS

Mountains are formed by the movement of geologic plates, which are rigid slabs of rocks beneath the earth's crust that float on a layer of partially molten rock in the earth's upper mantle. As the plates collide, they push up the crust to form mountains. This process is called **orogeny**. There are three basic forms of orogeny:

- If the collision of continental plates causes the crust to buckle and fold, a chain of **folded mountains**, such as the Appalachians, the Alps, or the Himalayas, is formed.
- If the collision of the plates causes a denser oceanic plate to go under a continental plate, a process called **subduction**; strong horizontal forces lift and fold the margin of the continent. A mountain range like the Andes is the result.
- If an oceanic plate is driven under another oceanic plate, **volcanic mountains** such as those in Japan and the Philippines are formed.

Coral Reefs

Coral reefs are formed from millions of tiny, tube-shaped **polyps**, an animal life form encased in tough limestone skeletons. Once anchored to a rocky surface, polyps eat plankton and miniscule shellfish caught with poisonous tentacles near their mouth. Polyps use calcium carbonate absorbed from chemicals given off by algae to harden their body armor and cement themselves together in fantastic shapes of many colors. Polyps reproduce through eggs and larvae, but the reef grows by branching out shoots of polyps. There are three types of coral reefs:

- **Fringing reefs** – These surround, or "fringe," an island.
- **Barrier reefs** – Over the centuries, a fringe reef grows so large that the island sinks down from the weight, and the reef becomes a barrier around the island. Water trapped between the island and the reef is called a lagoon.
- **Atolls** – Eventually, the sinking island goes under, leaving the coral reef around the lagoon.

Plains, Deserts, Deltas, and Basins

- **Plains** are extensive areas of low-lying, flat, or gently undulating land, and are usually lower than the landforms around them. Plains near the seacoast are called lowlands.
- **Deserts** are large, dry areas that receive less than 10 inches of rain per year. They are almost barren, containing only a few patches of vegetation.
- **Deltas** are accumulations of silt deposited at river mouths into the seabed. They are eventually converted into very fertile, stable ground by vegetation, becoming important crop-growing areas. Examples include the deltas of the Nile, Ganges, and Mississippi River.
- **Basins** come in various types. They may be low areas that catch water from rivers; large hollows that dip to a central point and are surrounded by higher ground, as in the Donets and Kuznetsk basins in Russia; or areas of inland drainage in a desert when the water can't reach the sea and flows into lakes or evaporates in salt flats as a result. An example is the Great Salt Lake in Utah.

Marshes and Swamps and Tundra and Taiga

Marshes and swamps are both **wet lowlands**. The water can be fresh, brackish, or saline. Both host important ecological systems with unique wildlife. There are, however, some major differences. **Marshes** have no trees and are always wet because of frequent floods and poor drainage that leaves shallow water. Plants are mostly grasses, rushes, reeds, typhas, sedges, and herbs. **Swamps** have trees and dry periods. The water is very slow-moving, and is usually associated with adjacent rivers or lakes.

Both taiga and tundra regions have many plants and animals, but they have few humans or crops because of their harsh climates. **Taiga** has colder winters and hotter summers than tundra because of its distance from the Arctic Ocean. Taiga is the world's largest forest region, located just south of the tundra line. It contains huge mineral resources and fur-bearing animals. **Tundra** is a Russian word describing marshy plain in an area that has a very cold climate but receives little snow. The ground is usually frozen, but is quite spongy when it is not.

HUMID CONTINENTAL, PRAIRIE, SUBTROPICAL, AND MARINE CLIMATES

- A **humid continental climate** is one that has four seasons, including a cold winter and a hot summer, and sufficient rainfall for raising crops. Such climates can be found in the United States, Canada, and Russia. The best farmlands and mining areas are found in these countries.
- **Prairie climates**, or steppe regions, are found in the interiors of Asia and North America where there are dry flatlands (prairies that receive 10-20 inches of rain per year). These dry flatlands can be grasslands or deserts.
- **Subtropical climates** are very humid areas in the tropical areas of Japan, China, Australia, Africa, South America, and the United States. The moisture, carried by winds traveling over warm ocean currents, produces long summers and mild winters. It is possible to produce a continuous cycle of a variety of crops.
- A **marine climate** is one near or surrounded by water. Warm ocean winds bring moisture, mild temperatures year-round, and plentiful rain. These climates are found in Western Europe and parts of the United States, Canada, Chile, New Zealand, and Australia.

ADAPTATION TO ENVIRONMENTAL CONDITIONS

The environment influences the way people live. People **adapt** to **environmental conditions** in ways as simple as putting on warm clothing in a cold environment; finding means to cool their surroundings in an environment with high temperatures; building shelters from wind, rain, and temperature variations; and digging water wells if surface water is unavailable. More complex adaptations result from the physical diversity of the earth in terms of soil, climate, vegetation, and topography. Humans take advantage of opportunities and avoid or minimize limitations. Examples of environmental limitations are that rocky soils offer few opportunities for agriculture and rough terrain limits accessibility. Sometimes, **technology** allows humans to live in areas that were once uninhabitable or undesirable. For example, air conditioning allows people to live comfortably in hot climates; modern heating systems permit habitation in areas with extremely low temperatures, as is the case with research facilities in Antarctica; and airplanes have brought people to previously inaccessible places to establish settlements or industries.

NATURAL RESOURCES, RENEWABLE RESOURCES, NONRENEWABLE RESOURCES, AND COMMODITIES

Natural resources are things provided by nature that have commercial value to humans, such as minerals, energy, timber, fish, wildlife, and the landscape. **Renewable resources** are those that can be replenished, such as wind, solar radiation, tides, and water (with proper conservation and clean-up). Soil is renewable with proper conservation and management techniques, and timber can be replenished with replanting. Living resources such as fish and wildlife can replenish themselves if they are not over-harvested. **Nonrenewable resources** are those that cannot be replenished. These include fossil fuels such as oil and coal and metal ores. These cannot be replaced or reused once they have been burned, although some of their products can be recycled. **Commodities** are natural resources that have to be extracted and purified rather than created, such as mineral ores.

HARMFUL OR POTENTIALLY HARMFUL INTERACTION WITH ENVIRONMENT

Wherever humans have gone on the earth, they have made **changes** to their surroundings. Many are harmful or potentially harmful, depending on the extent of the alterations. Some of the changes and activities that can harm the **environment** include:

- Cutting into mountains by machine or blasting to build roads or construction sites
- Cutting down trees and clearing natural growth
- Building houses and cities
- Using grassland to graze herds
- Polluting water sources
- Polluting the ground with chemical and oil waste
- Wearing out fertile land and losing topsoil
- Placing communication lines cross country using poles and wires or underground cable
- Placing railway lines or paved roads cross country
- Building gas and oil pipelines cross country
- Draining wetlands
- Damming up or re-routing waterways
- Spraying fertilizers, pesticides, and defoliants
- Hunting animals to extinction or near extinction

CARRYING CAPACITY AND NATURAL HAZARDS

Carrying capacity is the maximum, sustained level of use of an environment can incur without sustaining significant environmental deterioration that would eventually lead to environmental destruction. Environments vary in terms of their carrying capacity, a concept humans need to learn to measure and respect before harm is done. Proper **assessment of environmental conditions** enables responsible decision making with respect to how much and in what ways the resources of a particular environment should be consumed. **Energy and water conservation** as well as recycling can extend an area's carrying capacity. In addition to carrying capacity limitations, the physical environment can also have occasional extremes that are costly to humans. **Natural hazards** such as hurricanes, tornadoes, earthquakes, volcanoes, floods, tsunamis, and some forest fires and insect infestations are processes or events that are not caused by humans, but may have serious consequences for humans and the environment. These events are not preventable, and their precise timing, location, and magnitude are not predictable. However, some precautions can be taken to reduce the damage.

APPLYING GEOGRAPHY TO INTERPRETATION OF THE PAST

Space, environment, and chronology are three different points of view that can be used to study history. Events take place within **geographic contexts**. If the world is flat, then transportation choices are vastly different from those that would be made in a round world, for example. Invasions of Russia from the west have normally failed because of the harsh winter conditions, the vast distances that inhibit steady supply lines, and the number of rivers and marshes to be crossed, among other factors. Any invading or defending force anywhere must make choices based on consideration of space and environmental factors. For instance, lands may be too muddy or passages too narrow for certain equipment. Geography played a role in the building of the Panama Canal because the value of a shorter transportation route had to outweigh the costs of labor, disease, political negotiations, and equipment, not to mention a myriad of other effects from cutting a canal through an isthmus and changing a natural land structure as a result.

Applying Geography to Interpretation of the Present and Plans for the Future

The decisions that individual people as well as nations make that may **affect the environment** have to be made with an understanding of spatial patterns and concepts, cultural and transportation connections, physical processes and patterns, ecosystems, and the impact, or "footprint," of people on the physical environment. Sample issues that fit into these considerations are recycling programs, loss of agricultural land to further urban expansion, air and water pollution, deforestation, and ease of transportation and communication. In each of these areas, present and future uses have to be balanced against possible harmful effects. For example, wind is a clean and readily available resource for electric power, but the access roads to and noise of wind turbines can make some areas unsuitable for livestock pasture. Voting citizens need to have an understanding of **geographical and environmental connections** to make responsible decisions.

Cultural Studies

CULTURE

A **culture** is a comprehensive style of living that is developed in a society and maintained from generation to generation. Culture is manifested in a group's traditions, rituals, language, social norms, technology, and economic structures. Broadly speaking, culture is everything that is learned by a member of a particular society, though it may include things that an individual learns but which are never made explicit either in the individual's mind or in his or her social interactions. For this reason, many sociologists feel it is difficult to properly study one's own culture; they suggest that only the unclouded eyes of a foreign observer can perceive a society's most fundamental values.

SOCIOLOGY, PSYCHOLOGY, AND ANTHROPOLOGY

There are three branches of cultural studies known as psychology, sociology, and anthropology. Each of these categories deals with some form of studying humans and human behavior. **Anthropology** is the most material of the branches, as it deals with studying past and present ways of life for humans. It is an intersection between history, geography, technology, and art. Anthropology is the broadest of cultural studies and contains overlap with countless other disciplines. **Sociology** deals with social interaction and the cultures of human civilizations. Often, sociologists bring ethical, political, and historical matters into question. Sociology largely derives its viewpoints from principles of human interaction and external matters of life. **Psychology,** on the other hand, focuses mainly on the internal workings of the mind and the mental and biological processes involved in thinking.

MATERIAL CULTURE

A society's **material culture** is the set all of the physical objects that the people of that society have either created or to which they assign cultural meaning. Hence, material culture may include objects like books, jewelry, buildings, and furniture; but it may also include natural areas if those areas are assigned significance by the members of the society. As an example of this latter kind of material culture, a sociologist might point to the Native American society, in which the land itself held immense cultural value. Along with **verbal culture**, material culture makes up the sum total of what sociologists have at their disposal for study.

NONMATERIAL CULTURE

Nonmaterial culture is all of a society's customs, beliefs, political structures, languages, and ways of using material objects. In the United States, for instance, the emphasis placed on religious freedom and individual liberty might be considered an example of nonmaterial culture. The boundary between material and nonmaterial culture is never altogether clear; how, for instance, should one separate the American flag and what it stands for, namely the idea of freedom? **Values** and **norms**, as opposed to the physical things that are used to express values and norms, are what make up a society's nonmaterial culture. Typically, nonmaterial culture is more difficult to change than material culture, and its change is more difficult to observe.

VALUES

The **values** of a culture are its highest ideals. In the United States, for example, we would say that freedom and equality are two of our most important values. Values are usually very general concepts. They may be complementary, as for example the values of hard work and material success seem to go together. Values are quite fluid, and a major focus of sociology is observing how they change over time. Values may come into conflict with one another, which can create social conflict and disorganization. An example of this is the conflict in mid-twentieth-century America between the values of equal rights and segregation; ultimately, it was clear that only one of these values could remain.

SANCTIONS

In sociological terms, **sanctions** are any rewards or consequences given to an individual or group to pursue or renounce a certain course of behavior. Sanctions may be positive, as when a reward is promised for something done properly, or negative, as when a punishment is promised for something done improperly. Although the most common use of the word refers to *international economic pressures* (as in, for instance, the economic restrictions placed on Iraq during the 1990s), all societies place sanctions on their members in order to elicit approved behavior. People who uphold the values and norms of the society are rewarded with preferential treatment from their fellows, while those who transgress can be punished socially, economically, or legally.

NORMS

Norms are specific rules regulating behavior in a culture. Norms may or may not be directly codified in the law of a society, but they are intended to encourage behavior that promotes the society's values. Taking again the example of the United States, one might say that treating men and women equally is a social norm, insofar as equality between the sexes is a value aspired to by our culture. Norms, then, depend on values for their justification, and values depend on norms for their enactment. Norms may vary greatly from society to society, such that the same behavior may be approved or condemned depending on where it is performed. Most of the time, norms are so customary for the members of a society that they are performed automatically.

FORMAL NORMS AND INFORMAL NORMS

Norms may be considered formal or informal, depending on whether they are codified in the laws of the society in which they apply. **Formal norms** are written law; examples of formal norms include the prohibition of murder, the forced payment of taxes, and the sanctity of marriage. **Informal norms**, on the other hand, are unwritten codes of conduct. Examples of informal norms might include the prohibition of spitting in public or the encouragement of deference to women. Typically, a society formalizes the norms which are most important, and for which violators should be punished. Formal norms tend to be much more consistent among different societies than informal norms.

SOCIAL MARKERS, LAWS, AND FOLKWAYS

A **social marker** is any part of behavior that indicates the identity, character, or way of understanding of a particular group of people. Social markers can be laws, folkways, traditions, or other patterns of behavior. **Laws** are simply social norms that have been made explicit and are enforced by the government. There are plenty of norms, though, that are encoded in law but are also internalized-- the prohibition of murder, for instance. **Folkways** are social norms that have become habitual or traditional in a society. In the United States, we are accustomed to tipping a waiter or waitress for their service: that this is so ingrained in our daily life makes it an American folkway.

CULTURAL PLURALISM AND SUBCULTURE

Cultural pluralism exists when multiple distinct cultures exist within the same society after a process of accommodation. These self-contained cultures should not be confused with **subcultures**, which are smaller cultures within a large culture. Subcultures usually have a set of norms and values that are different from those held by the larger society of which they are a member. In the United States, we might consider punk rockers or hippies as subcultures, because they have different values than Americans on the whole, but do not really have a self-sustaining or separate society of their own.

Countercultures

A **counterculture** is any group whose values and norms challenge and seek to alter the values and norms of the dominant culture in their society. Although the term when used today evokes memories of the 1960s youth rebellion in Western Europe and the United States, earlier countercultural movements include the Bohemians in nineteenth century France, or even the early Christians. Countercultures typically appear at a time when traditional norms and values are felt to no longer be appropriate or helpful in making sense of the world. As in the case of a social movement, a counterculture tends to have more and stronger adherents at the beginning of its life; once the counterculture's norms have been partially co-opted by the larger society, countercultures tend to lose steam.

Dominant Culture and Ethnocentrism

In any society, the **dominant culture** is the group whose norms, values, and behavior patterns are most widespread and influential on the rest of the society. Many nations, including the United States, have laws to restrain the dominant culture from extinguishing minority cultures. **Ethnocentrism** describes the tendency to view one's own cultural patterns as superior and to judge all others only as they relate to one's own. This philosophy has been at the root of some of humanity's worst atrocities, including the Holocaust, which was perpetrated by Germans who believed they must maintain the purity of their race, and colonial conquests, in which Western nations brutally imposed their customs on various indigenous peoples.

Humanities and Fine Arts

Visual Arts

CREATIVE EXPRESSION

Creativity means the ability to produce or bring into existence a work of art (music, painting, sculpture, comedy, drama, and literature) that is original and imaginative. To express something is to convey an idea, an emotion or an opinion, or to depict a direct or indirect representation of an idea, an emotion or an opinion. The idea, emotion or opinion can be shown in words, pictures, gestures, signs and symbols. A person with **creative expression** has the burning need to bring forth a unique manifestation of his or her understanding and interpretation of mankind's primal desires. A soaring music score by Beethoven, a memorable scene by Grandma Moses, a gentle poem by Emily Dickinson, a moving performance by Sir Laurence Olivier are all examples of individual creative expression by artists of uncompromising vision.

ELEMENTS OF ART

There are seven basic **elements of art**: line, shape, space, texture, color, value, and form. Each has a specific function; each must be understood to truly appreciate the work of art being studied. The following definitions are composed from the *American Heritage College Dictionary*:

- **Line** is a continuous path made by a moving pen, pencil or brush that makes a real or imaginary mark in relation to a point of reference.
- **Shape** is the characteristic outline or contour of an object that is distinguished from its surroundings by its distinctive form.
- **Space** is a three-dimensional empty area with a specific outline that is reserved for a particular purpose.
- **Texture** is a surface of elements woven together that has distinctive or identifying characteristics.
- **Color** is the appearance of objects caused by different qualities of reflected light that involves hue, lightness, darkness, value and purity.
- **Value** is the quality of brightness in a particular color on a scale of white to black. Sometimes this element is grouped with color.
- **Form** is the element dealing with shape of three-dimensional figures. It is related to shape, which is made up of height and width, but also contains depth.

USE OF LIGHT AND DARK IN TWO- AND THREE-DIMENSIONAL ART FORMS

In western culture, the reaction to light and dark arouses strong, primitive emotions. **Light** suggests goodness, intelligence and wholeness. **Dark** expresses mystery, ignorance and evil. Contrasting these opposites in a work of art helps convey feelings and has a powerful psychological impact. Light and dark can also depict space and enhance form in two- and three-dimensional art. On a two-dimensional surface, the effects of light and shadow can be very dramatic. When light is blocked by different parts of a form and casts a shadow, the figures in a painting seem to come alive. This technique is called chiaroscuro. Light and shadow on sculpture and architecture define the form of the piece. As the contour fades away, the light grows dimmer causing changes in contrast and tonal value on the surface, which makes the object seem to swell and recede while enhancing the drama of its structural composition.

Principles of Art

In art, there are four basic **principles**: balance and harmony, proportion, unity, and variety. Each has a unique function and needs to be understood to appreciate the artist's vision whether it is shown in a painting, sculpture or a piece of architecture. The following definitions are composed from the *American Heritage College Dictionary*:

- **Balance and Harmony** is a state of equilibrium between parts that creates a pleasant arrangement in the whole and depicts a difference in dimension between opposing forces or influences.
- **Proportion** is the pleasing symmetry between objects or their parts with respect to comparative size, quantity or degree.
- **Unity** is the state of being in accord and having a continuity of purpose or action.
- **Variety**, the partner to Unity, is diversity in a collection that has specific characteristics.

Terms Associated with Color

- **Hue** — any specific color
- **Tone** — a color made by adding grey to a hue
- **Value** — the degree of light or darkness
- **Achromatic** — black, white and grays; artwork executed without color
- **Black** — the complete absence of light
- **Chroma** — the intensity, strength or purity of a color
- **Complementary Colors** — colors which appear opposite one another on a color wheel
- **Secondary colors** — orange, violet, green; each is midway between the Primaries from which it can be mixed
- **Shade** — mixing black with another color to make it darker; the opposite of shade is tint
- **Spectrum** — colors that are the result of a beam of white light that is broken by a prism into its hues
- **Tint** — the opposite of shade; combining white with a color to make it lighter

Terms Related to Positioning of Subject Matter Within a Painting

- **Background** — the part of the scene intended to be the most distant from the perspective of the viewer
- **Foreground** — the part of the scene intended to be nearest the viewer
- **Horizon** — the line where sky and earth meet; also referred to as "ground line"
- **Landscape** — a view of a section of country – applicable to outdoor scenes only
- **Middle ground** — the area between the foreground and the most distant part of a scene
- **Vertical lines** — lines that are painted straight up and down
- **Horizontal lines** — lines that are painted across the picture (90 degrees from straight up and down)
- **Point-of-view** — the angle from which the viewer is observing the work
- **Negative space** — the space behind and around an object; in two-dimensional art it is often synonymous with background
- **Overlapping** — occurs when one object partially covers another; usually done for compositional purposes
- **Design** — the arrangement of the elements of a picture

APPRECIATION OF VISUAL ART

The act of **appreciating visual art** is, in its simplest form, one of simply deriving satisfaction or pleasure from observing the beauty given to an artwork by its creator. Research has shown that a capacity for appreciating (or, alternatively, creating) aesthetically pleasing art appears to be present within every individual although it does seem to vary in terms of degrees. For most people, innate abilities remain untrained or underdeveloped – not so much in terms of the possession of individual tastes and opinions or in terms of an ability to find something beautiful, but rather in an ability to recognize artistic mastery with respect to technique or style. Education can reconcile such a deficiency. Therefore, anyone can truly appreciate art, but true "art appreciation" requires some understanding of the creative process involved in production, or perhaps, some particular insight into the thoughts and feelings of the creator. Ideally, art is best appreciated when one considers both dimensions.

WOOD CARVING AND ENGRAVING

Wood carving is an ancient art which has changed very little in its history. The process is relatively straightforward. After selecting a suitable wood, most carving is done with a limited set of tools to create works which don't typically exhibit an abundance of fine detail. Engraving is a more refined version of carving and is sometimes a preliminary step in other artistic activities such as printmaking, where fine detail and exacting shapes are desired. Several varieties of wood can be used successfully by the engraver, although boxwood is often preferred for its favorable characteristics. The wood is sawn cross-grain, which results in a block with both a tighter grain and better shape-holding ability. Due to its exacting nature, **engraving** often requires tools similar to those used by copper and steel workers. The tools are arranged into groups such as gravers, tint tools, scorpers, spit stickers, and small chisels. A typical beginning set includes flat, round, burin and lozenge, as well as both large and small U and V cutters.

PASTELS

Pastels are chemically pure pigments gently bound by gum or resin and are much softer than their harder chalk crayon cousins. Due to the nature of the pigment cohesion, durability is a primary concern when using them. The ability to correct mistakes is also severely limited. For this reason, pre-planning a work is crucial. A fairly recent addition to the arts, pastel work was pioneered mostly by French artists in the 18th century. Notable pastel artists of the era include Quentin de la Tour, Jean-Baptiste Perroneau and Jean-Baptiste Chardin. More recent artists include Odilon Redon and Mary Cassatt. Having never gained the popularity of other forms such as oils and watercolor, pastels remain one the less regarded mediums within the artistic community.

PEN AND INK

Pen and ink is one of the least demanding art forms in terms of equipment requirements. Pen and ink artists simply need the addition of virtually any kind of paper to produce their work. Historically, medieval monks employed pen and ink on prepared animal skins such as goat, sheep, calf, lamb, or kid using the quills of goose feathers. Pen use continued during the Renaissance and along with mixed media such as white highlighting, crayon and watercolors it flourished as an art form. It gained even more widespread use during the Post-Renaissance era by such artists as Rubens and Van Dyck. Hogarth is considered an exemplary penman of the 18th century while the advent of magazines and the mass production of books in the 19th century provided an outlet for notables such as Charles Keene and George du Maurier. By the 20th century, pen and ink luminaries included Matisse, Pascin and Picasso.

ELEMENTS OF SCULPTURE DESIGN

- **Mass** — The most influential element in sculpture, mass can have a dramatic effect upon interpretation, light reflectivity and symmetry.
- **Space** — Space in a multi-piece sculpture is an element that can be manipulated to effect interpretation by yielding clues with respect to the relationship between individual pieces.
- **Plane** — An element with two dimensions – length and width; plane thickness is typically minimized to provide the most dramatic differentiation between plane and volume.
- **Line** — Line lends an element of space to a sculpture; vertical lines belie support and strength lending a monumental quality while horizontal lines have a somewhat less dramatic effect. Convex lines can create tension while concave lines often indicate either real or implied forces.
- **Movement** — generally an implied effect; often a function of reflected light that can be altered through the manipulation of the sculpture's mass. Some sculptors, such as Alexander Calder, employ actual movement in their work through mobiles or similar effects.
- **Scale** — the relative size of the work; often a product of the manipulation of other elements such as mass.
- **Texture** — the surface quality of the work; primarily manipulated to either enhance or diminish light reflectivity and shadowing.
- **Color** — achieved through a variety of effects; can often add a sense of realism or a particular quality, such as age, to a work.

PERSPECTIVE

Perspective is a system of creating the illusion of three dimensions on a two-dimensional surface. There are two basic categories of perspective – aerial and linear. **Aerial perspective** refers to atmospheric effects on objects in space and can be seen as diminishing tones for objects which are receding from view. Put simply, **linear perspective** describes a process of seeing lines on objects from various angles converge and diverge. The position from which an object is seen and drawn is called the **station point** or **point of sight**. The **horizon** is represented by the eye level or horizon line. **Ground plane** refers to the horizontal plane where the artist is standing. The **center of vision** is the point on the horizon immediately opposite the eye. **Vanishing points** occur where parallel lines converge.

SHAPE, FORM, AND PROPORTION

Shape is an aspect of form which constitutes the individual masses, groupings or aesthetics that the artist uses to render the overall work. It is form, combined with content, which constitutes the basis of the art work itself. **Proportion** refers to the symmetrical three-dimensionality or solidity of a work. In representational art, the intent is to create an illusion of reality by rendering a work which is convincing in form. The mathematical concept known as the "**Golden Mean**" is often employed, either purposefully or incidentally, when rendering proportion. Put simply, the "Golden Mean" is the precept that the proportion of the smaller part to the larger part of a whole is equal to that of the larger to the whole. Perhaps the most well-known demonstration of the "Golden Mean" is the 1509 Leonardo da Vinci work titled "Divine Proportion."

PROTECTIVE APPAREL

Protective apparel such as gloves, long sleeves, long pants and boots or shoes rather than sandals help prevent contact of chemicals with the skin. The garments should be dedicated for use in the studio or work area and washed frequently in a separate load from other laundry. If skin contact does occur, flush immediately with soapy water or other suitable cleaners. Avoid the use of solvents or bleach to clean the skin as these will often absorb and enter the blood stream where they can accumulate in internal organs. If splashes or flying debris are concerns, goggles should be worn in the work area. Ear protection is generally advised when working with noisy equipment for extended periods. Wear a properly fitted respirator or dust mask if vapors or dust are present. Refrain from wearing jewelry when working and tie long hair back to prevent it from being caught in tools and equipment. Do not work when fatigued and always wash hands before drinking, eating or smoking.

Materials to Avoid When Children Are Participating in Art Projects

Numerous materials specially designed for **children** are available commercially. Adult supervision is also advisable when children are working with art materials. All adult materials should be avoided as these may contain toxic chemicals, including solvents, thinners, shellacs, acids, alkalis, bleaches, rubber cement and permanent markers. Materials which must be sprayed such as paints, fixatives, adhesives and airbrush paints should be avoided, as should pottery glazes, copper enamels, stained glass and pastels. Also, any materials requiring solvents for clean-up such as oil paint or oil-based printmaking inks should be substituted for water-based alternatives when available. It is often best to limit the amount or quantity of material given to very young children to reduce the risk should ingestion occur. Children should also be taught to wash their hands thoroughly after working with the materials.

Local Art and Architecture

The architecture of **home construction** is one obvious place. Although many newer areas around cities lack compelling diversity and creativity in home construction, there are almost always exceptions. This is particularly true of older areas with established traditions. **Churches** are another excellent place to discover art. The relationship between religion and art is as old as most religions themselves. Christianity is certainly no exception. Modern churches frequently have collections of paintings and sculpture consistent with the beliefs of their own individual congregations. For those fortunate enough to live in Europe or in the Eastern United States, numerous older churches are accessible. Many of these are exemplary works of art in themselves. A number of **businesses**, particularly large corporations, have substantial art collections in their common areas, many of which are accessible to visitors. Shopping centers, banks, and government buildings (particularly with respect to sculpture) are often rich resources for art seekers.

Art Forms

The following definitions are taken from *The American Heritage College Dictionary*:

- A **painting** is a picture or design created in oil or water-based paint.
- **Literature** is a body of creative writing that helps define a language, period or culture.
- **Music** is sounds arranged to produce a unified composition that has melody, rhythm and timber.
- A **sculpture** is an object created by chiseling marble, molding clay or casting in metal into a real or abstract figure.
- **Theater** is dramatic or comedic literature or other such material performed by actors impersonating characters through dialogue and action.
- **Drama** is verbal literature composed of serious subject matter written specifically to be performed by actors in the theater or on television, radio or film.
- **Comedy** is humorous or satirical verbal literature depicting funny themes, situations or characters that are written to be performed by actors in the theater or on television, radio or film.

Art Terms

These definitions are from the *New York City Public Library Desk Reference*, Second Edition:

- **Carving** means to cut hard material such as stone, wood or marble to create a form.
- In **casting**, the sculptor pours plaster or molten metal into a mold and lets the substance harden into the desired form.
- A **collage** is made of separate pieces of various materials and other objects glued to a surface.
- **Drypoint** is an engraving technique that uses a sharp steel needle to create a rough edge, which produces soft, velvety lines.
- **Engraving** is the art of carving, cutting or etching a design on a wood or metal surface then adding ink so the design can be printed.
- **Etching** is the art of cutting into a metal or glass surface then bathing the surface in acid, adding ink to the plate, and printing the design.
- In architecture, a **frieze** is a horizontal band of painted or sculpted decoration usually found at the top of a wall between the molding and the cornice.
- **Lithography** is a printing process in which a stone or metal plate has been treated with an oily substance so that the desired design retains ink while the rest of the surface is treated to repel ink.
- **Modeling** is when a sculptor uses clay or wax to build up a form. Using color and light to create the illusion of a three-dimensional plane in drawing and painting is also known as modeling.
- A **polyptych** is multiple scenes hinged together. A **diptych** has two panels; a triptych has three panels.
- In architecture, when a form sticks out from the background, depending on how far it protrudes, it is known as **high relief** or **low relief** (bas-relief). In painting or drawing, if an object appears to project out from the flat surface suggesting three dimensions, it is called relief.
- **Stenciling** is the technique of applying paint or ink to forms cut out of cardboard, metal, plastic or other flat materials to create letters, numbers and other images and designs.
- A **still life** is a study of ordinary objects in an every day setting in a painting, drawing or photograph. A still life can also be created on a tabletop or in a bookcase or a shadow box.
- **Woodcutting** is the art of carving an image on a wood block then using ink or paint to print the design.

Music

EMERGENCE OF MUSIC

Music as an artistic expression was not documented until the Middle Ages. Prior to that time, music was used as an equally contributing part of worship, poetry, and dance and served society by uniting a community to complete necessary labors, soothe mourners, express different emotions, and offer homage to a higher power. The older or ancient forms of musical expression set the foundation for the more disciplined arts of music, however, there was no musical notation for sharing these ideas until the Middle Ages. The Greeks, with their love of the lyre. established that musical foundation as surely as they did many modern theories regarding culture and philosophy. Greek musical theory introduced intervals, or relationships between pitches, using a tightened string to show how the shortening of the string to ⅔ or ¾ of the original length could change the tone when plucked.

STYLE OF MUSIC AND CHRONOLOGICAL CLASSIFICATIONS OF MUSIC

The **style** of music showcases not only the time and political or spiritual mood of the period, but also the composers and the mindset of the people. Music is meant to be listened to and, as such, can be repeated, expounded upon through different media, appreciated in different ways at different times, accepted as an individualistic part of the hearer, respected as a demonstration of a culture or belief system, and touted as a societal bragging right. Music offers these different abstract feelings, but its primary purpose and people's eternal fascination with it falls back on the fact that music is created for people's enjoyment. Styles of music are usually classified into chronological sections and referred to as Renaissance, Baroque, Classical, Romantic, and Twentieth Century.

QUALITY OF MUSIC

Music is difficult to label as good and bad since the biggest deciding factor of the quality of music is the **listener**. Defining any **greatness** in art by comparing the positive and negative aspects limits the artistic voice of the creator and the imagination of the audience. Critics have been in the business of defining the quality of art for centuries and have often made poor calls because of their inability to accept a new style or the enduring aspect of the composer and the audience's reception of that style. For any musician to become accepted, he or she must master a particular style or technique and perform or compose with a kind of genius that inspires others. To be considered great, music must be able to stand the test of time as being an indispensable example of a kind of work for the period, country, or composer.

SYMPHONY

As a work for an orchestra with multiple movements or multiple parts in one movement, the **symphony** contained three movements of fast-slow-fast and was named for the Italian opera *Sinfonia*. Performed with strings and winds, these musical pieces were enjoyed at private gatherings in palaces, monasteries, and residences, as well as civic functions and public concerts. The foundation for the symphony genre comes from Sammartini, whose works used the three-part movement with both strings and winds. As the Classical Period developed, the symphonic format increased to four parts or movements with an even greater transition in the third movement. After being expertly worked by Haydn, the symphony became a more celebrated style of music that allowed for greater freedom in composition and features.

BAROQUE STYLE AND CLASSICAL STYLE

While the stylistic choices for music differ between Baroque and Classical, an integrity and depth of composition is evident in both. Music requires a certain kind of simplicity for comprehension, and the simpler styles of the **Classical Period** did not take away that complexity. While Bach may create incredible musical feats on his polyphonic style, he incorporated a lucid design in his work. The surface sounds of works by Haydn and Mozart may appear simple but are in actuality incredibly organized and conceived, using a great amount of material and genius in that simplicity. The **Baroque** composers sought to express magnificence and grandeur in their music, while the Classical composers adopted an unpretentious format of hiding deep feelings. Baroque gave us the motet and opera, but from the Classical Period came the symphony, string quartet, and sonata.

INTERVALS

As the basis for any discussion of melodic or harmonic relationships, the **interval** refers to the measurement from pitch to pitch. The half step or **semitone** is the smallest movement and is the distance from one key to the next in the chromatic scale, such as C to C#. The whole step or **tone** refers to a full movement in which the notes are 2 keys apart, such as from C to D. The half step and whole step act as the basis of measurement for intervallic discussions. These intervals are defined by quantity and quality. The **quantity**, or numeric value assigned to the note, is established by the musical arrangement, such as C D E F G A B. Any interval created with C and G will always be a fifth, regardless of any sharps or flats.

SCALES

A **musical scale** is the sequenced arrangement of notes or pitches that are located within the octave. Both major and minor scales have seven different notes or scale degrees, and each scale degree is indicated by the Arabic number showing the position of the note as it appears in the scale. Each major scale has two similar units of four notes, or tetrachords, that are separated by a whole step where each tetrachord has two whole steps and one half step. **Minor scales** are classified as natural, harmonic, and melodic and all start with the same minor tetrachord of 1-2- b3-4 with variations occurring on degrees 6 and 7 in the upper tetrachord.

DYNAMICS

Dynamics is the degree of loudness or softness of a musical piece. Certain terms can indicate this degree, as well as specific abbreviations and symbols used within the music and at specific places. Dynamic marks can also indicate a change in volume or sound quality and usually suggest the character of the piece to be observed during its performance. Usually written in Italian, dynamic marks are often abbreviated and range from very soft pianissimo (pp) to mezzo piano (mp) to mezzo forte (mf) to fortissimo (ff) which is very loud. Gradual changes in volume can be represented by a < or the word **crescendo** for increasing in volume and by a > or the words **diminuendo** or **decrescendo** for decreasing in volume. These marks for the changing of volume can be several measures long or just a span of a few notes.

TEMPO

The **tempo** or speed of the piece of music can be designated by specific tempo marks as well as certain Italian words that describe the speed and also the character of the piece. The words used include *grave* for very slow and serious, *largo* for broad, *lento* for slow, *adagio* for slow and with ease, *andante* for steadily moving, *moderato* for moderate, *allegretto* for fast, *allegro* for fast and cheerful, *vivace* for lively, *presto* for very fast, and *prestissimo* for as fast as possible. Other relative changes in tempo can be described with the words *ritardando*, or rit., for slowing, as well as *accelerando* for quickening and *più mosso* for faster. The tempo markings are a guide for the performance and can be interpreted differently by different conductors.

LENGTH OF MUSICAL NOTES

Songs are often written using time signatures, measures, and beats. **Time signatures** are usually displayed as a fraction, such as $\frac{4}{4}$ or $\frac{6}{8}$. The numerator describes the number of beats per **measure**. If the numerator is four, then there will be four beats per measure. The denominator describes how to count the measure. If the denominator is four, then the count uses quarter notes, whereas if it is an eight, the measure will be counted with eighth notes.

Whole Note	Half Note	Quarter Note	Eighth Note	Whole Rest	Half Rest	Quarter Rest	Eighth Rest
o	♩	♩	♪	—	—	𝄽	𝄾
4 Beats	2 Beats	1 Beat	½ Beat	4 Beats	2 Beats	1 Beat	½ Beat

RHYTHM

As the pattern of movement in a particular time, **rhythm** has referred to both the flow of a piece and the ability of the piece to maintain or uphold the pulse. Rhythm can be generally assigned to cover any aspect of music that is not related to pitch, although it has also been used as another factor for consideration with melody and harmony. As an equal partner to meter and tempo, rhythm can describe a pattern of *stresses* and *retreats* that are defined by a particular tempo or meter and are composed of hazy pitches or subtle harmonies as well as percussive bursts. For rhythm to sustain, the stresses and retreats should be frequent enough to maintain the melodic or harmonic thought and have defined articulation.

ACOUSTICS

Acoustics refers to the study of the production and perception of sound within a particular room or area. By producing musical sound, musicians create mechanical vibrations from the stretching of strings or membranes, movement of wooden parts, and the oscillatory movement of air columns. This sound action affects the air, which carries the energy of the vibrations from the musician to the audience member. The sound is transmitted through to the brain where it is deciphered and interpreted. The perceived sound is referred to as a pure tone and has a frequency of full oscillations occurring each second. The human ear can perceive 20 to 20,000 cycles per second, or cps, and the corresponding frequency of the pure tone determines the pitch.

MUSIC EDUCATOR'S ROLE

Any **educator** of children is in a position to exert remarkable control and **influence** over these young lives. As such, educators are responsible in making that influence a positive one, so that the child can reach his or her fullest potential. All teachers should seek out ways to prepare for curriculum planning and designing instructions that are appropriate for the child's particular educational level. Music combines with all developmental, cognitive, language, physical, emotional, and social arenas of education and makes the music educator one of the most fundamental of teachers. Training is necessary for any teacher dealing with children; it is especially important for teachers dealing with children who are still young enough to be easily influenced. Music educators should be able to guide children in their musical experiences and encourage their progress as it occurs.

Singing and Chanting with Young Children

Young children explore their world with a different perspective than adults do, and their sense of **touch** is especially important when learning new things. Percussion and other simple instruments allow children to see and feel how an accented beat corresponds to music and the words in songs. Rhythmic songs and chants are important for children to understand the combination of sounds and beats and apply that process to their own sensory perceptions. When music educators participate in the singing or chanting, they can interact with the children, and show them how much fun moving to music and creating music can be for all ages. Through this type of exercise, children can learn how words work together and how they should sound by following the example of the music educator.

Teaching Songs to Young Children

Music educators must determine the best way to teach young children the **words** of songs, especially when those children cannot read and must learn songs by rote. The music educator can sing the same song repeatedly or incorporate different methods of participation for the children. Folk songs and nursery rhymes are easy to teach to children, since they are usually written in the limited vocal range of children and are composed of small segments. Parents may also be able to sing these songs with their children. Folk songs are usually specific to a culture or area and would probably be shared across generations. Music educators can also sing to children in order to teach them a new song that may be too complex for their abilities as yet or to show them how much fun music is.

Creative and Synchronized Movement

Movements that are associated with music and performed as dance or exercise by young children are classified as either creative movement or synchronized movement. **Creative movement** gives children a freer avenue for expression and allows them to improvise and enjoy the physical act itself. **Synchronized movement** follows an established routine and is choreographed to the rhythm and beat of the selected music. Synchronized movement helps children work as a group and realize the importance of teamwork, while creative movement allows them to freely express themselves to song. Both types of movement allow children to develop their listening skills and focus on what they are hearing. Focused listening is also considered perceptive or active listening.

Creative Movement

Creative movement involves a child's interpretation of the song without paying attention to the beat. Before a child can be expected to move freely, he or she must have a repertoire of movements already learned, and must feel comfortable choosing from that list. Before being allowed to move creatively, children should be familiar with walking, marching, running, galloping, dancing, clapping, hopping, sliding, and jumping to music. Music educators can help children expand their basis even more by suggesting **imagery exercises**, such as asking children to show how an ice cube melts or how a wind-up doll moves. Young children can also watch how older children and adults move and then attempt to duplicate those movements.

Benefits of Music Education

Combining music education with other facets of education improves the overall educational experience for children in many ways. One benefit is allowing them to learn about the use of symbols in different formats. Music education allows students to see the application of math in different subjects, learn the fulfillment of self-expression while developing creativity, and discover the fundamentals of self-image and self-discipline through music practice. Students of music education find their problem-solving skills becoming more advanced, as well as experience the intellectual satisfaction of sharing in the work required for a performance and of completing the challenge. Students do not suffer from music education and often broaden their own experiences with activities that are uplifting and wholesome.

INCLUDING MUSIC IN CURRICULUM

Music should be included in the **basic curriculum** for several reasons. As a topic and area of expression, music is worth learning about since it tells a lot about people and culture. Every person has the potential for musical abilities, as is evidenced in elementary classrooms, and school is the perfect place for a child to explore that possibility. By learning about music and how different voices depend on each other, students can view the interdependence of people of various backgrounds and cultures. The study of music improves other studies, especially for students who may have difficulty in some subjects. The hearing and creating of music inspires the listeners and the performers.

INCREASING FOCUS ON MUSIC AND THE ARTS

Music currently stands as a **sideline** to the major focus of science, math, and language regardless of the studies that show how music education can improve students' whole educational experience. An increased focus on music and the arts could motivate students to learn more in other areas, and all educational encouragement avenues should be considered for the changing student body. More researchers and educators are beginning to recognize music as a form of intellectual development along the same lines as Howard Gardner's multiple intelligence theory that encompasses linguistic, spatial, intra-personal, bodily-kinesthetic, logical-mathematical, inter-personal, naturalistic, musical, and possibly existential intelligences. These theoretical systems support the inclusion of music in the basic curriculum and argue that teaching music is only the first step to teaching all other subjects students must learn. Any learning that occurs can be fortified in other areas.

GOALS OF MUSIC EDUCATION

Music educators, parents, teachers, and other adults have witnessed an **improvement** in children who participate in instrumental and choral music education and practice, not only in their musical abilities, but also in their social skills and teamwork. These children learn about *self-discipline* while improving their *self-esteem* and enhancing their *self-expression* and *creativity*. The basic foundations of learning an instrument and then mastering that instrument to play a beginner piece and eventually an advanced piece serve to instill within the child a sense of accomplishment that correlates to improved self-image and greater confidence in an ability to complete other tasks and to persevere even when those tasks appear daunting. The goal, then, of music education should be to foster a sense of purpose and self-worth in the student.

INSTRUCTING YOUNG CHILDREN TO RECOGNIZE RHYTHM OF FAMILIAR SONGS

Once young children have grasped the concept of reading the rhythm and are comfortable with the musical notation, the music educator should lead them in the **clapping of the beats** for songs that are familiar to them, such as "Twinkle, Twinkle Little Star." This exercise will allow children to associate their lesson on rhythm with music they know. Music educators can also clap a measure or phrase and have the children clap the same pattern back. This will involve the children in the motor skills exercise of clapping with the perceptive listening of the rhythm and the particular emphasis as it is placed on the first note or another accented note within the phrase.

CHANGES TECHNOLOGY HAS MADE IN MUSIC

With different inventions and increases in technology, the music of the twentieth century and modern music can be **shared** on a grander scale and in more different formats than at any time before 1900. Whereas the music of the previous centuries was expressed from one person or ensemble to another person or audience, the twentieth century saw music disseminated to larger groups of people through radio and television broadcasts, as well as through pre-recorded sessions on other media. There has also been developments in the field of electronically-produced music.

Rise and Fall of Different Types of Music Within the Past 100 Years

America has seen different **styles of musical expression** rise and fall within the past 100 years. The African-American styles of ragtime, blues, and jazz appealed to listeners, just as the folk and classical traditions of music entertained audiences years before. Western popular culture and Rock 'n' Roll have permeated musical preferences worldwide. While composers of earlier periods had to please their audience to continue creating music, the Modern composers could alienate audience members since some will listen to music because of a popular trend. The composers from non-Western countries have also affected Western composers, so that Modern music may hearken to a traditional mode but incorporate the more rhythmic pulses of monophonic Indian music. With a larger choice for musical style, modern musicians have become better able to play many different styles and have improved their own techniques and performances. This expansion has allowed for more prominent composers than any other musical period.

Instructing Young Children to Read Measures

Music is written in **measures** within the staff. To introduce young children to the concept of the measure, the music educator should have the children count the measures or sections separated by bar lines. Much of today's sheet music provides a count for the measure so that professional musicians can follow along when they are not playing or so that the conductor can call attention to a particular part of the music. Music educators can ask children to count the measures and to locate a specific measure of the music. Once children are comfortable with the basic format for musical notation, they can be instructed more effectively on how to interpret other musical notations, such as the time signature or the rhythm.

Instructing Young Children to Read Time Signatures

Music educators can show children how each measure contains a specific number of beats and how that is indicated at the beginning of the first measure with the **time signature**. Music educators can show students that the top note of the time signature tells how many beats occur in the measure and the bottom note shows which note gets one beat. The music educator can explain how a 4/4 time signature shows that there are four beats in each measure, counted as 1, 2, 3, 4. Contrasting that with a 3/4 time signature, the music educator can show that there are only three beats in each measure, and can then ask students what other time signatures would show. Eventually, music educators can show students the mathematical relationship between quarter notes and half notes, whole notes, and sixteenth notes.

Instructing Young Children to Read Rhythm

The bottom number of the **time signature** becomes important when music educators try to teach children how to read rhythm. The bottom number shows which note gets one beat. In the 4/4 time signature, the quarter note gets one beat and is counted as 1, 2, 3, 4 within the measure. A mathematical explanation of how the bottom number relates to other notes can be incorporated into the lesson, and children can see how two half notes are counted as 1, 3 while eight eighth notes are counted as 1 &, 2 &, 3&, 4&. This exercise combines a study of math with the basic fundamentals of music, and music educators can lead the children toward reading combinations of the notes and playing or clapping those rhythms.

National Music Education Standards for Instructing Children in Grades K-4

The **National Music Education Standards** as outlined for music educators instructing students in grades K-4 as they read and notate music involve the following abilities:

- Ability of each child to **read** whole, half, dotted half, quarter, and eighth notes and rests in time signatures of 2/4, 3/4, 4/4, and others
- Ability of each child to incorporate the use of a system to determine basic **pitch notation** within the treble clef as it relates to major keys
- Ability of each child to identify traditional **terms and symbols** and differentiate their meanings in regards to articulation, dynamics, and tempo while correctly interpreting these symbols during Visual and Performing Arts
- Ability of each child to incorporate the use of standard **symbols** to indicate meter, pitch, rhythm, and dynamics in easy phrases as presented by the music educator

Assisting Children in Ability to Improve Motor Skills While Improvising or Singing New Songs

As children get older, there is an increase in their vocabulary and in their ability to add experiences and movements to their personal repertoire. Music educators can assist children in their ability to improve their motor skills while improvising or singing new songs. Children between five and nine enjoy games that involve rhythm and rhyme, so jump rope rhymes or chants are a great way to show children that music can be fun and entertaining. The music educator can show children a simple or even age-specific complex rhyme or chant, and the children can add clapping or stomping as they become more familiar with the rhyme and feel comfortable enough to improvise. Such rhymes include "Teddy Bear, Teddy Bear" and "The Lady with the Alligator Purse."

Encouraging Children's Music Education at Home

To continue a child's musical education outside of school, music educators should encourage parents to involve their children in **music outings**, such as free concerts or performances in outdoor theaters where children can listen to the music as well as to the sounds of the outdoors and the audience members. Parents can even plan to attend with other families, so that the children can enjoy the outing socially as well as musically. Music educators can also help parents locate musical instructors who would be willing to provide lessons for the children. As a limited option, music educators could create a marching band take-home box for parents that includes books on the music of marching bands or even composers like John Philip Sousa, CDs of marching band songs, index cards describing how to make small instruments, and party hats to remind the parents and children that music is fun.

Instructing Children on the Concept of Rests

Music is an important skill for music educators and parents to teach, and different children will be focused on certain sounds or the volume of those sounds. **Silences** or **rests** within the music can be the most difficult to teach young children who are interested in playing or singing continuously. Based on the same concept as the whole, half, quarter and eighth note beats, rests are set up with a corresponding count and also adhere to the restrictions put in place by the time signature. Children should be introduced to the **symbols** used to indicate rests and instructed how to count each rest. When interspersing beats with rests, some music educators find that clapping the beat and then turning the palms out for the rest is an easy way to show children how the rests function in relation to the beat.

Attitude of Music Educator

Music educators should always approach any musical assignment or practice with children with the right **attitude** of patience and exploration in order for the children to get the most out of their musical experience. The best equipment and the most up-to-date books will not guarantee that children have a good experience with musical instruments and music appreciation in general, so the attitude of the music educator is paramount to the children's success. Children learn best in a classroom and musical environment that includes structure even while fostering an individualized, creative movement format of learning. Music educators should adopt a philosophy of how to introduce children to music successfully that is based on core values and life experiences.

Accommodating Children Who Are Self-Conscious

Not all children between six and nine are comfortable dancing and moving in front of other children or the music educator unless they have been doing so since they were much younger. One of the easiest ways to foster an environment of acceptability is to sing and dance **alongside** the children, so that they can see others behaving in a particular way without being ostracized or ridiculed. Music educators could also provide areas for creative movement that have higher walls or are separated and somewhat shielded from the rest of the room. The music center can include headphones so that children do not feel they are encroaching on others' quiet time for homework. Room dividers combined with rugs and drapes can also provide some basic soundproofing.

Music Classrooms

Equipment

Music classrooms for children of all ages include different types of materials that are appropriate for the development of the children. Besides large **instruments** such as pianos and large or small keyboards, the music classroom will also include rhythm instruments, percussion instruments, string instruments, Orff instruments, Montessori sound cylinders and bells, guitar, and autoharp. Optional **hardware** includes tape recorders, headphones, tapes, CDs, players, and a karaoke machine. Some music educators like to provide specific furniture for the classroom, such as containers or shelving systems for storage, tables, tents, and rocking chairs. **Music boxes** are a nice addition to smaller sections, and computer **software** may be more appropriate for older children. Music-related **pictures** can be hung around the room as well as unbreakable **mirrors** for children to watch their own movements.

Materials

Music educators may have to create simple **instruments** or may find the children are creative enough to benefit from a more hands-on experience so as to appreciate this part of the work. The **construction materials** used in a music classroom may include paper, glue, and paint, as well as rubber bands, shoe boxes, and milk cartons of different sizes. Regular **household items** such as paper or disposable plastic plates, cans with lids, plastic bottles, toilet paper tubes, mailing tubes, and wrapping paper tubes act as containers and can be filled with such items as rocks, rice, beans, sand, or seeds. The containers can be further enhanced with guitar strings, bells, or brass pipes in different lengths. Scarves and ribbons can help with movement visualization, and drum heads and sandpaper samples can introduce different textures. As always, music educators can employ whatever materials imaginable to teach children about sound.

Singing

The **voice** can be used as a musical instrument through singing or humming. With a strong link to community relations predating recorded history, **singing** has been a task of the priest, healer, actor, poet, and entertainer. Greatly popular during the Middle Ages and the Renaissance, singing became less popular with the progression of instrumental music. Vocalists were encouraged to pursue musical instruction in how to use the voice as a musical instrument and not in the folk traditions enjoyed by previous audience members. As a result, music was composed to show off the vocal ranges of singers, and it was expected that vocalists would ornament their vocal pieces the same way instrumentalists would ornament theirs. Popular music and jazz have allowed singers to develop their voices more independently than the composers of the Romantic period did.

Performing Arts

TERMS RELATING TO DRAMATIC PERFORMANCES

- **Acting process**—refers to the methods and materials from which an actor draws his or her ability to perform; actors should be able to verbalize the tools they use in their acting processes.
- **Affective memory**—a technique in which an actor reactivates a past experience to gain the emotional and psychological feelings associated with those events and then transferring them to a performance; used when the actor believes the character they are portraying is undergoing an event that emotionally parallels that which the actor experienced in real life.
- **Atmospheres**—defined by Michael Chekhov as the inherent energy within a specific place; actors may imagine they are in a specific location while performing in order to depict the corresponding emotions and actions that would best suit that environment, thus creating an atmosphere.
- **Character acting**—occurs when an actor must make a change to their physical person in order to perform a role; may include the use of dialect or accents that are not part of the actor's real persona or using stage makeup to create a specific facial disfigurement.

TERMS USED IN THEATRE

- **Articulation**—the ability to clearly pronounce words while acting or performing.
- **Blocking**—developing the movements of actors on stage in relation to other actors, scenery, and props.
- **Catharsis**—the purging of an emotion, such as fear or grief, while performing on stage.
- **Concentration**—the ability of an actor to be in character through use of dialogue, attitude, voice, costume, expressions, and mannerisms.
- **Cold reading**—occurs when actors read a script for the first time.
- **Context**—the conditions or climate in which a play was written or meant to be performed.
- **Cue**—a signal that serves as an indicator of another action that is about to occur.

EXTERNALS

The elements that an actor can use in his or her environment to aid in creating specific characters are known as **externals**. An external can be a costume, a vocal change, makeup, or a set of mannerisms. For many actors, externals are the primary tool they use to create a character. By dressing or speaking in the way a character would, the actor can begin to relate to the feelings that the character would experience. Using externals to create a character is a method called **outside-in**. This means that the actor uses outside elements to cause internal changes. In order to be a character actor, one must be able to shed the restrictions of his or her everyday persona. In essence, her or she must be able to create a blank slate upon which the new character can be created.

CONSIDERATIONS FOR COSTUME DESIGNERS

The **costume designer's** role is very important in helping to achieve the director's vision because the costumes used should contribute to the tone and style of a production. It is important for costume designers to consult with the director in order to ensure that the costume designs will be consistent with the *theme* of the production. A costume designer must consider the *time period* in which the play is set. They must also consider the many facets of a character's *personality* and *lifestyle*, including his or her job and social status. The costumes also serve to *differentiate* and *unify* certain characters. For example, a play in which the characters are divided between servants and aristocracy should involve two distinct costuming groups. Costumes must also be practical for the actors and should allow them to move freely and change quickly.

Tools Used by Sound Technicians

In the early days of theatre, **sound** was created by any means available. For example, the sound of thunder was simulated by rolling a cannonball down a narrow trench carved into the roof of a theatre. Now, the sound of thunder can be created through the use of **digital sound equipment**. Technicians have the ability to reproduce sounds made by such things as door bells and telephones. Technicians can also reinforce these sounds through the use of amplification. The variety of technologies available in modern theatre allows for technicians to reproduce nearly any sound that might be needed for a performance. Background music and actors' voices can all be controlled through the use of speakers, microphones, and sound boards. **Sound quality** is a crucial part of any theatre experience, and a successful performance allows the audience to both see and hear the performance without distraction.

Lighting

Lighting in theatre can be used in several ways. The most basic purpose of theatre lighting is to allow the audience to see what is happening on stage. Lighting is also useful for providing depth to the stage and actors. The use of highlights and shadows, called modeling, create a three-dimensional effect. Lighting can serve an overall compositional purpose by helping to create a series of connected imagery that brings the director's *interpretation* to life. It can be used to give information about the *setting* of a play: time of day, season, and location. Light can also be used to focus the audience's attention on a particular *element* in the production. Lighting can be used to create a *mood* for a play. The proper lighting can reflect the *emotional content* of a performance, which leads to a cohesive and balanced production.

Goals for 9th-12th Grade Unit on Theatrical Presentation

Theatrical presentation involves familiarizing students with a broad range of activities that can be considered theatrical forms. Such forms include music, dance, performance, and visual arts. Students should examine the structure of each kind of dramatic form in order to determine how that particular form relates to the structure of all arts. Students should be given the opportunity to integrate their knowledge of various forms of theatre into an original performance they create themselves. Lessons should provide a means for students to study both traditional and non-traditional methods of artistic production. Lessons should also provide students with knowledge of and hands-on experience in emerging technology in theatrical productions including film, video, and computer applications.

Applying Lessons from Theatre Class to Other Subject Areas or Life Skills

In **first grade**, students can learn to cooperate in *group activities*. They also begin to understand the concept that all things in life have a beginning, a middle, and an end, just like they see in stories. In **second grade**, students learn *problem-solving skills*, which can be carried into other courses. In **third grade**, students are taught to question events and gain information through applying the 5 Ws (who, what, when, where and why). In **fourth grade**, students learn to use acting as a tool for *understanding local history*. They also learn to work with a *team* to accomplish a specific goal. In **fifth grade**, students learn about the various *career options* available to professional actors and theatrical technicians. In **sixth grade**, students learn how theatrical skills are used in the *social sciences*, such as advertising and marketing. In **seventh grade**, students learn how the voice can be used to project *confidence* during oral presentations. In **eighth grade**, students begin to understand the various *jobs* available in theatre, and they are encouraged to research the educational requirements necessary for those jobs.

Comprehending Dance Performance by Genre

Every form of dance has signature **characteristics** that identify and define it—and that make it beautiful and distinct from all other forms. An audience member can look for these when watching particular styles of dance, and can then discern whether those characteristics are present and strongly represented. For example, **tap** exemplifies rhythm and improvisation. If choreography ignores or contradicts the rhythm in an unpleasant way, or simply repeats time steps without ever choosing to improvise movements during the breaks, it could be considered an unsuccessful representation of its form. The same methods can be applied to evaluate modern dance's expressiveness and inquiry into creative movement types, ballet's fluidity and weightlessness, and flamenco's rhythm, passion, and footwork. It should be noted, however, that working contrary to form does not necessarily make a dance "bad." Looking at form is simply a place to start when considering the elements and effects of a dance.

Eliciting Particular Feelings or Reactions

Some dances are created to elicit an **emotional response** from audiences. They may represent characters, settings, or situations about which people already have strong feelings. For example, mythological stories have always been a favorite theme across many forms of dance, as the characters are strong, their defeats disheartening, and their triumphs inspiring. Dances with a **dramatic** or **comedic** objective often borrow methods from theater, such as staging, costumes, props, and sets. These methods help set the tone for bringing forth certain feelings. In these dances, dancers often portray more emotion than usual through facial expression, gestures, and a particular kind of energy in their movements. Whereas **formalistic dances** ask audiences to focus on the "what" and "how" of a dance, **dramatic pieces** draw the viewer into the humanity of the situation. They focus on the "why" or—in **comedic pieces** portraying the absurd behavior of a character—the "who."

Importance of the Audience Member's Experience and Perspective

The performance of any **dynamic** (moving) work of art involves three essential parties: the choreographer, who creates; the dancers, who perform; and the audience member, who receives and interprets. It is important for audience members to understand that their own perspectives will color their responses to a dance every bit as much as anything the choreographer or dancers do. **Choreographers** contribute intention, knowledge, and craft. **Dancers** supply their training, focus, interpretation, and energy. **Viewers** bring their own influential elements to a dance: past experiences; a sociopolitical orientation; aesthetic preferences; and a certain degree—or lack—of knowledge about dance in general and the specific choreographer, company, or presenting institution behind the dance. As the saying goes, "We can only see what we can see." Differing combinations of the viewer characteristics mentioned above create a different version of the dance for every viewer, shaping perception more strongly than any choreographic intention.

Design Elements in Formalistic Dance Pieces

A **choreographer** may create a dance to explore the relationship between floor patterns and the directions dancers face, or to explore patterns in time created by combining long delays and short bursts of movement. The choreographer might even include "what happens if" scenarios that are based on chance. In these dances, the **space** is quite visible in varying shapes made by bodies and the movements themselves, as well as levels, planes, facings, directions, and floor patterns in which the dancers move. **Time** can also be measured in the speed, duration, rhythms, arrangement, and sequencing of the movements. Choreographers can also explore **dynamics** by varying the weight put into the movements and the energy and timing with which the dancers approach, maintain, and release movements. Although **abstract dances** do not specifically aim to evoke viewers' emotions, they may still do so—and will certainly create impressions and elicit reactions of some kind.

QUESTIONS TO GAIN GREATER INSIGHT INTO A DANCE

Many viewers leave a dance performance asking one main **question**: "What was that all about?" However, there are other questions audience members can ask and answer for themselves or other spectators that are slightly smaller in scope and more likely to conjure up bits of understanding. These include: Did a clear message come through in the dance? What was that message? Did the dance tell a story, express feelings, solve a puzzle, comment on a situation, or just look pretty? Were there repeated movements or series that were easy to identify? Did specific images catch your attention? What images caught your attention, and what were they likely meant to express? What might the choreographer's intentions have been? What was the choreographer trying to say? Did the dance say it clearly? How did you feel after the dance? Can you distill the description of that feeling down to one sentence? Can you express that feeling using a single word?

CULTURAL CONTEXT OF A BODY OF WORK OR PARTICULAR DANCE

Cultural context—the time, place, cultural climate, and artistic influences surrounding artists and their work—can provide a strong set of clues to a viewer trying to analyze a dance or canon of work, and can be understood by using several methods. Comparing and contrasting a dance with other dances from the **same time period**—whether works made by the choreographer in question or several different choreographers—can give a clear "snapshot" of a certain era, especially if it is or was defined by particular historical or political events. Comparing and contrasting a dance with other forms of art from the same time period can provide an even clearer picture of the cultural climate of the time. Comparing and contrasting a dance with **earlier works** by the same choreographer can illustrate the development of the artist's canon throughout his or her career.

USING IMAGERY TO IMPROVE TECHNIQUE

Imagery connects the unfamiliar with the familiar, allowing a dancer to understand and feel the movement being performed. Following are some examples of imagery that could be used to improve technique, and their desired effects:

- **To improve balance**: The image of sand slowly falling and accumulating (as in an hourglass) to fill up a standing leg
- **To prolong lift in a leap**: The image of a gazelle leaping and remaining suspended for a second before landing
- **To achieve deeper abdominal contraction**: The image of a snail curling deep into its spiraling shell
- **To sharpen angular movement and shapes**: The image of skyscrapers that are full of hard lines and acute angles
- **To soften tension in port de bras**: The image of a soft blanket gently gliding over the skin, or of gentle waves washing the arms
- **To accelerate attack in an assemblé**: The image of stepping on a dollar bill before someone else gets it
- **To better employ plié in preparation for jumps:** The image of a floor made out of springs

CLASSICAL BALLET

Classical ballet technique revolves around a dancer's lifted, contracted torso. To provide stability, strength in the core muscles of the body is needed. The limbs are elevated from the core. Arms are typically extended away from the body in "airy" postures. The legs perform movements in a position rotated or "turned out" from the hips, requiring flexibility in the muscles of the hips and legs. Balances are often held upon the tips of the toes, known as "en pointe." The majority of movement is done in **upright positions**—balanced, locomoting upon, or jumping/leaping and landing upon the feet. This requires both flexibility and strength in the legs and feet. Movement is largely directed away from the floor, as the ballet dancer continually strives to create the illusion of weightlessness and effortlessness. The ultimate visual goal is elevation and elongation of the "lines" of the body, and of movement.

Modern Dance

Although **modern dance** shares some features with ballet, it was largely a response to—and rebellion against—ballet. It took shape under a banner of individual exploration into natural, instinctive, expressive movement styles, and has developed ever since into its own always-evolving entity that encompasses as many styles of movement as there are dancers. Movement philosophies prevalent in modern dance are: an emphasis on coordinating movement with the breath; a focus on shifting the weight freely across the feet, hands, shoulders, pelvis, spine, or any other body part that touches the floor; the use of an articulated spine and the limbs; a focus on working with the floor and the force of gravity; and an intention to explore or express a personal, intellectual, emotional, design, philosophical, or other concept through movement.

Terminology and Form in Modern Dance

Modern dance emphasizes the finding of an **individual, personally authentic movement style** over the codification of form and structure. Individual styles are often informed by the specific focus of a dancer's creative exploration and the needs of the physical body. Modern dance has **no standardized terminology**, so even though it uses many standard terms from its predecessor, ballet (plié, tendu, and battement, for example), these are augmented by countless other movement words that range from basic commands (bend, contract, and swing, for instance) to terms specific to each teacher's movement philosophy. Modern dance classes do not share a universally codified structure or sequence, although, like ballet classes, they begin with warm-up movements. Instead of being performed at a barre, however, they are usually performed at center, sometimes beginning from a supine position on the floor. From warm-ups, classes then progress through a series of increasingly demanding movements before finishing with the learning and performing of a choreographic combination.

Floor Work

Because of modern dance's emphasis on **groundedness**, a connection to the floor, and a working cooperation with gravity—as well as its openness to experimentation—the modern form of dance involves more **floor work** than other forms of dance, such as ballet or tap. In these forms, dancers usually stand on their feet. Floor work can be done while kneeling, crouching, on hands and knees, sitting, or lying on the floor. Combinations of these positions can also be used. Movements can include crawling, rolling, scooting, dragging, slithering, etc. Often, movements at this level can express ideas of earth, gravity, weight, debasement, filth, ugliness, evil, disadvantage, poverty, sadness, or dejection, among others. Floor work also supports the modern ethos by affording opportunities to use **unconventional body parts** for balance, locomotion, and pivoting (as in shoulder stands, dragging the prone body forward with the elbows, or spinning on one sitz bone), as well as to invert the body in unfamiliar orientations.

Social Dance and Other Traditional Dance Throughout the World

"**Folk dance**" is a catch-all term for any traditional dance participated in communally by non-professionals. Worldwide, these dances can be placed into two main categories: religious dance and social dance. Both are an effective way of transmitting culture and reinforcing a people's communal values and experiences.

Religious dances reflect a people's spiritual beliefs. They include storytelling dances to transfer knowledge, medicine dances for healing or protection, imitation dances (mimicking important animals or events), commemorative dances demarcating annual events (solstices, harvests, animal migrations, etc.) or personal landmarks in individuals' lives (birth, initiation, marriage, death, etc.), and dances to achieve a spiritual connection with deities.

Social dances are primarily for recreation and community. They include work dances (mimicking movements of a particular kind of labor); courtship dances (less prevalent in cultures that impose strict limitations on contact between the sexes); war dances to prepare, motivate, or intimidate before battle; and communal dances to enhance cooperation.

Social dance is, by definition, communal dance. It is created for the purpose of affirming a community's shared knowledge, culture, and experiences. The dance steps, as well as the music, costumes, and other accompanying traditions, are handed down from one generation to the next through observation and participation, rather than via a rigid scholastic format.

To best facilitate this informal learning, traditional dance steps are usually simple and somewhat natural. In many cases, steps are based on movements used in the work and daily lives of the people and their ancestors, and so are already familiar to the people learning them. Possible examples of familiar movements are fishermen pulling nets and farmers planting seeds.

Often, steps are rhythmic and feature set foot patterns, as rhythm and patterns are both easy devices for categorizing and recalling information. Most importantly, dances are taught in a fun, social environment, which motivates dancers to learn the dance steps, remember them, and look forward to performing them.

World Literature

AMERICAN LITERARY PERIODS
DARK ROMANTICS

In American literature, a group of late Romantic writers are recognized as **Dark Romantics**. These authors' works may be associated with both the Romantic and Gothic movements. These works emphasize nature and emotion, aligning them with Romanticism, and include dark themes and tones, aligning them with Gothic literature. However, these works do not all feature the historically inspired characteristics of Gothic literature, and their morals or outcomes more closely resemble those of Romantic literature. The Dark Romantics include writers such as Edgar Allan Poe, Nathaniel Hawthorne, Emily Dickinson, and Herman Melville.

TRANSCENDENTALISM

Transcendentalism was a smaller movement that occurred alongside the American Romantic movement. The **transcendentalists** shared the Romantic emphasis on emotion and also focused heavily on how a person experiences life through their senses. They extended these sentiments to suggest that through embracing one's senses, an individual could transcend, or experience a state of being above physical humanity. They also extended the Romantic emphasis on subjectivity through their praise of self-sufficiency, as exemplified through Ralph Waldo Emerson's *Self-Reliance*. Emerson was a prominent transcendentalist. His writings included an essay titled *Nature*, which explains a progression from the use of the senses to the achievement of transcendence. Transcendentalist literature includes several essays that discuss the value of the senses and emotions or the process of transcendence. Transcendentalists also wrote poetry that includes the frequent use of imagery, metaphors, and references to nature. These elements reflect the ideas of transcendentalism and create a resemblance to the alleged experience of transcendence. Ralph Waldo Emerson, Henry David Thoreau, and Walt Whitman were all prominent writers in this movement.

COLONIAL AMERICA

The **colonial era** in America was influenced by immigration from England to what is now New England. These immigrants were mainly Puritans who centered their society in New England on their religious beliefs, allowing those beliefs to inform all aspects of their lives. This is apparent in the literature of the time, as much of it includes essays and sermons that discuss religion or the way the Puritans believed one should live and conduct themselves. Colonial literature also includes many poems, and these works also discuss or reference religious ideas and themes. There was not much fiction written in Colonial America, as most of the literature was written to inform or persuade.

ROMANTIC PERIOD

The **American Romantic** movement is also known as the American Renaissance. This movement yielded several notable American writers and works that began characterizing American literature and differentiating it from British literature. This literature, written after the American Revolutionary War and until the end of the Civil War, praised individualism and featured an expression of national pride and patriotism. The transcendentalists' extreme ideas about self-sufficiency and subjectivity reiterated this individualism, and their recommendations about society and its structure furthered the separation of American literature from British literature. While this period shaped the definition of American literature, it is criticized for featuring a narrow view of

American politics and social issues at the time, as well as promoting a small group of similar writers.

> **Review Video: Authors in the Romantic Period**
> Visit mometrix.com/academy and enter code: 752719

HARLEM RENAISSANCE

The **Harlem Renaissance** took place in America during the 1920s and 1930s. The changing economy and opportunities led African Americans in the south to seek new lifestyles in other parts of America at the beginning of the 20th century. Many moved to Harlem, a small area in New York City. This group of African Americans yielded highly influential scholarly and artistic works, including poetry, fiction, music, and plays. The Harlem Renaissance marked an opportunity for these intellectuals and artists, who were largely ignored in the aftermath of the Civil War, to use their talents and express themselves through their works. While artists often featured personal expression in their works, the Harlem Renaissance was unique in its volume of culturally expressive works. This cultural expression and the movement's main ideas also contributed to the Civil Rights movement by promoting a spirit of unity among African Americans. The Harlem Renaissance eventually ended in the wake of the stock market crash in 1929. As the Great Depression began, financial support for the arts dwindled, making it difficult for many artists to succeed financially. Some members of the Harlem Renaissance who influenced American literature include Langston Hughes, Zora Neale Hurston, and Paul Robeson.

BRITISH LITERARY PERIODS

NEOCLASSICAL

The **British Neoclassical** period began in the middle of the 17th century and ended in the late 18th century. The latter part of the movement also took place alongside the Enlightenment, a period of scientific discovery and study that influenced many Western cultures. The Enlightenment's concern with intellectual pursuits and improvement increased discussions of introspection, or an individual's analysis of their own behavior, thoughts, and self. These ideas also affected society in England, as they contributed to a general attitude of complacency and a desire to ignore the past. The period saw a slightly increased acceptance of female writers, as their works were viewed as a method of self-reflection and improvement. The changes in British society allowed several new forms of literature to gain popularity and acceptance, usually for their introspective qualities. Essays, diaries, and letters all displayed the author's thoughts and experience, aligning them with the culture's values. Novels also gained popularity, as many were fictional diaries or epistolary novels. Journalism flourished during the Neoclassical period, leading to the creation of the newspaper. Literary criticism also gained popularity, though it was used to criticize an author and their style rather than examine or analyze the content of the work.

VICTORIAN

The **Victorian Era** in England was influenced by a variety of events and ideas, many of which were influenced by the Victorians' economy. The Industrial Revolution in England changed the circumstances of work for the Victorians. The changing industries and lack of labor laws led to several problems and a wide division between Victorian social classes. These factors inspired and saturated much of Victorian literature. Many novels' plots and characters were heavily influenced by social and economic issues, and many poems referenced and criticized specific events that occurred during this period.

While the structure of Victorian society was a major influence on literature, there were other popular topics that appeared in literature. Topics like evolution, psychology, and colonization frequently appeared in Victorian literature, reflecting the concerns and interests of the Victorian culture. The Victorian society was also characterized by a strict moral code that supported the view of women as homemakers and criticized the idea of female writers. Not only did this affect the portrayal of women in literature, but it also led some female novelists, such as the Bronte sisters, to write under a pseudonym and present their works as having been written by a man. Victorian literature also popularized forms of literature, including the novel and the dramatic monologue, a poetic form developed by Robert Browning. Victorian writers include Charles Dickens, Oscar Wilde, Elizabeth Barrett Browning, Emily Bronte, Matthew Arnold, and Thomas Hardy.

World Literary Characteristics and Periods

While many other nations shared literary movements with America and England, there are numerous literary movements that are unique to other countries and cultures. Some of these literary movements can be understood as variations of movements like Romanticism or modernism, since they occurred at similar times and feature similar elements, but the political and cultural events of each country shaped their version of each movement. Most regions also have some type of mythology, and while different mythologies have similar characters and events, each region's mythology is unique and significant to the region's literature. Another common feature of world literature is colonialism. Many nations are former colonies of European countries, and the effects of colonization are present in modern literature from countries worldwide, making it a key feature of many regions' body of literature.

African Literature

Literature from some cultures was not recorded until the 19th century, causing any movements and trends to be informed by ideas told aloud. This is true of African literature, where stories and ideas were spoken and passed down through the generations. Early African poetry was often metaphorical, structured or written to form a paradox, and included a riddle or puzzling statement. Proverbs and didactic tales were also told frequently, reflecting the dominant religions in a given region and time period. These poems and stories also reflect the variety of languages spoken in Africa and the shifts in each language's usage. Early African literature, once people began writing it down, included stories and proverbs that had been passed down, translations of religious texts, and descriptions of the way of life in different African cultures or groups. These cultures and the events specific to each of them produce a unique body of literature that places emphasis on certain topics and ideas. For example, much of the modern literature written in South Africa discusses politics and issues of race, since the country's history is characterized by events and movements that revolved around these topics.

Asian Literature

Asian literature features writings from several different countries and languages and has spanned many centuries. Many popular forms of writing have come from Asia, such as the haiku. A couple of significant literary movements include The Hungry Generation in South Asia and the Misty Poets in China. The Hungry Generation is a literary movement involving literature written in the Bengali language, spoken mainly in West Bengal and Bangladesh. The literature is characterized by unique and innovative writing, which impacted the use of figurative language in the region. The Hungry Generation also discussed cultural issues, particularly colonization in the region, and many participants were arrested for their work. The Misty Poets in China were characterized by their expressive use of abstractions. Their name, Misty Poets, comes from their writings, which were difficult to interpret due to their use of abstract language and ambiguity. This movement was partly inspired by the Misty Poets' distaste for literary realism, though its influence is detectable within their poetry. Many of the Misty Poets were punished for their poetry, since the poetry of this movement was also politically critical.

LATIN AMERICAN LITERATURE

Latin American literature has several literary movements, many of which occurred near the same time as American and British literary movements and share ideas and trends with their English counterparts. Despite these similarities, each of these movements is distinguishable as its own movement with unique impacts of Latin American literature. By the 17th century, written language was in use in Mexico, and Latin American literary trends and figures had been recognized. During the 18th century, Latin American literature featured a variety of ideas and themes within each form of literature. By the 19th century, literary themes were more unified throughout popular Latin American literature. In the early 19th century, Latin American literature embraced the Romantic movement as it came to an end in England and the United States. Several Latin American countries were also fighting for independence during this time, amplifying the Romantic idea of national pride and identity.

In the wake of the Romantic movement, Latin American literature introduced the unique *Modernismo* movement, which yielded a large volume of poetry and is characterized by the use of whimsical imagery and discussions of spiritual ideas. Following *Modernismo* was the *Vanguardia* movement, which was created to introduce diversity within Latin American literature after modernism permeated the literature of the time. *Vanguardia* involved writers taking risks in their writing and breaking the mold from typical Latin American literature. In the 20th century, *Estridentismo* followed the *Vanguardia* movement, marrying the *Vanguardia* movement with the European Avant-Garde movement. Other 20th century movements functioned similarly by adapting literary movements from other regions to suit the themes and trends in Latin American literature, reflect Latin American cultures, and set their literature apart from other cultures.

Literary Periods and Movements

OLD ENGLISH

The English language developed over a long period of time through interactions between different groups in Europe, including the Romans, the Germans, and the Celtics. The Anglo-Saxons, a group that left what is now Germany and settled in England, further established the English language by using what is now called **Old English**. While Old English laid foundations for modern English, its usage fundamentally differs from the way English is used today. For example, Old English relied on inflections to create meaning, placing little importance on the order of the words in the sentence. Its use of verbs and tenses also differs from modern English grammar. The Anglo-Saxons also used kennings, or compound words that functioned as figurative language.

Old English, as a language influenced by several cultures, had dialects from its inception. Differences in usage also came from the division between secular and religious cultures. This division heavily influenced Old English literature, as most of the literature from the time is categorized according to the set of beliefs it reflects. Most of the influential literature of the time includes riddles, poems, or translations of religious texts. Surviving Old English poetry mainly discusses real heroes and battles or provides a narrative about a fictional hero. Many of these fictional poems are considered *lays*, or *lais*, which are narrative poems that are structured using couplets of lines containing eight syllables each. The translations were often of passages from the Christian Bible, adaptations of Biblical passages, or copies of Christian hymns. Old English persisted until the 12th century, where it was eventually replaced with Middle English. Influential literature from this period includes *Beowulf*, "The Wanderer," "The Wife's Lament," and "The Seafarer."

MIDDLE ENGLISH

Old English was replaced by **Middle English**, which was used from the 12th century to the 16th century. Old English was not governed by a consistent set of grammatical rules until the Norse people, their language, and its structure influenced the integration of grammar into English, leading to Middle English. Middle English relied less on inflections than Old English, instead creating variations by using affixes and synonyms. The development of grammar was further facilitated by the printing press, which made it easier for writers to comply with grammar rules since the printing of identical copies reduced variation between texts.

Old English's evolution into Middle English can be narrowed down to three stages: Early, Central, and Late Middle English. Early Middle English, though it showed a change in the language, maintained the writing style of Old English. Central Middle English is characterized by the development of dialects within written communication, which is partly due to scribes who translated texts or parts of texts using terms from their own dialect, rather than the source. Late Middle English includes numerous developments that created the foundation for Modern English. *The Canterbury Tales*, "Sir Gawain and the Green Knight," and "Le Morte d'Arthur" are all Middle English texts that are still read and studied today.

THE RENAISSANCE

The **Renaissance** swept through Europe and lasted for multiple centuries, bringing many developments in culture, the arts, education, and philosophy. The Renaissance in England did not begin until the late 15th century. Though ideas and cultures of the past, especially those of the ancient Greeks and Romans, inspired the Renaissance, the period saw innumerable developments in the English language and literature. The Renaissance was characterized by a focus on the humanities, allowing the arts, including literature, to flourish. At the time, drama was possibly the most popular form of literature, as the popularity of plays and theatrical performances greatly increased. Much of Renaissance literature is still studied today, maintaining its influence on Western literature. Poetry was also popular, and the period saw the development of new forms of poetry, such as the sonnet. Sonnets are often recognized according to one of four styles, each of which was popularized by a Renaissance writer. Lyrical poetry, which discusses emotions and is often written using first-person point of view, was also popular during the Renaissance.

In addition to new forms and literary trends, the Renaissance period also impacted English literature by facilitating discussion over the translation of the Bible. Education at the time often included instruction in Greek and Latin, allowing those with an education to read ancient texts in their original language. However, this instruction did not reach the majority of the public. The Protestant Reformation encouraged discussions about translating the Bible to make it accessible to more people. This suggestion was challenged by those who doubted the ability of the English language to fully reflect the original text. Eventually, the Bible was translated to English, and William Tyndale's partial translation became especially influential for later translations and the continuing development of the English language. Influential writers of the English Renaissance include William Shakespeare, John Donne, John Milton, Edmund Spenser, and Christopher Marlowe.

GOTHIC

The Gothic literary movement, beginning in the 18th century and persisting through the 19th century, took inspiration from the architecture and cultures of the Late Middle Ages in Europe. The Late Middle Ages saw the popularity of Gothic architecture, most prominently in places of worship. These structures inspired many of the settings in **Gothic literature**, as a large volume of Gothic literature takes place in an impressive location, such as a castle or ornate mansion. Gothic works also are often set in the past, long before the time the story was written. This aligns with prominent themes in Gothic literature, as several pieces are informed by an event that occurred before the story begins or a character who died before the plot's first event.

Another common characteristic of Gothic literature is its eerie, dark, suspenseful tone. Authors of Gothic literature often created this tone by setting their works in secluded and strange locations and incorporating intense, unsettling, or even supernatural events and scenarios into the plot. This tone is also created through the theme of death or mortality that often appears in Gothic literature. These characteristics support the aim of many Gothic writers to create fiction that evokes a certain emotion from the reader or shapes their reading experience. Well-known authors of Gothic literature include Horace Walpole, Ann Radcliffe, Edgar Allan Poe, and Nathaniel Hawthorne. While the Gothic literary movement took place in the 18th and 19th centuries, many works have been published in more recent centuries that have several characteristics of Gothic literature and may be included within the overall Gothic genre.

NATURALISM

Naturalism was an active literary movement in the late 19th century, taking place alongside movements such as realism and modernism. **Naturalism**, like realism, rejected the emotional focus and sentimentality of Romanticism and provided a type of social commentary. However, the naturalist movement stretched the ideas of realism, promoting literature that authentically depicts the life of the common man and criticizing the influence of morality on such literature. Naturalist literature often includes characters who belong to a lower class and experience circumstances beyond their own control and takes place in urban settings. Prominent themes in naturalist literature include nature as an apathetic force, the influence of heredity, and life as something to be endured and survived. One of the most influential naturalist writers is French writer Emile Zola. Influential American Naturalists include Stephen Crane, Hamlin Garland, and Theodore Dreiser.

MODERNISM

The Modernist literary movement was largely influenced by industrialization, which heavily impacted both the Unites States and England, primarily in the 19th century. **Modernism** in literature was characterized by an attempt to turn away from the norms and traditions of literature and use new techniques and methods. Modernist literature was often written in first person and used literary devices and techniques to reveal problems within society. For the American modernists, these societal changes came from industrialization and the first World War, which effected the general view of human nature and reliability. In England, there were additional factors contributing to this shift. Modernism began during Queen Victoria's reign, which defined the period known as the Victorian Era. The Victorian society was characterized by a strict moral code that permeated England's society at the time. This moral code was incompatible with the Modernist's desire to turn away from tradition, but the changes that accompanied Victoria's death in 1901 enabled the Modernist movement to grow in England. American Modernist writers include Ezra Pound, William Carlos Williams, and Gertrude Stein. British Modernist writers include Matthew Arnold, William Butler Yeats, T. S. Eliot, and Joseph Conrad.

POSTMODERNISM

Postmodernism grew out of Modernism's reliance on science and universal assertions, but emphasized the individual's subjective perception of reality, as it is often more authentic to an individual's experience than a universally applied statement. Postmodernism asserts that since each person creates their own version of reality, fully and accurately defining reality is futile and impossible. Due to this skepticism, postmodern writers use many concrete details, rather than abstract details, because they can be objectively observed and are not left up to the individual. The postmodernist literary movement began around the 1960s. The literary movement included a variety of new genres and techniques, reflecting the postmodernist idea that things like art cannot be truly defined or simplified. Notable American writers of the postmodernist movement include Kurt Vonnegut, John Barth, and Thomas Pynchon. British postmodernist writers include John Fowles and Julian Barnes.

Public Speaking

SPEECHES

Speeches are written to be delivered in spoken language in public, to various groups of people, at formal or informal events. Some generic types include welcome speeches, thank-you speeches, keynote addresses, position papers, commemorative and dedication speeches, and farewell speeches. Speeches are commonly written in present tense and usually begin with an introduction greeting the audience. At official functions, specific audience members are named ("Chairperson [name]," "Principal [name], teachers, and students," etc.) and when audiences include a distinguished guest, he or she is often named as well. Then the speaker introduces him or herself by name, position, and department or organization as applicable. After the greeting, the speaker then introduces the topic and states the purpose of the speech. The body of the speech follows, similarly to the body of an essay, stating its main points, an explanation of each point, and supporting evidence. Finally, in the conclusion, the speaker states his or her hope for accomplishing the speech's purpose and thanks the audience for attending and listening to the speech.

CLEARLY WRITTEN PROSE AND SPEECHES

To achieve **clarity**, a writer or speaker must first define his or her purpose carefully. The speech should be organized logically, so that sentences make sense and follow each other in an understandable order. Sentences must also be constructed well, with carefully chosen words and structure. Organizing a speech in advance using an outline provides the writer or speaker with a blueprint, directing and focusing the composition to meet its intended purpose. Organized speeches enable audiences to comprehend and retain the presented information more easily. Humans naturally seek to impose order on the world by seeking patterns. Hence, when ideas in a speech are well-organized and adhere to a consistent pattern, the speaker communicates better with listeners and is more convincing. Speechwriters can use chronological patterns to organize events, sequential patterns to organize processes by their steps, and spatial patterns to help audiences visualize geographical locations and movements or physical scenarios. Also, comparison-contrast patterns give audiences insight about similarities and differences between and among topics, especially when listeners are more familiar with one than the other.

EVALUATING SPEECHES FOR CONCISE INFORMATION

To convince or persuade listeners or reinforce a message, speeches must be succinct. Audiences can become confused by excessive anecdotes and details. If a speaker takes three minutes or more to get to the point, audience members' attention will start to fade and will only worsen when details deviate from the main subject. When answering a question, the asker and speaker may even forget the original question if the speaker takes too long. Speakers should practice not only rehearsing written speeches, but also developing skill for spontaneous question-and-answer sessions after speeches. Speakers should differentiate necessary from simply interesting information because audiences can become overwhelmed by too much information. Speakers should know what points they wish to make. They should not be afraid to pause before responding to questions, which indicates thoughtfulness and control rather than lack of knowledge. Restating questions increases comprehension and appropriate responses, and allows time to form answers mentally.

ORGANIZATIONAL PATTERNS FOR SPEECHES

A speechwriter who uses an **advantages-disadvantages** pattern of organization presents the audience with the pros and cons of a topic. This aids writers in discussing two sides of an issue objectively without an argumentative position, enabling listeners to weigh both aspects. When a speechwriter uses a **cause-and-effect** pattern, it can help to persuade audiences to agree with an action or solution by showing significant relationships between factors. Writers may separate an outline into two main "cause" and "effect" sections or into separate sections for each cause, including the effect for each. Persuasive writing also benefits from **problem-solution** patterns: by establishing the existence of a problem, writers induce audiences to realize a need for change. By supplying a solution and supporting its superiority above other solutions, the writer convinces audiences of the value of that solution. When none of these patterns—or **chronological**, **sequential**, **spatial**, or **comparison-contrast** patterns—applies, speechwriters often use topical patterns. These organize information by various subtopics and types within the main topic or category.

EFFECTIVE SPEECH DELIVERY

Speakers should deliver speeches in a natural, conversational manner rather than being rigidly formal or theatrical. Effective delivery is also supported by confidence. Speakers should be direct, building audience rapport through personal connection and vivid imagery. Speakers should be mindful of the occasion, subject, and audience of their speeches and take care to use appropriate language. Good speakers learn vocal control, including volume, speed, pitch, use of pauses, tonal variety, correct pronunciation, and clear articulation. They can express enthusiasm and emphasize important points with their voices. Nonverbal behaviors, such as eye contact, facial expressions, gestures, good posture, and body movements clarify communication, stress important ideas, and influence perceptions that the speaker is trustworthy, competent, and credible. Nonverbal communications should seem as spontaneous and natural as vocal or verbal ones. Speakers should know their speeches well and practice frequently, taking care to avoid nervous or irrelevant movements such as tapping or pacing.

Unified, Coherent, and Effective Writing

The Writing Process

BRAINSTORMING

Brainstorming is a technique that is used to find a creative approach to a subject. This can be accomplished by simple **free-association** with a topic. For example, with paper and pen, write every thought that you have about the topic in a word or phrase. This is done without critical thinking. You should put everything that comes to your mind about the topic on your scratch paper. Then, you need to read the list over a few times. Next, look for patterns, repetitions, and clusters of ideas. This allows a variety of fresh ideas to come as you think about the topic.

FREE WRITING

Free writing is a more structured form of brainstorming. The method involves taking a limited amount of time (e.g., 2 to 3 minutes) to write everything that comes to mind about the topic in complete sentences. When time expires, review everything that has been written down. Many of your sentences may make little or no sense, but the insights and observations that can come from free writing make this method a valuable approach. Usually, free writing results in a fuller expression of ideas than brainstorming because thoughts and associations are written in complete sentences. However, both techniques can be used to complement each other.

PLANNING

Planning is the process of organizing a piece of writing before composing a draft. Planning can include creating an outline or a graphic organizer, such as a Venn diagram, a spider-map, or a flowchart. These methods should help the writer identify their topic, main ideas, and the general organization of the composition. Preliminary research can also take place during this stage. Planning helps writers organize all of their ideas and decide if they have enough material to begin their first draft. However, writers should remember that the decisions they make during this step will likely change later in the process, so their plan does not have to be perfect.

DRAFTING

Writers may then use their plan, outline, or graphic organizer to compose their first draft. They may write subsequent drafts to improve their writing. Writing multiple drafts can help writers consider different ways to communicate their ideas and address errors that may be difficult to correct without rewriting a section or the whole composition. Most writers will vary in how many drafts they choose to write, as there is no "right" number of drafts. Writing drafts also takes away the pressure to write perfectly on the first try, as writers can improve with each draft they write.

REVISING, EDITING, AND PROOFREADING

Once a writer completes a draft, they can move on to the revising, editing, and proofreading steps to improve their draft. These steps begin with making broad changes that may apply to large sections of a composition and then making small, specific corrections. **Revising** is the first and broadest of these steps. Revising involves ensuring that the composition addresses an appropriate audience, includes all necessary material, maintains focus throughout, and is organized logically. Revising may occur after the first draft to ensure that the following drafts improve upon errors from the first draft. Some revision should occur between each draft to avoid repeating these errors. The **editing** phase of writing is narrower than the revising phase. Editing a composition should include steps such as improving transitions between paragraphs, ensuring each paragraph is on topic, and improving the flow of the text. The editing phase may also include correcting grammatical errors that cannot be fixed without significantly altering the text. **Proofreading** involves fixing misspelled words, typos, other grammatical errors, and any remaining surface-level flaws in the composition.

RECURSIVE WRITING PROCESS

However you approach writing, you may find comfort in knowing that the revision process can occur in any order. The **recursive writing process** is not as difficult as the phrase may make it seem. Simply put, the recursive writing process means that you may need to revisit steps after completing other steps. It also implies that the steps are not required to take place in any certain order. Indeed, you may find that planning, drafting, and revising can all take place at about the same time. The writing process involves moving back and forth between planning, drafting, and revising, followed by more planning, more drafting, and more revising until the writing is satisfactory.

> Review Video: Recursive Writing Process
> Visit mometrix.com/academy and enter code: 951611

TECHNOLOGY IN THE WRITING PROCESS

Modern technology has yielded several tools that can be used to make the writing process more convenient and organized. Word processors and online tools, such as databases and plagiarism detectors, allow much of the writing process to be completed in one place, using one device.

TECHNOLOGY FOR PLANNING AND DRAFTING

For the planning and drafting stages of the writing process, word processors are a helpful tool. These programs also feature formatting tools, allowing users to create their own planning tools or create digital outlines that can be easily converted into sentences, paragraphs, or an entire essay draft. Online databases and references also complement the planning process by providing convenient access to information and sources for research. Word processors also allow users to keep up with their work and update it more easily than if they wrote their work by hand. Online word processors often allow users to collaborate, making group assignments more convenient. These programs also allow users to include illustrations or other supplemental media in their compositions.

TECHNOLOGY FOR REVISING, EDITING, AND PROOFREADING

Word processors also benefit the revising, editing, and proofreading stages of the writing process. Most of these programs indicate errors in spelling and grammar, allowing users to catch minor errors and correct them quickly. There are also websites designed to help writers by analyzing text for deeper errors, such as poor sentence structure, inappropriate complexity, lack of sentence variety, and style issues. These websites can help users fix errors they may not know to look for or may have simply missed. As writers finish these steps, they may benefit from checking their work for any plagiarism. There are several websites and programs that compare text to other documents and publications across the internet and detect any similarities within the text. These websites show the source of the similar information, so users know whether or not they referenced the source and unintentionally plagiarized its contents.

TECHNOLOGY FOR PUBLISHING

Technology also makes managing written work more convenient. Digitally storing documents keeps everything in one place and is easy to reference. Digital storage also makes sharing work easier, as documents can be attached to an email or stored online. This also allows writers to publish their work easily, as they can electronically submit it to other publications or freely post it to a personal blog, profile, or website.

Outlining and Organizing Ideas

MAIN IDEAS, SUPPORTING DETAILS, AND OUTLINING A TOPIC

A writer often begins the first paragraph of a paper by stating the **main idea** or point, also known as the **topic sentence**. The rest of the paragraph supplies particular details that develop and support the main point. One way to visualize the relationship between the main point and supporting information is by considering a table: the tabletop is the main point, and each of the table's legs is a supporting detail or group of details. Both professional authors and students can benefit from planning their writing by first making an outline of the topic. Outlines facilitate quick identification of the main point and supporting details without having to wade through the additional language that will exist in the fully developed essay, article, or paper. Outlining can also help readers to analyze a piece of existing writing for the same reason. The outline first summarizes the main idea in one sentence. Then, below that, it summarizes the supporting details in a numbered list. Writing the paper then consists of filling in the outline with detail, writing a paragraph for each supporting point, and adding an introduction and conclusion.

INTRODUCTION

The purpose of the introduction is to capture the reader's attention and announce the essay's main idea. Normally, the introduction contains 50-80 words, or 3-5 sentences. An introduction can begin with an interesting quote, a question, or a strong opinion—something that will **engage** the reader's interest and prompt them to keep reading. If you are writing your essay to a specific prompt, your introduction should include a **restatement or summarization** of the prompt so that the reader will have some context for your essay. Finally, your introduction should briefly state your **thesis or main idea**: the primary thing you hope to communicate to the reader through your essay. Don't try to include all of the details and nuances of your thesis, or all of your reasons for it, in the introduction. That's what the rest of the essay is for!

> **Review Video: Introduction**
> Visit mometrix.com/academy and enter code: 961328

THESIS STATEMENT

The thesis is the main idea of the essay. A temporary thesis, or working thesis, should be established early in the writing process because it will serve to keep the writer focused as ideas develop. This temporary thesis is subject to change as you continue to write.

The temporary thesis has two parts: a **topic** (i.e., the focus of your essay based on the prompt) and a **comment**. The comment makes an important point about the topic. A temporary thesis should be interesting and specific. Also, you need to limit the topic to a manageable scope. These three questions are useful tools to measure the effectiveness of any temporary thesis:

- Does the focus of my essay have enough interest to hold an audience?
- Is the focus of my essay specific enough to generate interest?
- Is the focus of my essay manageable for the time limit? Too broad? Too narrow?

The thesis should be a generalization rather than a fact because the thesis prepares readers for facts and details that support the thesis. The process of bringing the thesis into sharp focus may help in outlining major sections of the work. Once the thesis and introduction are complete, you can address the body of the work.

> **Review Video: Thesis Statements**
> Visit mometrix.com/academy and enter code: 691033

SUPPORTING THE THESIS

Throughout your essay, the thesis should be **explained clearly and supported** adequately by additional arguments. The thesis sentence needs to contain a clear statement of the purpose of your essay and a comment about the thesis. With the thesis statement, you have an opportunity to state what is noteworthy of this particular treatment of the prompt. Each sentence and paragraph should build on and support the thesis.

When you respond to the prompt, use parts of the passage to support your argument or defend your position. Using supporting evidence from the passage strengths your argument because readers can see your attention to the entire passage and your response to the details and facts within the passage. You can use facts, details, statistics, and direct quotations from the passage to uphold your position. Be sure to point out which information comes from the original passage and base your argument around that evidence.

BODY

In an essay's introduction, the writer establishes the thesis and may indicate how the rest of the piece will be structured. In the body of the piece, the writer **elaborates** upon, **illustrates**, and **explains** the **thesis statement**. How writers arrange supporting details and their choices of paragraph types are development techniques. Writers may give examples of the concept introduced in the thesis statement. If the subject includes a cause-and-effect relationship, the author may explain its causality. A writer will explain or analyze the main idea of the piece throughout the body, often by presenting arguments for the veracity or credibility of the thesis statement. Writers may use development to define or clarify ambiguous terms. Paragraphs within the body may be organized using natural sequences, like space and time. Writers may employ **inductive reasoning**, using multiple details to establish a generalization or causal relationship, or **deductive reasoning**, proving a generalized hypothesis or proposition through a specific example or case.

> **Review Video: Drafting Body Paragraphs**
> Visit mometrix.com/academy and enter code: 724590

PARAGRAPHS

After the introduction of a passage, a series of body paragraphs will carry a message through to the conclusion. Each paragraph should be **unified around a main point**. Normally, a good topic sentence summarizes the paragraph's main point. A topic sentence is a general sentence that gives an introduction to the paragraph.

The sentences that follow support the topic sentence. However, though it is usually the first sentence, the topic sentence can come as the final sentence to the paragraph if the earlier sentences give a clear explanation of the paragraph's topic. This allows the topic sentence to function as a concluding sentence. Overall, the paragraphs need to stay true to the main point. This means that any unnecessary sentences that do not advance the main point should be removed.

The main point of a paragraph requires adequate development (i.e., a substantial paragraph that covers the main point). A paragraph of two or three sentences does not cover a main point. This is especially true when the main point of the paragraph gives strong support to the argument of the thesis. An occasional short paragraph is fine as a transitional device. However, a well-developed argument will have paragraphs with more than a few sentences.

METHODS OF DEVELOPING PARAGRAPHS

Common methods of adding substance to paragraphs include examples, illustrations, analogies, and cause and effect.

- **Examples** are supporting details to the main idea of a paragraph or a passage. When authors write about something that their audience may not understand, they can provide an example to show their point. When authors write about something that is not easily accepted, they can give examples to prove their point.
- **Illustrations** are extended examples that require several sentences. Well-selected illustrations can be a great way for authors to develop a point that may not be familiar to their audience.
- **Analogies** make comparisons between items that appear to have nothing in common. Analogies are employed by writers to provoke fresh thoughts about a subject. These comparisons may be used to explain the unfamiliar, to clarify an abstract point, or to argue a point. Although analogies are effective literary devices, they should be used carefully in arguments. Two things may be alike in some respects but completely different in others.
- **Cause and effect** is an excellent device to explain the connection between an action or situation and a particular result. One way that authors can use cause and effect is to state the effect in the topic sentence of a paragraph and add the causes in the body of the paragraph. This method can give an author's paragraphs structure, which always strengthens writing.

TYPES OF PARAGRAPHS

A **paragraph of narration** tells a story or a part of a story. Normally, the sentences are arranged in chronological order (i.e., the order that the events happened). However, flashbacks (i.e., an anecdote from an earlier time) can be included.

A **descriptive paragraph** makes a verbal portrait of a person, place, or thing. When specific details are used that appeal to one or more of the senses (i.e., sight, sound, smell, taste, and touch), authors give readers a sense of being present in the moment.

A **process paragraph** is related to time order (i.e., First, you open the bottle. Second, you pour the liquid, etc.). Usually, this describes a process or teaches readers how to perform a process.

Comparing two things draws attention to their similarities and indicates a number of differences. When authors contrast, they focus only on differences. Both comparing and contrasting may be done point-by-point, noting both the similarities and differences of each point, or in sequential paragraphs, where you discuss all the similarities and then all the differences, or vice versa.

Breaking Text into Paragraphs

For most forms of writing, you will need to use multiple paragraphs. As such, determining when to start a new paragraph is very important. Reasons for starting a new paragraph include:

- To mark off the introduction and concluding paragraphs
- To signal a shift to a new idea or topic
- To indicate an important shift in time or place
- To explain a point in additional detail
- To highlight a comparison, contrast, or cause and effect relationship

Paragraph Length

Most readers find that their comfort level for a paragraph is between 100 and 200 words. Shorter paragraphs cause too much starting and stopping and give a choppy effect. Paragraphs that are too long often test the attention span of readers. Two notable exceptions to this rule exist. In scientific or scholarly papers, longer paragraphs suggest seriousness and depth. In journalistic writing, constraints are placed on paragraph size by the narrow columns in a newspaper format.

The first and last paragraphs of a text will usually be the introduction and conclusion. These special-purpose paragraphs are likely to be shorter than paragraphs in the body of the work. Paragraphs in the body of the essay follow the subject's outline (e.g., one paragraph per point in short essays and a group of paragraphs per point in longer works). Some ideas require more development than others, so it is good for a writer to remain flexible. A paragraph of excessive length may be divided, and shorter ones may be combined.

Coherent Paragraphs

A smooth flow of sentences and paragraphs without gaps, shifts, or bumps will lead to paragraph **coherence**. Ties between old and new information can be smoothed using several methods:

- **Linking ideas clearly**, from the topic sentence to the body of the paragraph, is essential for a smooth transition. The topic sentence states the main point, and this should be followed by specific details, examples, and illustrations that support the topic sentence. The support may be direct or indirect. In **indirect support**, the illustrations and examples may support a sentence that in turn supports the topic directly.
- The **repetition of key words** adds coherence to a paragraph. To avoid dull language, variations of the key words may be used.
- **Parallel structures** are often used within sentences to emphasize the similarity of ideas and connect sentences giving similar information.
- Maintaining a **consistent verb tense** throughout the paragraph helps. Shifting tenses affects the smooth flow of words and can disrupt the coherence of the paragraph.

> **Review Video: How to Write a Good Paragraph**
> Visit mometrix.com/academy and enter code: 682127

Sequence Words and Phrases

When a paragraph opens with the topic sentence, the second sentence may begin with a phrase like *first of all*, introducing the first supporting detail or example. The writer may introduce the second supporting item with words or phrases like *also*, *in addition*, and *besides*. The writer might introduce succeeding pieces of support with wording like, *another thing*, *moreover*, *furthermore*, or *not only that, but*. The writer may introduce the last piece of support with *lastly*, *finally*, or *last but not least*. Writers get off the point by presenting off-target items not supporting the main point. For example, a main point *my dog is not smart* is supported by the statement, *he's six years old and still doesn't answer to his name.* But *he cries when I leave for school* is not supportive, as it does not indicate lack of intelligence. Writers stay on point by presenting only supportive statements that are directly relevant to and illustrative of their main point.

> **Review Video: Sequence**
> Visit mometrix.com/academy and enter code: 489027

TRANSITIONS

Transitions between sentences and paragraphs guide readers from idea to idea and indicate relationships between sentences and paragraphs. Writers should be judicious in their use of transitions, inserting them sparingly. They should also be selected to fit the author's purpose—transitions can indicate time, comparison, and conclusion, among other purposes. Tone is also important to consider when using transitional phrases, varying the tone for different audiences. For example, in a scholarly essay, *in summary* would be preferable to the more informal *in short*.

When working with transitional words and phrases, writers usually find a natural flow that indicates when a transition is needed. In reading a draft of the text, it should become apparent where the flow is disrupted. At this point, the writer can add transitional elements during the revision process. Revising can also afford an opportunity to delete transitional devices that seem heavy handed or unnecessary.

> **Review Video: Transitions in Writing**
> Visit mometrix.com/academy and enter code: 233246

TYPES OF TRANSITIONAL WORDS

Time	Afterward, immediately, earlier, meanwhile, recently, lately, now, since, soon, when, then, until, before, etc.
Sequence	too, first, second, further, moreover, also, again, and, next, still, besides, finally
Comparison	similarly, in the same way, likewise, also, again, once more
Contrasting	but, although, despite, however, instead, nevertheless, on the one hand... on the other hand, regardless, yet, in contrast.
Cause and Effect	because, consequently, thus, therefore, then, to this end, since, so, as a result, if... then, accordingly
Examples	for example, for instance, such as, to illustrate, indeed, in fact, specifically
Place	near, far, here, there, to the left/right, next to, above, below, beyond, opposite, beside
Concession	granted that, naturally, of course, it may appear, although it is true that
Repetition, Summary, or Conclusion	as mentioned earlier, as noted, in other words, in short, on the whole, to summarize, therefore, as a result, to conclude, in conclusion
Addition	and, also, furthermore, moreover
Generalization	in broad terms, broadly speaking, in general

> **Review Video: Transitional Words and Phrases**
> Visit mometrix.com/academy and enter code: 197796
>
> **Review Video: Transitions**
> Visit mometrix.com/academy and enter code: 707563
>
> **Review Video: How to Effectively Connect Sentences**
> Visit mometrix.com/academy and enter code: 948325

CONCLUSION

Two important principles to consider when writing a conclusion are strength and closure. A strong conclusion gives the reader a sense that the author's main points are meaningful and important, and that the supporting facts and arguments are convincing, solid, and well developed. When a conclusion achieves closure, it gives the impression that the writer has stated all necessary information and points and completed the work, rather than simply stopping after a specified length. Some things to avoid when writing concluding paragraphs include:

- Introducing a completely new idea
- Beginning with obvious or unoriginal phrases like "In conclusion" or "To summarize"
- Apologizing for one's opinions or writing
- Repeating the thesis word for word rather than rephrasing it
- Believing that the conclusion must always summarize the piece

> **Review Video: Drafting Conclusions**
> Visit mometrix.com/academy and enter code: 209408

Writing Style and Form

WRITING STYLE AND LINGUISTIC FORM

Linguistic form encodes the literal meanings of words and sentences. It comes from the phonological, morphological, syntactic, and semantic parts of a language. **Writing style** consists of different ways of encoding the meaning and indicating figurative and stylistic meanings. An author's writing style can also be referred to as his or her **voice**.

Writers' stylistic choices accomplish three basic effects on their audiences:

- They **communicate meanings** beyond linguistically dictated meanings,
- They communicate the **author's attitude**, such as persuasive or argumentative effects accomplished through style, and
- They communicate or **express feelings**.

Within style, component areas include:

- Narrative structure
- Viewpoint
- Focus
- Sound patterns
- Meter and rhythm
- Lexical and syntactic repetition and parallelism
- Writing genre
- Representational, realistic, and mimetic effects
- Representation of thought and speech
- Meta-representation (representing representation)
- Irony
- Metaphor and other indirect meanings
- Representation and use of historical and dialectal variations
- Gender-specific and other group-specific speech styles, both real and fictitious
- Analysis of the processes for inferring meaning from writing

LEVEL OF FORMALITY

The relationship between writer and reader is important in choosing a **level of formality** as most writing requires some degree of formality. **Formal writing** is for addressing a superior in a school or work environment. Business letters, textbooks, and newspapers use a moderate to high level of formality. **Informal writing** is appropriate for private letters, personal emails, and business correspondence between close associates.

For your exam, you will want to be aware of informal and formal writing. One way that this can be accomplished is to watch for shifts in point of view in the essay. For example, unless writers are using a personal example, they will rarely refer to themselves (e.g., "*I* think that *my* point is very clear.") to avoid being informal when they need to be formal.

Also, be mindful of an author who addresses his or her audience **directly** in their writing (e.g., "Readers, *like you*, will understand this argument.") as this can be a sign of informal writing. Good writers understand the need to be consistent with their level of formality. Shifts in levels of formality or point of view can confuse readers and cause them to discount the message.

Clichés

Clichés are phrases that have been **overused** to the point that the phrase has no importance or has lost the original meaning. These phrases have no originality and add very little to a passage. Therefore, most writers will avoid the use of clichés. Another option is to make changes to a cliché so that it is not predictable and empty of meaning.

Examples:

> When life gives you lemons, make lemonade.
>
> Every cloud has a silver lining.

Jargon

Jargon is **specialized vocabulary** that is used among members of a certain trade or profession. Since jargon is understood by only a small audience, writers will use jargon in passages that will only be read by a specialized audience. For example, medical jargon should be used in a medical journal but not in a New York Times article. Jargon includes exaggerated language that tries to impress rather than inform. Sentences filled with jargon are not precise and are difficult to understand.

Examples:

> "He is going to *toenail* these frames for us." (Toenail is construction jargon for nailing at an angle.)
>
> "They brought in a *kip* of material today." (Kip refers to 1000 pounds in architecture and engineering.)

Slang

Slang is an **informal** and sometimes private language that is understood by some individuals. Slang terms have some usefulness, but they can have a small audience. So, most formal writing will not include this kind of language.

Examples:

> "Yes, the event was a blast!" (In this sentence, *blast* means that the event was a great experience.)
>
> "That attempt was an epic fail." (By *epic fail*, the speaker means that his or her attempt was not a success.)

Colloquialism

A colloquialism is a word or phrase that is found in informal writing. Unlike slang, **colloquial language** will be familiar to a greater range of people. However, colloquialisms are still considered inappropriate for formal writing. Colloquial language can include some slang, but these are limited to contractions for the most part.

Examples:

> "Can *y'all* come back another time?" (Y'all is a contraction of "you all.")

"Will you stop him from building this *castle in the air*?" (A "castle in the air" is an improbable or unlikely event.)

ACADEMIC LANGUAGE

In educational settings, students are often expected to use academic language in their schoolwork. Academic language is also commonly found in dissertations and theses, texts published by academic journals, and other forms of academic research. Academic language conventions may vary between fields, but general academic language is free of slang, regional terminology, and noticeable grammatical errors. Specific terms may also be used in academic language, and it is important to understand their proper usage. A writer's command of academic language impacts their ability to communicate in an academic or professional context. While it is acceptable to use colloquialisms, slang, improper grammar, or other forms of informal speech in social settings or at home, it is inappropriate to practice non-academic language in academic contexts.

TONE

Tone may be defined as the writer's **attitude** toward the topic, and to the audience. This attitude is reflected in the language used in the writing. The tone of a work should be **appropriate to the topic** and to the intended audience. While it may be fine to use slang or jargon in some pieces, other texts should not contain such terms. Tone can range from humorous to serious and any level in between. It may be more or less formal, depending on the purpose of the writing and its intended audience. All these nuances in tone can flavor the entire writing and should be kept in mind as the work evolves.

WORD SELECTION

A writer's choice of words is a signature of their style. Careful thought about the use of words can improve a piece of writing. A passage can be an exciting piece to read when attention is given to the use of vivid or specific nouns rather than general ones.

Example:

General: His kindness will never be forgotten.

Specific: His thoughtful gifts and bear hugs will never be forgotten.

Attention should also be given to the kind of verbs that are used in sentences. Active verbs (e.g., run, swim) are about an action. Whenever possible, an **active verb should replace a linking verb** to provide clear examples for arguments and to strengthen a passage overall. When using an active verb, one should be sure that the verb is used in the active voice instead of the passive voice. Verbs are in the active voice when the subject is the one doing the action. A verb is in the passive voice when the subject is the recipient of an action.

Example:

Passive: The winners were called to the stage by the judges.

Active: The judges called the winners to the stage.

CONCISENESS

Conciseness is writing that communicates a message in the fewest words possible. Writing concisely is valuable because short, uncluttered messages allow the reader to understand the author's message more easily and efficiently. Planning is important in writing concise messages. If you have in mind what you need to write beforehand, it will be easier to make a message short and to the point. Do not state the obvious.

Revising is also important. After the message is written, make sure you have effective, pithy sentences that efficiently get your point across. When reviewing the information, imagine a conversation taking place, and concise writing will likely result.

APPROPRIATE KINDS OF WRITING FOR DIFFERENT TASKS, PURPOSES, AND AUDIENCES

When preparing to write a composition, consider the audience and purpose to choose the best type of writing. Three common types of writing are persuasive, expository, and narrative. **Persuasive**, or argumentative writing, is used to convince the audience to take action or agree with the author's claims. **Expository** writing is meant to inform the audience of the author's observations or research on a topic. **Narrative** writing is used to tell the audience a story and often allows more room for creativity. While task, purpose, and audience inform a writer's mode of writing, these factors also impact elements such as tone, vocabulary, and formality.

For example, students who are writing to persuade their parents to grant them some additional privilege, such as permission for a more independent activity, should use more sophisticated vocabulary and diction that sounds more mature and serious to appeal to the parental audience. However, students who are writing for younger children should use simpler vocabulary and sentence structure, as well as choose words that are more vivid and entertaining. They should treat their topics more lightly, and include humor when appropriate. Students who are writing for their classmates may use language that is more informal, as well as age-appropriate.

> **Review Video: Writing Purpose and Audience**
> Visit mometrix.com/academy and enter code: 146627

Modes of Writing

Essays

Essays usually focus on one topic, subject, or goal. There are several types of essays, including informative, persuasive, and narrative. An essay's structure and level of formality depend on the type of essay and its goal. While narrative essays typically do not include outside sources, other types of essays often require some research and the integration of primary and secondary sources.

The basic format of an essay typically has three major parts: the introduction, the body, and the conclusion. The body is further divided into the writer's main points. Short and simple essays may have three main points, while essays covering broader ranges and going into more depth can have almost any number of main points, depending on length.

An essay's introduction should answer three questions:

1. What is the **subject** of the essay?

    If a student writes an essay about a book, the answer would include the title and author of the book and any additional information needed—such as the subject or argument of the book.

2. How does the essay **address** the subject?

    To answer this, the writer identifies the essay's organization by briefly summarizing main points and the evidence supporting them.

3. What will the essay **prove**?

    This is the thesis statement, usually the opening paragraph's last sentence, clearly stating the writer's message.

The body elaborates on all the main points related to the thesis, introducing one main point at a time, and includes supporting evidence with each main point. Each body paragraph should state the point in a topic sentence, which is usually the first sentence in the paragraph. The paragraph should then explain the point's meaning, support it with quotations or other evidence, and then explain how this point and the evidence are related to the thesis. The writer should then repeat this procedure in a new paragraph for each additional main point.

The conclusion reiterates the content of the introduction, including the thesis, to remind the reader of the essay's main argument or subject. The essay writer may also summarize the highlights of the argument or description contained in the body of the essay, following the same sequence originally used in the body. For example, a conclusion might look like: Point 1 + Point 2 + Point 3 = Thesis, or Point 1 → Point 2 → Point 3 → Thesis Proof. Good organization makes essays easier for writers to compose and provides a guide for readers to follow. Well-organized essays hold attention better and are more likely to get readers to accept their theses as valid.

Informative vs. Persuasive Writing

Informative writing, also called explanatory or expository writing, begins with the basis that something is true or factual, while **persuasive** writing strives to prove something that may or may not be true or factual. Whereas argumentative text is written to **persuade** readers to agree with the author's position, informative text merely **provides information and insight** to readers. Informative writing concentrates on **informing** readers about why or how something is as it is. This can include offering new information, explaining how a process works, and developing a concept for readers. To accomplish these objectives, the essay may name and distinguish various things within a category, provide definitions, provide details about the parts of something, explain a particular function or behavior, and give readers explanations for why a fact, object, event, or process exists or occurs.

Narrative Writing

Put simply, **narrative** writing tells a story. The most common examples of literary narratives are novels. Non-fictional biographies, autobiographies, memoirs, and histories are also narratives. Narratives should tell stories in such a way that the readers learn something or gain insight or understanding. Students can write more interesting narratives by describing events or experiences that were meaningful to them. Narratives should start with the story's actions or events, rather than long descriptions or introductions. Students should ensure that there is a point to each story by describing what they learned from the experience they narrate. To write an effective description, students should include sensory details, asking themselves what they saw, heard, felt or touched, smelled, and tasted during the experiences they describe. In narrative writing, the details should be **concrete** rather than **abstract**. Using concrete details enables readers to imagine everything that the writer describes.

> **Review Video: Narratives**
> Visit mometrix.com/academy and enter code: 280100

Sensory Details

Students need to use vivid descriptions when writing descriptive essays. Narratives should also include descriptions of characters, things, and events. Students should remember to describe not only the visual detail of what someone or something looks like, but details from other senses, as well. For example, they can contrast the feeling of a sea breeze to that of a mountain breeze, describe how they think something inedible would taste, and compare sounds they hear in the same location at different times of day and night. Readers have trouble visualizing images or imagining sensory impressions and feelings from abstract descriptions, so concrete descriptions make these more real.

Concrete vs. Abstract Descriptions in Narrative

Concrete language provides information that readers can grasp and may empathize with, while **abstract language**, which is more general, can leave readers feeling disconnected, empty, or even confused. "It was a lovely day" is abstract, but "The sun shone brightly, the sky was blue, the air felt warm, and a gentle breeze wafted across my skin" is concrete. "Ms. Couch was a good teacher" uses abstract language, giving only a general idea of the writer's opinion. But "Ms. Couch is excellent at helping us take our ideas and turn them into good essays and stories" uses concrete language, giving more specific examples of what makes Ms. Couch a good teacher. "I like writing poems but not essays" gives readers a general idea that the student prefers one genre over another, but not why. But when reading, "I like writing short poems with rhythm and rhyme, but I hate writing five-page essays that go on and on about the same ideas," readers understand that the student prefers the brevity, rhyme, and meter of short poetry over the length and redundancy of longer prose.

Autobiographical Narratives

Autobiographical narratives are narratives written by an author about an event or period in their life. Autobiographical narratives are written from one person's perspective, in first person, and often include the author's thoughts and feelings alongside their description of the event or period. Structure, style, or theme varies between different autobiographical narratives, since each narrative is personal and specific to its author and his or her experience.

REFLECTIVE ESSAY

A less common type of essay is the reflective essay. **Reflective essays** allow the author to reflect, or think back, on an experience and analyze what they recall. They should consider what they learned from the experience, what they could have done differently, what would have helped them during the experience, or anything else that they have realized from looking back on the experience. Reflection essays incorporate both objective reflection on one's own actions and subjective explanation of thoughts and feelings. These essays can be written for a number of experiences in a formal or informal context.

JOURNALS AND DIARIES

A **journal** is a personal account of events, experiences, feelings, and thoughts. Many people write journals to express their feelings and thoughts or to help them process experiences they have had. Since journals are **private documents** not meant to be shared with others, writers may not be concerned with grammar, spelling, or other mechanics. However, authors may write journals that they expect or hope to publish someday; in this case, they not only express their thoughts and feelings and process their experiences, but they also attend to their craft in writing them. Some authors compose journals to record a particular time period or a series of related events, such as a cancer diagnosis, treatment, surviving the disease, and how these experiences have changed or affected them. Other experiences someone might include in a journal are recovering from addiction, journeys of spiritual exploration and discovery, time spent in another country, or anything else someone wants to personally document. Journaling can also be therapeutic, as some people use journals to work through feelings of grief over loss or to wrestle with big decisions.

EXAMPLES OF DIARIES IN LITERATURE

The Diary of a Young Girl by Dutch Jew Anne Frank (1947) contains her life-affirming, nonfictional diary entries from 1942-1944 while her family hid in an attic from World War II's genocidal Nazis. *Go Ask Alice* (1971) by Beatrice Sparks is a cautionary, fictional novel in the form of diary entries by Alice, an unhappy, rebellious teen who takes LSD, runs away from home and lives with hippies, and eventually returns home. Frank's writing reveals an intelligent, sensitive, insightful girl, raised by intellectual European parents—a girl who believes in the goodness of human nature despite surrounding atrocities. Alice, influenced by early 1970s counterculture, becomes less optimistic. However, similarities can be found between them: Frank dies in a Nazi concentration camp while the fictitious Alice dies from a drug overdose. Both young women are also unable to escape their surroundings. Additionally, adolescent searches for personal identity are evident in both books.

> **Review Video: Journals, Diaries, Letters, and Blogs**
> Visit mometrix.com/academy and enter code: 432845

LETTERS

Letters are messages written to other people. In addition to letters written between individuals, some writers compose letters to the editors of newspapers, magazines, and other publications, while some write "Open Letters" to be published and read by the general public. Open letters, while intended for everyone to read, may also identify a group of people or a single person whom the letter directly addresses. In everyday use, the most-used forms are business letters and personal or friendly letters. Both kinds share common elements: business or personal letterhead stationery; the writer's return address at the top; the addressee's address next; a salutation, such as "Dear [name]" or some similar opening greeting, followed by a colon in business letters or a comma in personal letters; the body of the letter, with paragraphs as indicated; and a closing, like "Sincerely/Cordially/Best regards/etc." or "Love," in intimate personal letters.

Early Letters

The Greek word for "letter" is *epistolē*, which became the English word "epistle." The earliest letters were called epistles, including the New Testament's epistles from the apostles to the Christians. In ancient Egypt, the writing curriculum in scribal schools included the epistolary genre. Epistolary novels frame a story in the form of letters. Examples of noteworthy epistolary novels include:

- *Pamela* (1740), by 18th-century English novelist Samuel Richardson
- *Shamela* (1741), Henry Fielding's satire of *Pamela* that mocked epistolary writing.
- *Lettres persanes* (1721) by French author Montesquieu
- *The Sorrows of Young Werther* (1774) by German author Johann Wolfgang von Goethe
- *The History of Emily Montague* (1769), the first Canadian novel, by Frances Brooke
- *Dracula* (1897) by Bram Stoker
- *Frankenstein* (1818) by Mary Shelley
- *The Color Purple* (1982) by Alice Walker

Blogs

The word "blog" is derived from "weblog" and refers to writing done exclusively on the internet. Readers of reputable newspapers expect quality content and layouts that enable easy reading. These expectations also apply to blogs. For example, readers can easily move visually from line to line when columns are narrow, while overly wide columns cause readers to lose their places. Blogs must also be posted with layouts enabling online readers to follow them easily. However, because the way people read on computer, tablet, and smartphone screens differs from how they read print on paper, formatting and writing blog content is more complex than writing newspaper articles. Two major principles are the bases for blog-writing rules: The first is while readers of print articles skim to estimate their length, online they must scroll down to scan; therefore, blog layouts need more subheadings, graphics, and other indications of what information follows. The second is onscreen reading can be harder on the eyes than reading printed paper, so legibility is crucial in blogs.

Rules and Rationales for Writing Blogs

1. Format all posts for smooth page layout and easy scanning.
2. Column width should not be too wide, as larger lines of text can be difficult to read
3. Headings and subheadings separate text visually, enable scanning or skimming, and encourage continued reading.
4. Bullet-pointed or numbered lists enable quick information location and scanning.
5. Punctuation is critical, so beginners should use shorter sentences until confident in their knowledge of punctuation rules.
6. Blog paragraphs should be far shorter—two to six sentences each—than paragraphs written on paper to enable "chunking" because reading onscreen is more difficult.
7. Sans-serif fonts are usually clearer than serif fonts, and larger font sizes are better.
8. Highlight important material and draw attention with **boldface**, but avoid overuse. Avoid hard-to-read *italics* and ALL CAPITALS.
9. Include enough blank spaces: overly busy blogs tire eyes and brains. Images not only break up text but also emphasize and enhance text and can attract initial reader attention.
10. Use background colors judiciously to avoid distracting the eye or making it difficult to read.
11. Be consistent throughout posts, since people read them in different orders.
12. Tell a story with a beginning, middle, and end.

Specialized Modes of Writing

Editorials

Editorials are articles in newspapers, magazines, and other serial publications. Editorials express an opinion or belief belonging to the majority of the publication's leadership. This opinion or belief generally refers to a specific issue, topic, or event. These articles are authored by a member, or a small number of members, of the publication's leadership and are often written to affect their readers, such as persuading them to adopt a stance or take a particular action.

Resumes

Resumes are brief, but formal, documents that outline an individual's experience in a certain area. Resumes are most often used for job applications. Such resumes will list the applicant's work experience, certification, and achievements or qualifications related to the position. Resumes should only include the most pertinent information. They should also use strategic formatting to highlight the applicant's most impressive experiences and achievements, to ensure the document can be read quickly and easily, and to eliminate both visual clutter and excessive negative space.

Reports

Reports summarize the results of research, new methodology, or other developments in an academic or professional context. Reports often include details about methodology and outside influences and factors. However, a report should focus primarily on the results of the research or development. Reports are objective and deliver information efficiently, sacrificing style for clear and effective communication.

Memoranda

A memorandum, also called a memo, is a formal method of communication used in professional settings. Memoranda are printed documents that include a heading listing the sender and their job title, the recipient and their job title, the date, and a specific subject line. Memoranda often include an introductory section explaining the reason and context for the memorandum. Next, a memorandum includes a section with details relevant to the topic. Finally, the memorandum will conclude with a paragraph that politely and clearly defines the sender's expectations of the recipient.

Research Writing

RESEARCH WRITING

Writing for research is essentially writing to answer a question or a problem about a particular **research topic**. A **problem statement** is written to clearly define the problem with a topic before asking about how to solve the problem. A **research question** serves to ask what can be done to address the problem. Before a researcher should try to solve a problem, the researcher should spend significant time performing a **literature review** to find out what has already been learned about the topic and if there are already solutions in place. The literature review can help to re-evaluate the research question as well. If the question has not been thoroughly answered, then it is proper to do broader research to learn about the topic and build up the body of literature. If the literature review provides plenty of background, but no practical solutions to the problem, then the research question should be targeted at solving a problem more directly. After the research has been performed, a **thesis** can act as a proposal for a solution or as a recommendation to future researchers to continue to learn more about the topic. The thesis should then be supported by significant contributing evidence to help support the proposed solution.

EXAMPLE OF RESEARCH WRITING ELEMENTS

Topic	The general idea the research is about. This is usually broader than the problem itself. Example: Clean Water
Problem Statement	A problem statement is a brief, clear description of a problem with the topic. Example: Not all villages in third-world countries have ready access to clean water.
Research Question	A research question asks a specific question about what needs to be learned or done about the problem statement. Example: What can local governments do to improve access to clean water?
Literature Review	A review of the body of literature by the researcher to show what is already known about the topic and the problem. If the literature review shows that the research question has already been thoroughly answered, the researcher should consider changing problem statements to something that has not been solved.
Thesis	A brief proposal of a solution to a problem. Theses do not include their own support, but are supported by later evidence. Example: Local governments can improve access to clean water by installing sealed rain-water collection units.
Body Paragraphs	Paragraphs focused on the primary supporting evidence for the main idea of the thesis. There are usually three body paragraphs, but there can be more if needed.
Conclusion	A final wrap-up of the research project. The conclusion should reiterate the problem, question, thesis, and briefly mention how the main evidences support the thesis.

THE RESEARCH PROCESS

Researchers should prepare some information before gathering sources. Researchers who have chosen a **research question** should choose key words or names that pertain to their question. They should also identify what type of information and sources they are looking for. Researchers should consider whether secondary or primary sources will be most appropriate for their research project. As researchers find credible and appropriate sources, they should be prepared to adjust the scope of their research question or topic in response to the information and insights they gather.

Using Sources and Synthesizing Information

As researchers find potential sources for their research project, it is important to keep a **record** of the material they find and note how each source may impact their work. When taking these notes, researchers should keep their research question or outline in mind and consider how their chosen references would complement their discussion. **Literature reviews** and **annotated bibliographies** are helpful tools for evaluating sources, as they require the researcher to consider the qualities and offerings of the sources they choose to use. These tools also help researchers synthesize the information they find.

Synthesizing Information

Synthesizing information requires the researcher to integrate sources and their own thoughts by quoting, paraphrasing, or summarizing outside information in their research project. Synthesizing information indicates that the research complements the writer's claims, ensures that the ideas in the composition flow logically, and makes including small details and quotes easier. Paraphrasing is one of the simplest ways to integrate a source. **Paraphrasing** allows the writer to support their ideas with research while presenting the information in their own words, rather than using the source's original wording. Paraphrasing also allows the writer to reference the source's main ideas instead of specific details. While paraphrasing does not require the writer to quote the source, it still entails a direct reference to the source, meaning that any paraphrased material still requires a citation.

Citing Sources

While researchers should combine research with their own ideas, the information and ideas that come from outside sources should be attributed to the author of the source. When conducting research, it is helpful to record the publication information for each source so that **citations** can be easily added within the composition. Keeping a close record of the source of each idea in a composition or project is helpful for avoiding plagiarism, as both direct and indirect references require documentation.

Plagiarism

Understanding what is considered to be plagiarism is important to preventing unintentional plagiarism. Using another person's work in any way without proper attribution is **plagiarism**. However, it is easy to mistakenly commit plagiarism by improperly citing a source or creating a citation that is not intended for the way the source was used. Even when an honest attempt to attribute information is made, small errors can still result in plagiarized content. For this reason, it is important to create citations carefully and review citations before submitting or publishing research. It is also possible to plagiarize one's own work. This occurs when a writer has published work with one title and purpose and then attempts to publish it again as new material under a new title or purpose.

Literature Review

One of the two main parts of a literature review is searching through existing literature. The other is actually writing the review. Researchers must take care not to get lost in the information and inhibit progress toward their research goal. A good precaution is to write out the research question and keep it nearby. It is also wise to make a search plan and establish a time limit in advance. Finding a seemingly endless number of references indicates a need to revisit the research question because the topic is too broad. Finding too little material means that the research topic is too narrow. With new or cutting-edge research, one may find that nobody has investigated this particular question. This requires systematic searching, using abstracts in periodicals for an overview of available literature, research papers or other specific sources to explore its reference, and references in books and other sources.

When searching published literature on a research topic, one must take thorough notes. It is common to find a reference that could be useful later in the research project, but is not needed yet. In situations like this, it is helpful to make a note of the reference so it will be easy to find later. These notes can be grouped in a word processing document, which also allows for easy compiling of links and quotes from internet research. Researchers should explore the internet regularly, view resources for their research often, learn how to use resources correctly and efficiently, experiment with resources available within the disciplines, open and examine databases, become familiar with reference desk materials, find publications with abstracts of articles and books on one's topic, use papers' references to locate the most useful journals and important authors, identify keywords for refining and narrowing database searches, and peruse library catalogues online for available sources—all while taking notes.

As one searches for references, one will gradually develop an overview of the body of literature available for his or her subject. This signals the time to prepare for writing the literature review. The researcher should assemble his or her notes along with copies of all the journal articles and all the books he or she has acquired. Then one should write the research question again at the top of a page and list below it all of the author names and keywords discovered while searching. It is also helpful to observe whether any groups or pairs of these stand out. These activities are parts of structuring one's literature review—the first step for writing a thesis, dissertation, or research paper. Writers should rewrite their work as necessary rather than expecting to write only one draft. However, stopping to edit along the way can distract from the momentum of writing the first draft. If the writer is dissatisfied with a certain part of the draft, it may be better to skip to a later portion of the paper and revisit the problem section at another time.

BODY AND CONCLUSION IN LITERATURE REVIEW

The first step of a literature review paper is to create a rough draft. The next step is to edit: rewrite for clarity, eliminate unnecessary verbiage, and change terminology that could confuse readers. After editing, a writer should ask others to read and give feedback. Additionally, the writer should read the paper aloud to hear how it sounds, editing as needed. Throughout a literature review, the writer should not only summarize and comment on each source reviewed, but should also relate these findings to the original research question. The writer should explicitly state in the conclusion how the research question and pertinent literature interaction is developed throughout the body, reflecting on insights gained through the process.

SUMMARIES AND ABSTRACTS

When preparing to submit or otherwise publish research, it may be necessary to compose a summary or abstract to accompany the research composition.

A summary is a brief description of the contents of a longer work that provides an overview of the work and may include its most important details. One common type of summary is an abstract. Abstracts are specialized summaries that are most commonly used in the context of research. Abstracts may include details such as the purpose for the research, the researcher's methodology, and the most significant results of the research. Abstracts sometimes include sections and headings, where most summaries are limited to one or a few paragraphs with no special groupings.

EDITING AND REVISING

After composing a rough draft of a research paper, the writer should **edit** it. The purpose of the paper is to communicate the answer to one's research question in an efficient and effective manner. The writing should be as **concise** and **clear** as possible, and the style should also be consistent. Editing is often easier to do after writing the first draft rather than during it, as taking time between writing and editing allows writers to be more objective. If the paper includes an abstract and an introduction, the writer should compose these after writing the rest, when he or she will have a better grasp of the theme and arguments. Not all readers understand technical terminology or long words, so writers should use these sparingly. Finally, writers should consult a writing and style guide to address any industry- or institution-specific issues that may arise as they edit.

> **Review Video: Revising and Editing**
> Visit mometrix.com/academy and enter code: 674181

MOGEA Practice Test

Want to take this practice test in an online interactive format? Check out the bonus page, which includes interactive practice questions and much more: **mometrix.com/bonus948/mogea081**

Communications

Refer to the following for questions 1 - 3:

>   Jo's face was a study next day, for the secret rather weighed upon her, and she found it hard not to look mysterious and important. Meg observed it, but did not trouble herself to make inquiries, for she had learned that the best way to manage Jo was by the law of contraries, so she felt sure of being told everything if she did not ask. She was rather surprised, therefore, when the silence remained unbroken, and Jo assumed a patronizing air, which decidedly aggravated Meg, who in turn assumed an air of dignified reserve and devoted herself to her mother. This left Jo to her own devices, for Mrs. March had taken her place as nurse, and bade her rest, exercise, and amuse herself after her long confinement. Amy being gone, Laurie was her only refuge, and much as she enjoyed his society, she rather dreaded him just then, for he was an incorrigible tease, and she feared he would coax the secret from her.
>
>   (*Little Women* by Louisa May Alcott)

1. From what point of view is this passage written?
   a. First person
   b. Second person
   c. Third person
   d. Fourth person

2. The phrase "was a study" implies that
   a. Jo looked jubilant.
   b. Jo looked secretive.
   c. Jo looked disheveled.
   d. Jo looked angry.

3. What can you infer about Laurie?
   a. He was stoic.
   b. He was taciturn.
   c. He was unruly.
   d. He was uncanny.

Refer to the following for questions 4 - 7:

By Sara Teasdale

> There will come soft rains and the smell of the ground,
> And swallows circling with their shimmering sound;
>
> And frogs in the pools singing at night,
> And wild plum trees in tremulous white;
>
> 5 Robins will wear their feathery fire
> Whistling their whims on a low fence-wire;
>
> And not one will know of the war, not one
> Will care at last when it is done.
>
> Not one would mind, neither bird nor tree
> 10 If mankind perished utterly;
>
> And Spring herself, when she woke at dawn,
> Would scarcely know that we were gone

4. Which line uses personification?
- a. Line 2
- b. Line 4
- c. Line 10
- d. Line 11

5. The "we" used in line 12 refers to
- a. all of mankind.
- b. the victors of the war.
- c. Americans.
- d. the poet and the reader.

6. This poem is an example of a(n)
- a. sonnet.
- b. rhymed verse.
- c. free verse.
- d. lyric.

7. Which of these statements offers the best summary of the poem?
- a. Nature does not care about the affairs of mankind.
- b. It is the government's responsibility to fight a war.
- c. War has a devastating impact on nature.
- d. Wars should not be fought in the spring.

Refer to the following for questions 8 - 10:

Archaeological Sites are concentrations of artifacts, rock art or features that reflect activities conducted by past human cultures. Archaeological sites are also areas or buildings where historic human events occurred, such as mining camps or railroad construction sites. These areas are usually, but not always, accompanied by artifacts.

Cultural Resources are usually archaeological sites. They are also *areas* or *localities* that are considered by Native Americans to have been or are presently significant in the exercise of their respective Native American religions or traditional lifeway customs.

Artifacts are objects that show evidence of use or alteration by humans. There are three kinds of artifacts:

- Prehistoric artifacts were used prior to written history, which is considered in North America to have been before the arrival of Europeans. Examples of prehistoric artifacts are arrowheads, manos and metates, and ceramic materials.
- Historic artifacts were used during written history, but more than 50 years ago. Historic artifacts include purple glass bottles, tin cans sealed with solder, and parts of wagons.
- Recent artifacts were used within the last 50 years and are generally not considered of archaeological significance. (U.S. Department of the Interior)

8. What is a prehistoric artifact?
a. An artifact found on an archaeological site
b. A purple glass bottle
c. An item used within the last 50 years
d. An item used prior to written history

9. What is the main idea of the first paragraph?
a. Archaeological sites are areas of artifacts, rock art or features that reflect activities of past human cultures.
b. Artifacts are objects that show evidence of use by humans.
c. Artifacts include purple glass bottles, tin cans sealed with solder, and parts of wagons.
d. Archaeological sites can include mining camps and railroad construction sites.

10. What would be a logical implication based on this passage?
a. Cultural Resources always contain recent artifacts.
b. A site that contains recent artifacts would not be of interest to an archaeologist.
c. Arrowheads can be found in mining camps and railroad construction sites.
d. Prehistoric artifacts are the most important of the three types of artifacts.

Refer to the following for questions 11 - 14:

Mary Ainsworth described three major categories of infant attachment: secure, anxious/avoidant, and anxious/ambivalent. After years of additional research by many investigators, Mary Main and Judith Solomon in 1986 identified a fourth pattern: anxious/disorganized/disoriented.

These four major patterns of attachment describe unique sets of behavior:

Secure: Securely attached babies are able to use the attachment figure as an effective secure base from which to explore the world. When such moderately stressful events as brief (3-minute) separations in an unfamiliar environment occur, these securely attached babies approach or signal to the attachment figure at reunion and achieve a degree of proximity or contact which suffices to terminate attachment behavior. They accomplish this with little or no open or masked anger, and soon return to exploration or play.

Avoidant: Babies with avoidant attachments are covertly anxious about the attachment figure's responsiveness and have developed a defensive strategy for managing their anxiety. Upon the attachment figure's return after the same moderately stressful events, these avoidant babies show mild version of the "detachment" behavior which characterizes many infants after separations of two or three weeks; that is, they fail to greet the mother, ignore her overtures and act as if she is of little importance.

Ambivalent: In babies with anxious/ambivalent attachments, both anxiety and mixed feelings about the attachment figure are readily observable. At reunion after brief separations in an unfamiliar environment, they mingle openly angry behavior with their attachment behavior.

Disorganized/Disoriented: Babies classified in this group appear to have no consistent strategy for managing separation from and reunion with the attachment figure. Some appear to be clinically depressed; some demonstrate mixtures of avoidant behavior, openly angry behavior and attachment behavior. Others show odd, often uncomfortable and disturbing behaviors. These infant are often seen in studies of high-risk samples of severely maltreated, very disturbed or depressed babies, but also appear in normal middle-class samples. (U.S. Department of Health and Human Services)

11. It can be inferred from this passage that Mary Ainsworth is a
   a. Botanist
   b. Biologist
   c. Psychologist
   d. Entomologist

12. This passage is mainly about
   a. three categories of infant attachment.
   b. four major patterns of infant attachment.
   c. secure infant attachment.
   d. high risk babies.

13. This passage would most likely be found in a
   a. human resources handbook.
   b. human development textbook.
   c. philosophy textbook.
   d. physiology textbook.

14. Babies with avoidant attachments
   a. show odd, uncomfortable behaviors.
   b. are openly angry.
   c. show masked anger.
   d. act as if the mother is of no importance.

15. Which author's works have explored the experience and roles of black women in American society?
    a. Toni Morrison
    b. Washington Irving
    c. Richard Wright
    d. Flannery O'Conner

16. Which author is associated with the Contemporary movement?
    a. Homer
    b. Henry David Thoreau
    c. George Orwell
    d. William Shakespeare

17. Catherine and Heathcliff are main characters from which novel?
    a. Jane Eyre
    b. Wuthering Heights
    c. The Awakening
    d. The Scarlett Letter

18. What is one strategy for prewriting?
    a. Clustering
    b. Reconsidering arguments
    c. Retell, Recite, Relate
    d. Getting the reader's attention

19. The main difference between a topic outline and a sentence outline is
    a. a topic outline helps arrange ideas.
    b. ideas are numbered or lettered in a sentence outline.
    c. ideas are fully stated in a sentence outline.
    d. a sentence outline only uses brief phrases or single words.

20. If a student is writing a thesis on brain disorders, the best source of information would be a(n):
    a. medical journals.
    b. encyclopedia.
    c. webpage.
    d. newspaper.

21. Which is the best revision of this sentence?
    I will start the music after the guests have arrived.
    a. After the guests have arrived, I will start the music.
    b. I will start the music after the guests arrive.
    c. I start the music when the guests have arrived.
    d. I will have started the music when the guests have arrived.

22. Which sentence is incorrect?
   a. Shawna graduated from college.
   b. Shawna graduated college.
   c. The college graduated Shawna.
   d. Shawna was graduated from college.

23. Which is not a main step in the writing process?
   a. Revising
   b. Editing
   c. Publishing
   d. Brainstorming

24. What is the goal of the drafting stage of the writing process?
   a. Correcting work before publication
   b. Making content clear, interesting and complete
   c. Getting ideas down on paper without undue concern for mechanics
   d. Brainstorming ideas

25. When creating an outline, it is important to use
   a. prepositions.
   b. progressivism.
   c. abbreviation.
   d. subordination.

26. What takes place in the revision stage of the writing process?
   a. Correcting errors in grammar, spelling and punctuation
   b. Making major changes in content and structure
   c. Brainstorming ideas
   d. Getting ideas down on paper

27. Which sentence is an example of passive voice?
   a. Debbie Knuteson won the award.
   b. The doctor admitted Joan to the hospital yesterday.
   c. James was released from prison in 1951.
   d. The veterinarian injected the puppy with three vaccines.

28. Which of the following is a compound-complex sentence?
   a. The dog lived in the backyard, but the cat, who knew he was superior, lived inside the house.
   b. She ate her breakfast, and then brushed her teeth.
   c. When she arrived, the train had already left.
   d. Facts can be proven.

29. Which of the following is the best example of parallel sentence structure?
   a. She enjoys dessert, walking on the beach, and songs from the 1980s.
   b. I like to eat pies, playing soccer games, and mysteries.
   c. The sheriff tried to make the law explicit, accurate, and fair.
   d. He is adorable, wears a feather in his hat, and has a cunning way about him.

30. **Which correction, if any, should be made in this sentence?**

    Servicing the air conditioner every summer, the appliance seemed to run better.
    a. Servicing the air conditioner every summer, there is an easy way to keep your appliance cooling your home.
    b. Servicing the air conditioner every summer, Joan found she could have a much lower electric bill.
    c. Servicing the air conditioner every summer, the appliance was kept in excellent condition.
    d. No correction is required.

31. **Identify the error in this sentence:**

    The baking of homemade meals have increased during the current economy.
    a. of
    b. have
    c. during
    d. current

32. **Identify the error in this sentence.**

    No matter how diligent Jonas tries, he still fails to complete his homework.
    a. Adjective and adverb error
    b. Antecedent agreement error
    c. Dangling modifier
    d. Verb tense error

33. **Which correction should be made in this sentence?**

    After the new neighbors moved in, Russell found there excessively loud music very aggravating.
    a. Russell found their excessively loud music very aggravating.
    b. Russell was aggravated by their excessively loud music.
    c. Russell found their excessively loud music very annoying.
    d. Russell found them aggravating.

34. **What correction, if any, should be made in this sentence?**

    Major remodeling is necessary, in instances where mold and dry rot, have destroyed infrastructure.
    a. Major remodeling is necessary in instances where mold and dry rot have destroyed infrastructure.
    b. Major remodeling is necessary, in instances where mold and dry rot have destroyed infrastructure.
    c. Major remodeling is necessary in instances where mold, and dry rot, have destroyed infrastructure.
    d. No correction is required.

35. **Which sentence is incorrectly punctuated?**
    a. My son's smile reminds me of his father.
    b. I drove to the grocery store, the Laundromat, and the library that is just down the street.
    c. "I am going to lunch," she said. "I haven't finished my work, but I need to eat now."
    d. They drove all day to see the snow, however, it had all melted by the time they got there.

36. Identify the error in this sentence.

The teacher gave stickers to whomever had stood in line quietly.

a. Punctuation error
b. Verb tense error
c. Subject and object form error
d. Dangling modifier

37. Which title is not punctuated correctly?

a. A Christmas Carol, by Charles Dickens
b. "The Road Not Taken," by Robert Frost
c. "The Raven," by Edgar Allan Poe
d. "The Heart of Darkness," by Joseph Conrad

Mathematical Sciences

1. A blouse normally sells for $138, but is on sale for 25% off. What is the cost of the blouse?
   a. $67
   b. $103.50
   c. $34.50
   d. $113

2. The following table shows the distance from a point to a moving car at various times.

d	Distance	50	70	110
t	Time	2	3	5

   If the speed of the car is constant, which of the following equations describes the distance from the point to the car?
   a. $d = 25t$
   b. $d = 35t$
   c. $d = 55t$
   d. $d = 20t + 10$

3. Which of the following is an example of an irrational number?
   a. -8
   b. 1/4
   c. $\sqrt{2}$
   d. 28

4. Which of the following is an example of the commutative property?
   a. 8 + 12 = 12 + 8
   b. 20 + 0 = 20
   c. 9(3 + 6) = 9 • 3 + 9 • 6
   d. 2 + -2 = 0

5. To determine a student's grade, a teacher throws out the lowest grade obtained on 5 tests, averages the remaining grades, and rounds up to the nearest integer. If Betty scored 72, 75, 88, 86, and 90 on her tests, what grade will she receive?
   a. 68
   b. 85
   c. 88
   d. 84.8

6. What is the value of the expression $-3 \times 5^2 + 2(4-18) + 33$?
   a. -130
   b. -70
   c. -20
   d. 74

7. A box of laundry detergent contains 16.5 oz of product. What is the maximum number of loads that can be washed if each load requires a minimum of ¾ oz of detergent?
   a. 10
   b. 50
   c. 22
   d. 18

8. A crane raises one end of a 3300 lb steel beam. The other end rests upon the ground. If the crane supports 30% of the beam's weight, how many pounds does it support?
   a. 330 lbs
   b. 990 lbs
   c. 700 lbs
   d. 1100 lbs

9. A taxi service charges $5.50 for the first $\frac{1}{5}$ of a mile, $1.50 for each additional $\frac{1}{5}$ of a mile, and 20¢ per minute of waiting time. Joan took a cab from her place to a flower shop 8 miles away, where she bought a bouquet, then another 3.6 miles to her mother's place. The driver had to wait 9 minutes while she bought the bouquet. What was the fare?
   a. $20
   b. $120.20
   c. $92.80
   d. $91

10. Solve the following equation: $x + 16 = 3x + 32$.
    a. $-16 = 2x$
    b. $x = -8$
    c. $x = -16$
    d. $x = -32$

11. Translate the following into mathematical symbols:

    46 is less than the difference of 17 and a number
    a. 46 < x - 17
    b. 46 > 17 - x
    c. 46 < 17 – x
    d. 17 – x < 46

12. What geometric figure is this?

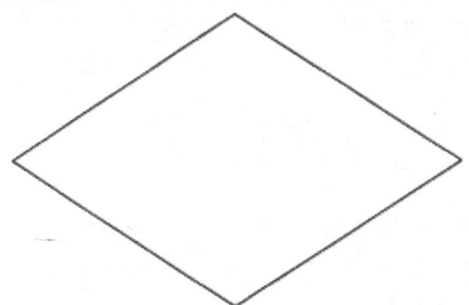

a. rhombus
b. trapezoid
c. pentagon
d. square

13. How are the following polygons related?

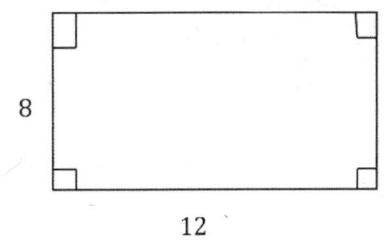

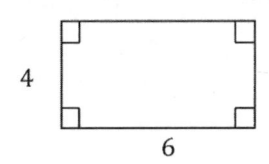

a. They are congruent.
b. They are acute.
c. They are similar.
d. They are adjacent.

14. Find the perimeter of a triangle with sides measuring 6 centimeters, 12 centimeters and 14 centimeters.

a. 18 cm
b. 24 cm
c. 28 cm
d. 32 cm

15. The radius of a circle is 6 inches. What is the area?

a. 18.84 in²
b. 37.68 in²
c. 87.98 in²
d. 113.04 in²

16. Find the volume of a cube with the length of each side as 12 cm.

a. 36 cm³
b. 650 cm³
c. 1,728 cm³
d. 2,421 cm³

17. Find the surface area of a sphere with the radius of 1.5 cm.
    a. 28.26 cm²
    b. 7.065 cm²
    c. 18.84 cm²
    d. 14.13 cm²

18. Find the length of c based on the right triangle below.

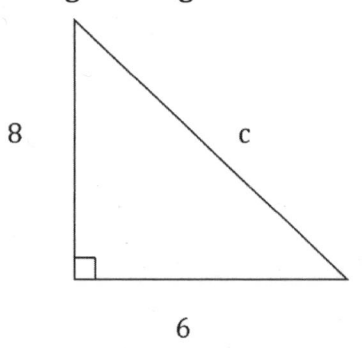

    a. 7 cm
    b. 10 cm
    c. 14 cm
    d. 20 cm

19. What is the surface area, in square inches, of a cube if the length of one side is 3 inches?
    a. 9
    b. 27
    c. 54
    d. 21

20. Which of the following values is closest to the diameter of a circle with an area of 314 square inches?
    a. 20 inches
    b. 10 inches
    c. 100 inches
    d. 31.4 inches

21. The town of Fram will build a water storage tank on a hill overlooking the town. The tank will be a right circular cylinder of radius R and height H. The plot of ground selected for the installation is large enough to accommodate a circular tank 60 feet in diameter. The planning commission wants the tank to hold 1,000,000 cubic feet of water, and they intend to use the full area available. Which of the following is the minimum acceptable height?
    a. 655 ft
    b. 455 ft
    c. 355 ft
    d. 255 ft

22. A teacher can grade 20 math tests per hour. If she starts grading test at 10:30 a.m., which of the following is the best estimate as to when she will be done grading 134 tests?
    a. 3:00 p.m.
    b. 4:00 p.m.
    c. 4:30 p.m.
    d. 5:00 p.m.

23. What is the next number in the series?
    132, 123, 115, 108, 102
    a. 82
    b. 87
    c. 92
    d. 97

24. What is the mode of the following numbers?
    37, 46, 52, 52, 61, 63
    a. 37
    b. 52
    c. 55
    d. 311

25. If a = 3 and b = 4, simplify the following expression: 6a + b -7
    a. 12
    b. 15
    c. 20
    d. 22

Natural Sciences

1. If you were testing the effectiveness of a cream that reduced the signs of wrinkles around women's eyes, which of the following would be a good control group?

    a. Rats with no wrinkles
    b. A group of women with no wrinkles around their eyes who are given the cream
    c. A group of women with wrinkles who are given a harmless cream that has no effect
    d. A group of women with wrinkles around their eyes

2. Which step of the scientific method involves independent variables?

    a. Make an observation
    b. Ask a question
    c. Formulate a hypothesis
    d. Conduct an experiment

3. Which of these units of measurement is used to measure bicyclist's energy expenditure?

    a. ergs
    b. nanometers
    c. milligrams
    d. cubic centimeters

4. Convert 0.0000000736 to scientific notation.

    a. $7.36 \times 10 8$
    b. $736 \times 10 - 8$
    c. 7.36×10^{-8}
    d. $736 \times 10 - 8$

5. The true diameter of electrical wire 3.67 cm. Three measurements of the wire produce the following values: 3.9 cm, 3.9 cm, and 3.9 cm. Which of the following statements is true concerning the measurements?

    a. They are neither precise nor accurate.
    b. They are precise and accurate.
    c. They are precise but not accurate.
    d. They are accurate but not precise.

6. Science can be differentiated from non-science because scientific results

    a. are repeatable.
    b. always take place in a laboratory.
    c. are based on single events.
    d. are formed from opinions.

7. Which of the following is formed by meiosis?

    a. spores
    b. embryos
    c. DNA
    d. chromosomes

8. Most of the energy in a food chain is concentrated in the level of the
    a. primary producers.
    b. primary consumers.
    c. secondary consumers.
    d. tertiary consumers.

9. In a mixture of NaCl and H₂O, what piece of equipment should be used to separate the mixture?
    a. magnet
    b. hotplate
    c. funnel
    d. drill

10. A scientist wants to measure the direction and duration of the movement of the ground. Which of the following instruments will the scientist most likely use?
    a. A laser light with holograph
    b. A seismograph
    c. An electron microscope
    d. A stereoscope

11. The major advantage of sexual reproduction over asexual forms is that
    a. it requires two individuals.
    b. it promotes diversity.
    c. it produces more offspring.
    d. it involves chromosomes.

12. A solar eclipse is
    a. when the moon comes between the sun and the earth
    b. the path of the sun across the celestial sphere
    c. a geometrical curve
    d. when the earth comes between the moon and the sun

13. Pollination involves which plant parts?
    a. Xylem and petiole
    b. Apical meristem and floral meristem
    c. Anther and stigma
    d. Root hairs and stroma

14. Which agricultural product takes the most energy to produce?
    a. rice
    b. potatoes
    c. beef
    d. wheat

15. Read the following paragraph:

An experiment was conducted to determine whether taking an aspirin every day could reduce the chance of a heart attack. Scientists gave a group of 600 heart attack survivors who were in a health and fitness program one aspirin per day for three years. The study found that the people in the study had a much smaller chance of having another heart attack than the national average for heart attack survivors. The scientists concluded that taking aspirin lowers your risk of a heart attack.

What is the main flaw of this study?
   a. The number of people examined in the study was too small.
   b. The results of the study may be due to the health regimen the participants were on, not the aspirin.
   c. The study did not have a long enough duration to have accurate results.
   d. There was no control group.

16. The pilot of an eastbound plane determines wind speed relative to his aircraft. He measures a wind velocity of 320 km/h, with the wind coming from the east. An observer on the ground sees the plane pass overhead, and measures its velocity as 290 km/h. What is the wind velocity relative to the observer?
   a. 30 km/h east-to-west
   b. 30 km/h west-to-east
   c. 320 km/h east-to-west
   d. 290 km/h east-to-west

17. During periods that are unfavorable for growth, some plants become dormant. Which season would these plants most likely lie dormant in North America?
   a. Summer
   b. Fall
   c. Winter
   d. Spring

18. Which is the smallest unit of measure, out of the following choices?
   a. microliter
   b. megaliter
   c. deciliter
   d. milliliter

19. Put 9×10^6 in standard notation.
   a. 9,000,000
   b. 90,000,000
   c. 0.000009
   d. 0.0000009

20. What is oxidation?
   a. The exchange of carbon dioxide for oxygen
   b. The reduction of the number of chromosomes per cell
   c. Cave formations resulting from the dripping of mineralized water
   d. A change in the chemical composition of iron

Refer to the following for question 21:

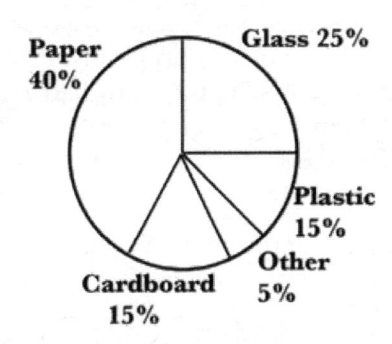

Paper 40%
Glass 25%
Plastic 15%
Other 5%
Cardboard 15%

21. A recycling company collects sorted materials from its clients. The materials are weighed and then processed for re-use. The chart shows the weights of various classes of materials that were collected by the company during a representative month. Which of the following statements is NOT supported by the data in the chart?

    a. Paper products, including cardboard, make up a majority of the collected materials.
    b. One quarter of the materials collected are made of glass.
    c. More plastic is collected than cardboard.
    d. Plastic and cardboard together represent a larger portion of the collected materials than glass bottles.

22. A Tsunami may be caused by

    a. earthquakes
    b. volcanoes
    c. landslides
    d. A, B and C

23. What is the best use for a barometer?

    a. measuring temperature
    b. measuring atmospheric pressure
    c. observing remote objects
    d. viewing objects too small for the naked eye to see

24. Sn is the symbol for which element?

    a. Sulfur
    b. Selenium
    c. Scandium
    d. Tin

25. What is often used to transport a measured volume of liquid?

    a. a pipette
    b. a graduated cylinder
    c. a beaker
    d. a slide

Social and Behavioral Sciences

1. Which list is in the correct chronological order?
   a. Great Schism, Norman Conquest, French Revolution
   b. Great Schism, French Revolution, Norman Conquest
   c. Norman Conquest, Great Schism, French Revolution
   d. French Revolution, Norman Conquest, Great Schism

2. Marxism had a profound influence on the development of
   a. the Bolshevik political movement.
   b. Autumn Harvest Uprising.
   c. the National Socialist German Workers' Party
   d. the Greek Civil war

3. The Lincoln-Douglas debates resulted in
   a. the declaration of Illinois as a slave state.
   b. the split of the Democratic Party.
   c. the election of Douglas as president in 1860.
   d. the election of Lincoln to the senate in 1858.

4. What major U.S. event took place around the same time that the Judiciary Act set up the federal judiciary system?
   a. The Neutrality Act was passed.
   b. The United States entered WWII.
   c. The Korean War ended.
   d. George Washington was inaugurated president.

5. What invention increased the value and demand for slaves in the South?
   a. the combine
   b. the steam engine
   c. the cotton gin
   d. the automobile

6. What significance did *Brown* v. *Board of Education of Topeka* have on the system if education in the United States?
   a. Students were educated separately but equally.
   b. Students were taught creationism.
   c. Students were taught evolution.
   d. The "separate but equal" ruling was reversed.

7. What was generally the sentiment towards Chinese laborers in the United States in 1882?
   a. Chinese laborers were viewed as cheap laborers and were generally discriminated against.
   b. Chinese laborers were highly valued members of the United States society.
   c. Chinese laborers were forced out of the country.
   d. Chinese laborers were welcomed through several immigration laws.

8. Iran, Iraq, and Kuwait all border what body of water?
   a. Indian Ocean
   b. Red Sea
   c. Persian Gulf
   d. Caspian Sea

9. The majority of residents of Brazil identify themselves as
   a. Roman Catholic
   b. Buddhist
   c. Muslim
   d. Jewish

10. Which economic/political system has the following characteristics:
    - private ownership of property
    - property and capital provides income for the owner
    - freedom to compete for economic gain
    - profit motive driving the economy.

    a. Fascism
    b. Capitalism
    c. Communism
    d. Marxism

11. Which of these would not be found in a democracy?
    a. a congress
    b. a parliament
    c. a prime minister
    d. a dictator

12. A researcher is collecting data for her study on parenting. She hypothesized that countries where mothers carry their infants on their person have children who have more secure attachments as toddlers. Which method would be the most helpful in collecting data for this study?
    a. Interviewing parents in the United States about their methods of carrying babies.
    b. Determining methods of carrying babies and studying the toddlers in several countries.
    c. Researching popular methods of carrying infants on the internet.
    d. Collecting data on the number of strollers sold in several countries.

13. **Based on the chart, which of the following statements is NOT accurate?**

Jail Inmates by Sex and Race				
Year	1990	1995	2000	2005
Male	365,821	448,000	543,120	646,807
Female	37,198	51,300	70,414	93,963
Juveniles	2,301	7,800	7,613	6,759
White	169,600	203,300	260,500	331,000
Black	172,300	220,600	256,300	290,500
Hispanic	58,100	74,400	94,100	111,900

[Source: U.S. Dept. of Justice; does not include federal or state prisons.]

a. Fewer women than men are incarcerated in each year sampled.
b. The rate of jail incarceration rose for every subgroup of prisoner.
c. In 2000 and in 2005, more whites were incarcerated in jails than any other race.
d. Rate of Hispanic jailing has steadily increased over the fifteen years represented.

14. **ARTICLE XXVI (Ratified July 1, 1971) of the United States Constitution states:**

Section 1. The right of citizens of the United States, who are eighteen years of age or older, to vote shall not be denied or abridged by the United States or by any State on account of age.

This amendment to the Constitution was ratified in part because of what historical reality?

a. Women gained the right to vote.
b. Suffrage was extended to all African Americans.
c. Young men were being drafted to serve in the Vietnam War.
d. The number of people under 21 years of age increased.

15. **Who became the commander of the Confederate army of northern Virginia at the beginning of the Civil War?**

a. Abraham Lincoln
b. Thomas "Stonewall" Jackson
c. Robert E. Lee
d. Jefferson Davis

16. **Which invention had a major role in communication during the Civil War?**

a. Morse Code
b. Telephone
c. Radio
d. Computer

17. **The Dred Scott case involved the Supreme Court ruling on**

a. Women's voting rights
b. Civil rights
c. Miranda Rights
d. Right to an attorney

18. The Andes Mountain Range is located on which continent?
   a. North America
   b. South America
   c. Australia
   d. Asia

19. What effect does the Sahara Desert have on trade?
   a. Caravans have to skirt the desert.
   b. Oases make trade possible.
   c. Due to massive amounts of rain, trade routes are unpredictable.
   d. Trade across the Sahara Desert has never existed due to the inhospitable conditions.

20. India's economy can be best described as
   a. a third-world country.
   b. one of the lowest producing economies in the world.
   c. a market-based system.
   d. an agricultural stronghold.

21. Which of the following countries can be described as a constitutional democratic monarchy?
   a. Thailand
   b. Mexico
   c. Australia
   d. South Africa

22. Read the following passage:

> Islam spread to Europe during the medieval period, bringing scientific and technological insights. The Muslim emphasis on knowledge and learning can be traced to an emphasis on both in the Qur'an [Koran], the holy book of Islam. Because of this emphasis, scholars preserved some of the Greek and Roman texts that were lost to the rest of Europe. The writings of Aristotle, among others, were saved by Muslim translators. Islamic scholars modified a Hindu number system, which became the more commonly used Arabic system, which replaced Roman numerals. They also developed algebra and invented the astrolabe, a device for telling time that also helped sailors to navigate. In medicine, Muslim doctors cleaned wounds with antiseptics, closed the wounds with gut and silk sutures, and were among the first to use sedatives.

Based on the information above, which of the following conclusions is likely true?
   a. People of Muslim faith were braver than others when facing surgery.
   b. Fewer Muslim patients died of wound infections than did their European counterparts.
   c. The silk market expanded because of the Muslim use of silk sutures.
   d. No one would read Aristotle today had the Muslims not saved the translations.

23. Which of the following countries is NOT located along the Indian Ocean?
   a. Cameroon
   b. Somalia
   c. Mozambique
   d. Kenya

Humanities and Fine Arts

1. What literary movement is a type of realistic fiction that developed in France, America and England in late the 19th century?

    a. Romanticism
    b. Realism
    c. Naturalism
    d. Classicism

2. What ornamental figures are found in Gothic architecture?

    a. dragons
    b. phoenixes
    c. gargoyles
    d. Tuscan columns

3. In social sciences, reification is best understood as:

    a. using qualitative data instead of quantitative data.
    b. treating an abstraction as a concrete thing.
    c. the use of heuristic devices.
    d. mistaking subjectivity for objectivity.

4. A distinguishing feature of the form known as haiku is...

    a. 5/7/5 syllables per line
    b. An ABA rhyme scheme
    c. Perfectly regular meter
    d. Lengthy epic narratives

5. Analyzing each character in a script, studying biographical information, and understanding each characters' strengths and weaknesses are important aspects of:

    a. Developing character relationships
    b. Script analysis
    c. Plot development
    d. Psychological dissection

6. All of the following are examples of widely studied ancient theatre forms except:

    a. Greek.
    b. Roman
    c. English Renaissance
    d. Medieval

7. Which theatrical term best describes a dramatic outburst or a release of strong emotion by an actor or an audience member?

    a. Catharsis
    b. Alienation effect
    c. Performance purification
    d. Ablution

8. Which of the following describes the placing of two visual elements next to each other to create the effect of contrast?
   a. Juxtaposition
   b. Appropriation
   c. Transformation
   d. Extrusion

9. An artwork is analyzed by the recognition of the subject as being important to the viewer's perception. This artwork is being analyzed using which of the following aesthetic theories of art criticism?
   a. Emotionalism
   b. Formalism
   c. Deconstructivism
   d. Representationalism

10. Which of the following best describes a way that visual art has influenced popular culture?
   a. Artists appropriated images from comic books to use in their artwork.
   b. The bright colors and repetition of Pop art were subsequently used in fashion and advertising.
   c. Mass-produced objects were a subject in the artworks.
   d. Artists used commercial methods such as screen-printing.

Writing Prompt

1. Imagine you are attending a college that is contemplating a change to electronic textbooks. All students who attend the school will be offered the opportunity to access their textbooks through an electronic textbook search engine. Supporters argue that switching to the e-textbooks will save students money and will be a more environmentally friendly choice over traditional printed textbooks.

The Student Council has asked students to submit statements expressing their opinions on the issue, and you have decided to submit a statement.

In an organized, coherent, and supported essay directed to the Student Council, explain what you think the college should do and why it should do so. Address the pros and cons of switching to an electronic textbook system.

Answer Key and Explanations

Communications

1. C: Point of view refers to the vantage point from which a story is written. First person uses the pronoun *I*. Second person uses the pronoun *you*. Third person uses the pronouns *he/she/they*. There is no fourth person point of view. This passage was written in the third person.

2. B: The words "mysterious" and "important" used in the sentence help the reader deduce that Jo looked secretive. Jo neither looked jubilant, or joyful; disheveled, or disarrayed; or angry.

3. C: The last sentence states that Laurie was "an incorrigible tease." From this statement you can infer that Laurie was unruly or unmanageable. Stoic means not showing passion or emotion. Taciturn means silent. Uncanny means supernatural. There is nothing in the passage to imply he had any of these characteristics.

4. D: Personification is a metaphor in which a thing or abstraction is represented as a person. Personification is used throughout this poem. However, of the answer choices given, line 11 is the best choice. The author personifies spring as a female.

5. A: The fifth stanza gives clues to whom "we" refers.

> "Not one would mind, neither bird nor tree
> If mankind perished utterly"

"We" is referencing mankind.

6. B: This is an example of a rhymed verse poem. The last two words of each line rhymes in every stanza. A sonnet is a poem of fourteen lines following a set rhyme scheme and logical structure. Often, poets use iambic pentameter when writing sonnets. A free verse poem is written without using strict meter or rhyme. A lyric poem is a short poem that expresses personal feelings, which may or may not be set to music.

7. A: Answer choice A gives the best summary of the poem. The poem imagines nature reclaiming the earth after humanity has been wiped out by a war. The poet imagines how little the human race will be missed.

8. D: According to the passage, a prehistoric artifact is an item used by humans prior to written history. The other answer choices are details included in the passage, but not the definition of prehistoric artifacts.

9. A: The first paragraph gives the definition of an archaeological site, choice A. The other answer choices are details covered in the passage, but not the main idea of the first paragraph.

10. B: Since the passage states that recent artifacts are not of archaeological significance, a logical implication is that a site containing recent artifacts would not be of interest to an archaeologist. Answer choices A, C, and D are not true based on the information given in the passage.

11. C: Since this passage is about the characteristics of human behavior, it can be inferred that Mary Ainsworth is a psychologist. A botanist studies plants. A biologist studies plant and animal life. An entomologist studies insects.

12. B: This passage describes four major patterns of infant attachment.

13. B: This passage addresses infant behavior and would most likely be found in a human development textbook.

14. D: The paragraph that describes the avoidant attachment pattern states that the infant acts as if the mother is of no importance.

15. A: Toni Morrison's novels focus on black women and their search for a place within American culture and society. She often uses fantasy to explore the themes of racism, gender bias, and class conflict. She is both a Nobel Prize and Pulitzer Prize winner. Her novels include *The Bluest Eye*, *Sula*, *Song of Solomon*, and *Beloved*.

16. C: Authors of the Contemporary movement wrote from 1945 to the present. George Orwell wrote *Animal Farm* in 1945 and *1984* in 1949.

17. B: Heathcliff and Catherine are main characters in *Wuthering Heights*, written by Emily Bronte in 1847.

18. A: Clustering is a prewriting strategy. The writer starts with a circle in the middle that contains a main idea and then draws lines to other, smaller circles that contain sub-ideas or issues related to the main idea. Other prewriting strategies include free-writing, brainstorming, tagmemics, and journalistic techniques.

19. C: The headings and subheadings of a topic outline are words or phrases, and it is brief. The headings and subheadings of a sentence outline are full sentences, and it is longer and more detailed.

20. A: The best source for information would be a medical journal. While the other sources may have information on the topic, the medical journal would have the most reliable information.

21. B: No matter what the tense of the main part of a sentence, the verb that follows *after* should be in the simple present (*arrive*) or the simple past (*arrived*). In this case, it should be the simple present.

22. B: Use *graduate* with the preposition *from*, unless the noun comes first in the sentence.

23. D: Although brainstorming can be used as part of the prewriting step, it is not main step in the writing process. The five steps of the writing process are Prewriting, Drafting, Revising, Editing, and Publishing.

24. C: The goal of the drafting stage is to get ideas down on paper without undue concern for mechanics. Errors will be corrected in the editing stage.

25. D: There are four main components to an effective outline. Subordination means that the information in the heading is more general, while the subheadings are more specific. For example:

I. Visit and Evaluate College Websites

    A. Note important statistic

    B. Look for interesting classes

The other three components of an effective outline include parallelism, coordination, and division.

26. B: Revising is the time to reconsider the topic, the audience, and the purpose of writing. Rethinking the approach may lead to major changes in content and structure.

27. C: The passive voice is used to eliminate the necessity of naming the agent of the action when the agent is unknown or unimportant. Here is an example of this sentence using the active voice:

Prison authorities released James from prison in 1951.

28. A: A compound-complex sentence has two or more independent clauses and one or more dependent clauses.

29. C: Parallel sentence structure uses parallel grammatical form between coordinated elements. Option C uses the following grammatical structure after the word law: adjective--adjective--adjective.

30. B: When a sentence begins with a modifying word, phrase, or clause, the subject must be modified by that modifier. When a modifier improperly modifies something, it is called a "dangling modifier." Option B introduces a person into the subject position and corrects the dangling modifier.

31. B: The subject of this sentence is *the baking* and the verb is *have increased*. However, *baking* is a singular subject, so the correct verb form is *has* increased. This is an example of incorrect subject-verb agreement.

32. A: This is an adjective and adverb error. Adjectives modify nouns and pronouns; adverbs modify verbs, adjectives, and other adverbs. *Attentive* is modifying Jonas' diligence. *Tries* is a verb, so *diligent* needs to be an adverb to make this sentence grammatically correct.

No matter how diligently Jonas tries, he still fails to complete his homework.

33. C: This sentence contains both a homonym error (their/there) and a confused pair (annoy/aggravate). The use of *aggravate* to mean *annoy* is sometimes objected to because it departs from the etymological meaning "to make heavier."

34. A: This is an example of superfluous commas.

35. D: When conjunctive adverbs (*however, furthermore,* and *therefore*) are used in place of coordinating conjunctions to combine two sentences into one a semicolon is needed before the conjunctive adverb.

36. C: "Who" is the subject form of the pronoun and "whom" is the object form. This sentence should read:

"The teacher gave stickers to whoever had stood in line quietly."

37. D: The titles of books, movies, plays, magazines and newspapers are written in italics. The titles of poems, stories, and paintings are written with quotation marks.

Mathematical Sciences

1. B: 25% off is equivalent to, $25 * \frac{\$138}{100} = \$34.50$, and therefore the sale price becomes:

$138 - $34.50 = $103.50.

2. D: Inspection of the data shows that the distance traveled by the car during any 1-unit interval (velocity) is 20 units. However, the first data point shows that the car is 50 units from the point of origin at time 2, so it had a 10-unit head start before time measurement began.

3. C: An irrational number is a real number that cannot be expressed as a ratio of two integers.

4. A: The commutative property states that changing the order of something does not change the end result.

5. B: The lowest score, 68, is eliminated. The average of the remaining four grades is:

$$Avg = \frac{75 + 88 + 86 + 90}{4} = 84.75$$

Rounding up to the nearest integer gives a final grade of 85.

6. B: Use the order of operations to find the value for this expression: parentheses, exponents, multiplication and division, addition and subtraction:

$$-3 \times 5^2 + 2(4-18) + 33$$
$$= -3 \times 5^2 + 2(-14) + 33$$
$$= -3 \times 25 + 2(-14) + 33$$
$$= -75 + (-28) + 33$$
$$= -70$$

7. C: Recall that dividing by a fraction is the same as multiplying by its reciprocal: $16.5 \times \frac{4}{3} = 22$.

8. B: It is helpful to recall that percentages can be converted to decimals: 30% of 3300 is 0.3×3300 lbs = 990 lbs

9. C: The total distance traveled was $8 + 3.6 = 11.6$ miles. The first $\frac{1}{5}$ of a mile is charged at the higher rate. Since $\frac{1}{5} = 0.2$, the remainder of the trip is 11.4 miles. Thus, the fare for the distance traveled is computed as $\$5.50 + 5 \times 11.4 \times \$1.50 = \$91$. To this the charge for waiting time must be added, which is simply $9 \times 20¢ = 180¢ = \$1.80$. Finally, add the two charges, $\$91 + \$1.80 = \$92.80$.

10. B: To solve the equation, isolate the variable on one side.

Subtract x from each side:

$$16 = 2x + 32$$

Subtract 32 from each side.

$$-16 = -2x$$

Divide both sides by 2:

$$x = -8$$

11. C: First write "46 is less than" using 46 and the less than symbol:

$$46 <$$

Difference means subtract. When "difference of" is used, write the numbers in the same order as they appear in the sentence:

$$17 - x$$

The sentence should read:

$$46 < 17 - x$$

12. A: A rhombus is four-sided polygon having all four sides of equal length. The sum of the angles of a rhombus is 360 degrees.

13. C: Similar polygons are polygons for which all corresponding angles are congruent and all corresponding sides are proportional.

14. D: To find the perimeter of a triangle, take the sum of the length of each side.

15. D: The formula for the area of a circle is $A = \pi r^2$.

$$A = \pi \cdot r \cdot r$$
$$A = 3.14 \cdot (6 \text{ in}) \cdot (6 \text{in})$$
$$A = 3.14 \cdot (36 \text{ in}^2)$$
$$A = 113.04 \text{ in}^2$$

16. C: The formula for the volume of a cube is $V = L^3$.

$$12^3 = 1,728 \text{ cm}^3$$

17. A: The formula for the surface area of a sphere is $A = 4\pi r^2$.

$$A = 4 \cdot \pi \cdot r \cdot r$$
$$A = 4 \cdot 3.14 \cdot (1.5 \text{ cm}) \cdot (1.5 \text{ cm})$$
$$A = 12.56 \cdot (2.25 \text{ cm}^2)$$
$$A = 28.26 \text{ cm}^2$$

18. B: Use the Pythagorean Theorem to solve this problem: $a^2 + b^2 = c^2$

$$8^2 + 6^2 = c^2$$
$$64 + 36 = c^2$$
$$100 = c^2$$
$$\sqrt{100} = 10$$

19. C: The surface area of a cube is obtained by multiplying the area of each face by 6, since there are 6 faces. The area of each face is the square of the length of one edge:

$$A = 6 \times 3^2 = 6 \times 9 = 54$$

20. A: The area A of a circle is given by $A = \pi \times r^2$, where r is the radius. Since π is approximately 3.14, we can solve for $r = \sqrt{\frac{A}{\pi}} = \sqrt{\frac{314 \text{ inches}^2}{3.14}} = \sqrt{100 \text{ inches}^2} = 10$ inches. Now, the diameter d is twice the radius, or 2×10 inches $= 20$ inches.

21. C: The volume of a right circular cylinder is equal to its height multiplied by the area of its base, A. Since the base is circular, $A = \pi R^2$, where R, the radius, is half the diameter, or 30 feet. Therefore: $V = H \times \pi R^2$.

Solving for H,

$$H = \frac{V}{\pi R^2} = \frac{1{,}000{,}000}{\pi \times 30^2} = \frac{1{,}000{,}000}{\pi \times 900} = 353.7 ft$$

22. D: The teacher is grading 134 tests, which can be estimated at 130 tests. Divide the total number of tests by the number of tests she can grade in an hour to determine how many hours it will take to grade the tests:

$$130 \div 20 = 6.5 \text{ hours}$$

She started grading at 10:30 a.m., so 6.5 hours later will be 5:00 p.m.

23. D: The pattern is subtracting one less number each time:

$$132 - 9 = 123$$
$$123 - 8 = 115$$
$$115 - 7 = 108$$
$$108 - 6 = 102$$

The next number to be subtracted is 5, so $102 - 5 = 97$

24. B: The mode is the number that appears the most. 52 appears the most in this series of numbers.

25. B: $6 \cdot 3 + 4 - 7$

$$= 18 + 4 - 7$$
$$= 15$$

Natural Sciences

1. C: The best control group would be women with wrinkles around their eyes using a harmless cream that has no effect. A scientific control group is used to minimize the unintended influence of other variables on a scientific study. Such extraneous variables include researcher bias, environmental changes, and biological variation. Scientific controls ensure that data are valid and are a vital part of the scientific method.

2. D: The Scientific method is set of steps used to solve scientific problems. The steps are making an observation, asking a question, formulating a hypothesis, conducting an experiment, analyzing data, and drawing a conclusion. Independent variables are used in experiments to ensure that only a single variable is tested.

3. A: An erg is a centimeter-gram-second unit of energy. An ergometer is used to measure ergs. They are often used on exercise equipment. Portable ergometers can be mounted on bicycles to measure the rider's energy expenditure. A nanometer is a measurement of length. A milligram is a unit of mass or weight. A cubic centimeter is measurement of volume.

4. C: In scientific notation, the numerical portion will be "7.36". Count how many places the decimal point has to move to get from where it is now to where it needs to be. The power on 10 has to be –8 because that's how many places the decimal point needs to be moved.

5. C: All three measurements differ in value from the true length. This means they are not accurate. However, all three the measurements are equal in, so they are precise.

6. A: In order for something to be considered scientific fact, the results must be repeatable. Scientific study does not always take place in a laboratory. Scientific fact is never based on a single event. Only after the same experiments are conducted numerous times with the same results is the hypothesis accepted as fact. Science is not based on opinions.

7. A: Meiosis is a process that cuts the number of chromosomes per cell is cut in half. In animals, meiosis results in the formation of gametes, while in other organisms it results in spores.

8. A: A food chain shows how energy is transferred from one organism to another. A producer uses the energy from the sun to make its own food. Most of the energy in a food chain is in the level of the producer.

9. B: A mixture of NaCl and H_2O is salt and water. The only way to separate salt from water is to boil the mixture which evaporates the water, leaving the salt behind.

10. B: Movement of the ground, or an earthquake, generates seismic waves. These movements can be detected with a sensitive instrument called a seismograph.

11. B: Sexual reproduction allows the genetic information from two parents to mix. Recombination events between the two parental copies of individual genes may occur, creating new genes. The production of new genes and of new gene combinations leads to an increase in diversity within the population, which is a great advantage in terms of adapting to changes in the environment.

12. A: A solar eclipse is when the moon moves between the Sun and the Earth. When viewed from the Earth, the moon and the Sun are about the same size, and thus the moon can completely block the sun.

13. C: Pollination is the fertilization of plants. It involves the transfer of pollen from the anther to the stigma, either by wind or by insects.

14. C: Energy is lost when matter is transferred from one trophic level to another. It requires energy to produce the food for the cattle, and therefore it takes more energy to produce beef than any of the plant crops.

15. B: The flaw in this study is that it does not observe a single variable, but several variables at the same time. The participants were taking aspirin and participating in a health regime.

16. A: The velocities of both the wind and the aircraft can be represented by vectors, with the length of the vector representing the speed, and the direction of the vector representing the direction of either the wind or the airplane. Since the wind speed opposes that of the plane, the pilot will measure the sum of the actual wind speed plus that of his aircraft:

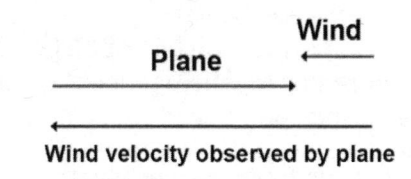

```
                    Wind
         Plane     ←——
         ——————→
         ←————————————
         Wind velocity observed by plane
```

17. C: Since the winter is most unfavorable for plant growth in North America, some plants go dormant during this season.

18. A: A microliter is a millionth of a liter.

19. A: Move the decimal point six positions to the right.

20. D: Oxidation, also known as rusting, is the result of a change in the chemical composition of the iron.

21. C: The chart shows that plastic and cardboard materials both comprise 15% of the collected materials, and therefore it is incorrect to say that there is more plastic than cardboard. They are present in equal quantities.

22. D: A tsunami, sometimes referred to as a tidal wave, is a large wave or series of waves caused by the displacement of a large volume of water. While the most common cause is an earthquake, large landslides (either falling into the sea or taking place under water) or explosive volcanic action may also result in a tsunami.

23. B: A barometer is an instrument for measuring atmospheric pressure, used especially in weather forecasting.

24. D: Sn is the symbol for tin.

25. D: A pipette is used to transport a measured volume of liquid. Graduated cylinders are used to measure liquids. A beaker is used for stirring, mixing, or heating liquids. They can be used to measure liquids, but are less accurate than a graduated cylinder. A slide holds objects for examination under a microscope.

Social and Behavioral Sciences

1. C: The Norman Conquest was the English historical period beginning in 1066. It began with the defeat of Anglo-Saxon King Harold II. With this defeat, the customs, laws, and language of the Normans was introduced in England. The Great Schism was the division in the Roman Catholic Church from 1378–1417 when two rival popes emerged.

The French Revolution was the prolonged political and social struggle between 1789 and 1799 in France. It encompassed the regicide of the king, Louis XVI, and the queen, Marie-Antoinette, included the Reign of Terror, the establishment of the First Republic, and led to the rise of Napoleon Bonaparte as Emperor of France, leading Europe to war.

2. A: Marxism is a term applied to the political, economic, and social theories advanced by Marx and Engels. Marx's theories had a profound influence on the development of Socialist movements and were the basis for the Bolshevik political movement lead by Lenin.

3. B: The debates between Lincoln, a Republican, and Douglas, a Democrat, resulted in Douglas making statements about slavery that the South would not accept. This resulted in the split of the Democratic Party and the defeat of Douglas in the presidential election in 1860.

4. D: The Judiciary Act established the Supreme Court, district courts, circuit courts, and the office of attorney general in 1789. George Washington was inaugurated president in 1789.

5. C: Eli Whitney invented the cotton gin in 1794. The gin enabled one worker to produce 50 pounds of cleaned cotton in one day. This made cotton a profitable crop and increased the demand for and value of slaves in the South.

6. D: In 1954 the Warren Court unanimously reversed the separate but equal ruling of *Plessy* v. *Ferguson* in 1896.

7. A: In 1880, ill sentiment was high against Chinese laborers. This sentiment lead to the reversal of the Burlingame Treaty of 1868, and thus legal immigration was stopped for a period of 10 years.

8. C: Iran, Iraq, and Kuwait all border the Persian Gulf.

9. A: The national religion of Brazil is Roman Catholicism.

10. B: These characteristics describe capitalism.

11. D: A dictator is a leader with absolute power without respect to constitutional limitations. This would not be found in a democracy. Democracy is rule by the people; government by the consent of the governed.

12. B: Determining methods of carrying babies and studying the toddlers in several countries would be the best method for gathering data for this study.

13. B: The rate of incarceration for juveniles did decrease after 1995. Answer A is a correct statement. Fewer women than men are incarcerated in each year sampled, even though the number of females incarcerated is growing. Response C is also accurate; in the years specified, more whites were incarcerated in jails than any other race. The chart clearly shows an increase in the number of Hispanics being jailed, making response D an accurate statement.

14. C: Young people protested being old enough to fight and die for their country while being denied voting rights. Choice A is incorrect because women had gained the right to vote with passage of the Nineteenth Amendment in 1920. Choice B is also wrong. African American males were guaranteed suffrage following the Civil War; African American females gained the right in 1920. The baby boom ended in 1964, so Choice D is not correct.

15. C: Robert E. Lee declined Lincoln's offer to command the U.S. Army at the outbreak of the Civil War. He instead chose to become the commander of the Confederate army of northern Virginia. In the final phases of the war, he was the commander of all Confederate forces.

16. A: Samuel Morse invented a code of dots and dashes that became known as Morse Code, and in 1844 the first message was transmitted over a telegraph line. Morse code played an important role in communications during the Civil War.

17. B: In the Dred Scot case of 1857, the Supreme Court ruled that Dred Scott was not a citizen and had no right to bring his case to court.

18. B: The Andes mountain range is the world's longest continental mountain range. It lies as a continuous chain of mountains along the western coast of South America.

19. B: Trade has been a part of the Sahara desert for centuries. Without the oases, this would have been impossible. An oasis is an area fed by an underground spring. Where oases were found in the Sahara, communities were established. This allowed traders to cross the desert by traveling from one oasis to another.

20. C: In recent years, India's economy has been shaping into a market-based economy. This is an economic system that relies on supply and demand to set prices, rather than having prices set by the government.

21. A: A constitutional democratic monarchy is a country where the head of state is a monarch. The monarch shares power with a government that is organized by a constitution. Thailand's government meets this definition.

22. B: By using antiseptics, Muslim doctors prevented the infection that often led to loss of limbs or life among Europeans. The other responses are opinion or not supported by the paragraph. We have no way of comparing the bravery of Muslim people with those of other faiths when facing surgery, so Choice A can be eliminated. Likewise, Choice C is incorrect; there would not be sufficient rise in silk use for sutures to account for an expanded silk market. It is not clear that the Muslims were the only people to have translations of the works of Aristotle, nor does the passage suggest such.

23. A: Cameroon is on the Atlantic coast, south of Nigeria and north of Gabon. Choice B is not accurate. Somalia is bordered by both the Indian Ocean and the Gulf of Aden; its capital, Mogadishu, is on the Indian Ocean. Choice C is incorrect; Mozambique, near the southern part of the continent, is bordered by the Indian Ocean. Choice D, Kenya, near the middle of the African continent, likewise, is an inaccurate choice. Kenya is also bordered by the Indian Ocean.

Humanities and Fine Arts

1. C: Naturalism is a type of realistic fiction. The Naturalist movement took place in France, America, and England in the late 19th and early 20th centuries. Naturalists believed that people were controlled by both outer and inner forces.

2. C: Gothic architecture often uses gargoyles, grotesque creatures with open mouths. They served as gutters, directing water away from walls.

3. B: Reification is the act of treating an abstraction as a real, concrete thing. For example, the concept of society might be useful, but it is not an actual, concrete thing separate from the components (such as people and infrastructure) that make up society. Options A, C, and D can all be rejected because none accurately capture the concept of reification. Social scientists might indeed be concerned with the relative appropriateness of qualitative data and quantitative data, but using one over the other is not reification. Social scientists might use heuristic devices, but this is not simply reification (not all cases of reification are cases of using heuristic devices). Reification is not mistaking subjectivity for objectivity.

4. A: The haiku, originating in Japanese poetry and since adopted in English-language poetry, is a short poem of only three lines, often with 17 syllables, with the first and third lines having five syllables and the second line having seven syllables. (In Japanese there are many other rules, which become very complicated.) Haiku are typically unrhymed, so they do not have a rhyme scheme. Similarly, they do not employ any regular meter. Because haiku are typically 17 syllables or fewer, they do not involve long narratives.

5. A: Analyzing and studying characters are important aspects of script analysis, but script analysis is much too broad to be the correct choice here. Plot development focuses on the storyline and occurs during the developmental stages before the script is complete. Psychological dissection is not a term that is used in theatre. The question is clearly asking for a choice that is related to better understanding a work's characters and their relationships with one another.

6. C: The first form of theatre originated in ancient Greece. Some experts believe this happened as far back as 500 BC. The Romans developed their own form of theatre shortly after the decline of the Greek government, imitating many aspects of Greek theatre. Medieval theatre, which relied heavily on religious undertones, came next. There are other forms of ancient theatre, but Greek, Roman, and Medieval are the most commonly studied. The English Renaissance is too young to be considered "ancient," as it originated in the 16th century.

7. A: As it relates to theatre, catharsis is a term that means "to purge the emotions." The terms *purification* and *ablution* have similar connotations, meaning "to cleanse or purify," but neither term is commonly used in the theatre industry. Therefore, answer choices C and D are incorrect. The alienation effect is when a director wants to distance the audience from the characters so they can be observed and critiqued from a non-emotional standpoint. Therefore, answer choice B is incorrect.

8. A: Juxtaposition describes a method of placing two visual elements next to each other to create a contrasting effect. This can help draw attention to the elements, or it can help one stand out more. Juxtaposing two complementary colors can make the colors stand out and can create a jarring effect. Juxtaposing light and dark values, different textures, and other visually opposing elements can draw the viewer's eye and help the artist create a focal point.

9. D: The representationalism aesthetic theory states the importance of the viewer understanding and recognizing the subject of an artwork. For example, if an artist wishes to show the subject of a landscape or a person sitting in a chair, he or she will clearly express this subject, and the viewer will be able to clearly receive this message from the artist. The artist will be able to represent the message to the viewer.

10. B: Pop art was an art movement that used comic images, and items from popular culture. This movement subsequently influenced popular culture with its bright colors and designs, as well as its use of mass-produced items in the artwork.

How to Overcome Test Anxiety

Just the thought of taking a test is enough to make most people a little nervous. A test is an important event that can have a long-term impact on your future, so it's important to take it seriously and it's natural to feel anxious about performing well. But just because anxiety is normal, that doesn't mean that it's helpful in test taking, or that you should simply accept it as part of your life. Anxiety can have a variety of effects. These effects can be mild, like making you feel slightly nervous, or severe, like blocking your ability to focus or remember even a simple detail.

If you experience test anxiety—whether severe or mild—it's important to know how to beat it. To discover this, first you need to understand what causes test anxiety.

Causes of Test Anxiety

While we often think of anxiety as an uncontrollable emotional state, it can actually be caused by simple, practical things. One of the most common causes of test anxiety is that a person does not feel adequately prepared for their test. This feeling can be the result of many different issues such as poor study habits or lack of organization, but the most common culprit is time management. Starting to study too late, failing to organize your study time to cover all of the material, or being distracted while you study will mean that you're not well prepared for the test. This may lead to cramming the night before, which will cause you to be physically and mentally exhausted for the test. Poor time management also contributes to feelings of stress, fear, and hopelessness as you realize you are not well prepared but don't know what to do about it.

Other times, test anxiety is not related to your preparation for the test but comes from unresolved fear. This may be a past failure on a test, or poor performance on tests in general. It may come from comparing yourself to others who seem to be performing better or from the stress of living up to expectations. Anxiety may be driven by fears of the future—how failure on this test would affect your educational and career goals. These fears are often completely irrational, but they can still negatively impact your test performance.

> **Review Video: 3 Reasons You Have Test Anxiety**
> Visit mometrix.com/academy and enter code: 428468

Elements of Test Anxiety

As mentioned earlier, test anxiety is considered to be an emotional state, but it has physical and mental components as well. Sometimes you may not even realize that you are suffering from test anxiety until you notice the physical symptoms. These can include trembling hands, rapid heartbeat, sweating, nausea, and tense muscles. Extreme anxiety may lead to fainting or vomiting. Obviously, any of these symptoms can have a negative impact on testing. It is important to recognize them as soon as they begin to occur so that you can address the problem before it damages your performance.

> **Review Video: 3 Ways to Tell You Have Test Anxiety**
> Visit mometrix.com/academy and enter code: 927847

The mental components of test anxiety include trouble focusing and inability to remember learned information. During a test, your mind is on high alert, which can help you recall information and stay focused for an extended period of time. However, anxiety interferes with your mind's natural processes, causing you to blank out, even on the questions you know well. The strain of testing during anxiety makes it difficult to stay focused, especially on a test that may take several hours. Extreme anxiety can take a huge mental toll, making it difficult not only to recall test information but even to understand the test questions or pull your thoughts together.

> **Review Video: How Test Anxiety Affects Memory**
> Visit mometrix.com/academy and enter code: 609003

Effects of Test Anxiety

Test anxiety is like a disease—if left untreated, it will get progressively worse. Anxiety leads to poor performance, and this reinforces the feelings of fear and failure, which in turn lead to poor performances on subsequent tests. It can grow from a mild nervousness to a crippling condition. If allowed to progress, test anxiety can have a big impact on your schooling, and consequently on your future.

Test anxiety can spread to other parts of your life. Anxiety on tests can become anxiety in any stressful situation, and blanking on a test can turn into panicking in a job situation. But fortunately, you don't have to let anxiety rule your testing and determine your grades. There are a number of relatively simple steps you can take to move past anxiety and function normally on a test and in the rest of life.

> **Review Video: How Test Anxiety Impacts Your Grades**
> Visit mometrix.com/academy and enter code: 939819

Physical Steps for Beating Test Anxiety

While test anxiety is a serious problem, the good news is that it can be overcome. It doesn't have to control your ability to think and remember information. While it may take time, you can begin taking steps today to beat anxiety.

Just as your first hint that you may be struggling with anxiety comes from the physical symptoms, the first step to treating it is also physical. Rest is crucial for having a clear, strong mind. If you are tired, it is much easier to give in to anxiety. But if you establish good sleep habits, your body and mind will be ready to perform optimally, without the strain of exhaustion. Additionally, sleeping well helps you to retain information better, so you're more likely to recall the answers when you see the test questions.

Getting good sleep means more than going to bed on time. It's important to allow your brain time to relax. Take study breaks from time to time so it doesn't get overworked, and don't study right before bed. Take time to rest your mind before trying to rest your body, or you may find it difficult to fall asleep.

> **Review Video: The Importance of Sleep for Your Brain**
> Visit mometrix.com/academy and enter code: 319338

Along with sleep, other aspects of physical health are important in preparing for a test. Good nutrition is vital for good brain function. Sugary foods and drinks may give a burst of energy but this burst is followed by a crash, both physically and emotionally. Instead, fuel your body with protein and vitamin-rich foods.

Also, drink plenty of water. Dehydration can lead to headaches and exhaustion, especially if your brain is already under stress from the rigors of the test. Particularly if your test is a long one, drink water during the breaks. And if possible, take an energy-boosting snack to eat between sections.

> **Review Video: How Diet Can Affect your Mood**
> Visit mometrix.com/academy and enter code: 624317

Along with sleep and diet, a third important part of physical health is exercise. Maintaining a steady workout schedule is helpful, but even taking 5-minute study breaks to walk can help get your blood pumping faster and clear your head. Exercise also releases endorphins, which contribute to a positive feeling and can help combat test anxiety.

When you nurture your physical health, you are also contributing to your mental health. If your body is healthy, your mind is much more likely to be healthy as well. So take time to rest, nourish your body with healthy food and water, and get moving as much as possible. Taking these physical steps will make you stronger and more able to take the mental steps necessary to overcome test anxiety.

Mental Steps for Beating Test Anxiety

Working on the mental side of test anxiety can be more challenging, but as with the physical side, there are clear steps you can take to overcome it. As mentioned earlier, test anxiety often stems from lack of preparation, so the obvious solution is to prepare for the test. Effective studying may be the most important weapon you have for beating test anxiety, but you can and should employ several other mental tools to combat fear.

First, boost your confidence by reminding yourself of past success—tests or projects that you aced. If you're putting as much effort into preparing for this test as you did for those, there's no reason you should expect to fail here. Work hard to prepare; then trust your preparation.

Second, surround yourself with encouraging people. It can be helpful to find a study group, but be sure that the people you're around will encourage a positive attitude. If you spend time with others who are anxious or cynical, this will only contribute to your own anxiety. Look for others who are motivated to study hard from a desire to succeed, not from a fear of failure.

Third, reward yourself. A test is physically and mentally tiring, even without anxiety, and it can be helpful to have something to look forward to. Plan an activity following the test, regardless of the outcome, such as going to a movie or getting ice cream.

When you are taking the test, if you find yourself beginning to feel anxious, remind yourself that you know the material. Visualize successfully completing the test. Then take a few deep, relaxing breaths and return to it. Work through the questions carefully but with confidence, knowing that you are capable of succeeding.

Developing a healthy mental approach to test taking will also aid in other areas of life. Test anxiety affects more than just the actual test—it can be damaging to your mental health and even contribute to depression. It's important to beat test anxiety before it becomes a problem for more than testing.

Review Video: Test Anxiety and Depression
Visit mometrix.com/academy and enter code: 904704

Study Strategy

Being prepared for the test is necessary to combat anxiety, but what does being prepared look like? You may study for hours on end and still not feel prepared. What you need is a strategy for test prep. The next few pages outline our recommended steps to help you plan out and conquer the challenge of preparation.

STEP 1: SCOPE OUT THE TEST

Learn everything you can about the format (multiple choice, essay, etc.) and what will be on the test. Gather any study materials, course outlines, or sample exams that may be available. Not only will this help you to prepare, but knowing what to expect can help to alleviate test anxiety.

STEP 2: MAP OUT THE MATERIAL

Look through the textbook or study guide and make note of how many chapters or sections it has. Then divide these over the time you have. For example, if a book has 15 chapters and you have five days to study, you need to cover three chapters each day. Even better, if you have the time, leave an extra day at the end for overall review after you have gone through the material in depth.

If time is limited, you may need to prioritize the material. Look through it and make note of which sections you think you already have a good grasp on, and which need review. While you are studying, skim quickly through the familiar sections and take more time on the challenging parts. Write out your plan so you don't get lost as you go. Having a written plan also helps you feel more in control of the study, so anxiety is less likely to arise from feeling overwhelmed at the amount to cover.

STEP 3: GATHER YOUR TOOLS

Decide what study method works best for you. Do you prefer to highlight in the book as you study and then go back over the highlighted portions? Or do you type out notes of the important information? Or is it helpful to make flashcards that you can carry with you? Assemble the pens, index cards, highlighters, post-it notes, and any other materials you may need so you won't be distracted by getting up to find things while you study.

If you're having a hard time retaining the information or organizing your notes, experiment with different methods. For example, try color-coding by subject with colored pens, highlighters, or post-it notes. If you learn better by hearing, try recording yourself reading your notes so you can listen while in the car, working out, or simply sitting at your desk. Ask a friend to quiz you from your flashcards, or try teaching someone the material to solidify it in your mind.

STEP 4: CREATE YOUR ENVIRONMENT

It's important to avoid distractions while you study. This includes both the obvious distractions like visitors and the subtle distractions like an uncomfortable chair (or a too-comfortable couch that makes you want to fall asleep). Set up the best study environment possible: good lighting and a comfortable work area. If background music helps you focus, you may want to turn it on, but otherwise keep the room quiet. If you are using a computer to take notes, be sure you don't have any other windows open, especially applications like social media, games, or anything else that could distract you. Silence your phone and turn off notifications. Be sure to keep water close by so you stay hydrated while you study (but avoid unhealthy drinks and snacks).

Also, take into account the best time of day to study. Are you freshest first thing in the morning? Try to set aside some time then to work through the material. Is your mind clearer in the afternoon or evening? Schedule your study session then. Another method is to study at the same time of day that you will take the test, so that your brain gets used to working on the material at that time and will be ready to focus at test time.

Step 5: Study!

Once you have done all the study preparation, it's time to settle into the actual studying. Sit down, take a few moments to settle your mind so you can focus, and begin to follow your study plan. Don't give in to distractions or let yourself procrastinate. This is your time to prepare so you'll be ready to fearlessly approach the test. Make the most of the time and stay focused.

Of course, you don't want to burn out. If you study too long you may find that you're not retaining the information very well. Take regular study breaks. For example, taking five minutes out of every hour to walk briskly, breathing deeply and swinging your arms, can help your mind stay fresh.

As you get to the end of each chapter or section, it's a good idea to do a quick review. Remind yourself of what you learned and work on any difficult parts. When you feel that you've mastered the material, move on to the next part. At the end of your study session, briefly skim through your notes again.

But while review is helpful, cramming last minute is NOT. If at all possible, work ahead so that you won't need to fit all your study into the last day. Cramming overloads your brain with more information than it can process and retain, and your tired mind may struggle to recall even previously learned information when it is overwhelmed with last-minute study. Also, the urgent nature of cramming and the stress placed on your brain contribute to anxiety. You'll be more likely to go to the test feeling unprepared and having trouble thinking clearly.

So don't cram, and don't stay up late before the test, even just to review your notes at a leisurely pace. Your brain needs rest more than it needs to go over the information again. In fact, plan to finish your studies by noon or early afternoon the day before the test. Give your brain the rest of the day to relax or focus on other things, and get a good night's sleep. Then you will be fresh for the test and better able to recall what you've studied.

Step 6: Take a practice test

Many courses offer sample tests, either online or in the study materials. This is an excellent resource to check whether you have mastered the material, as well as to prepare for the test format and environment.

Check the test format ahead of time: the number of questions, the type (multiple choice, free response, etc.), and the time limit. Then create a plan for working through them. For example, if you have 30 minutes to take a 60-question test, your limit is 30 seconds per question. Spend less time on the questions you know well so that you can take more time on the difficult ones.

If you have time to take several practice tests, take the first one open book, with no time limit. Work through the questions at your own pace and make sure you fully understand them. Gradually work up to taking a test under test conditions: sit at a desk with all study materials put away and set a timer. Pace yourself to make sure you finish the test with time to spare and go back to check your answers if you have time.

After each test, check your answers. On the questions you missed, be sure you understand why you missed them. Did you misread the question (tests can use tricky wording)? Did you forget the information? Or was it something you hadn't learned? Go back and study any shaky areas that the practice tests reveal.

Taking these tests not only helps with your grade, but also aids in combating test anxiety. If you're already used to the test conditions, you're less likely to worry about it, and working through tests until you're scoring well gives you a confidence boost. Go through the practice tests until you feel comfortable, and then you can go into the test knowing that you're ready for it.

Test Tips

On test day, you should be confident, knowing that you've prepared well and are ready to answer the questions. But aside from preparation, there are several test day strategies you can employ to maximize your performance.

First, as stated before, get a good night's sleep the night before the test (and for several nights before that, if possible). Go into the test with a fresh, alert mind rather than staying up late to study.

Try not to change too much about your normal routine on the day of the test. It's important to eat a nutritious breakfast, but if you normally don't eat breakfast at all, consider eating just a protein bar. If you're a coffee drinker, go ahead and have your normal coffee. Just make sure you time it so that the caffeine doesn't wear off right in the middle of your test. Avoid sugary beverages, and drink enough water to stay hydrated but not so much that you need a restroom break 10 minutes into the test. If your test isn't first thing in the morning, consider going for a walk or doing a light workout before the test to get your blood flowing.

Allow yourself enough time to get ready, and leave for the test with plenty of time to spare so you won't have the anxiety of scrambling to arrive in time. Another reason to be early is to select a good seat. It's helpful to sit away from doors and windows, which can be distracting. Find a good seat, get out your supplies, and settle your mind before the test begins.

When the test begins, start by going over the instructions carefully, even if you already know what to expect. Make sure you avoid any careless mistakes by following the directions.

Then begin working through the questions, pacing yourself as you've practiced. If you're not sure on an answer, don't spend too much time on it, and don't let it shake your confidence. Either skip it and come back later, or eliminate as many wrong answers as possible and guess among the remaining ones. Don't dwell on these questions as you continue—put them out of your mind and focus on what lies ahead.

Be sure to read all of the answer choices, even if you're sure the first one is the right answer. Sometimes you'll find a better one if you keep reading. But don't second-guess yourself if you do immediately know the answer. Your gut instinct is usually right. Don't let test anxiety rob you of the information you know.

If you have time at the end of the test (and if the test format allows), go back and review your answers. Be cautious about changing any, since your first instinct tends to be correct, but make sure you didn't misread any of the questions or accidentally mark the wrong answer choice. Look over any you skipped and make an educated guess.

At the end, leave the test feeling confident. You've done your best, so don't waste time worrying about your performance or wishing you could change anything. Instead, celebrate the successful completion of this test. And finally, use this test to learn how to deal with anxiety even better next time.

> **Review Video: 5 Tips to Beat Test Anxiety**
> Visit mometrix.com/academy and enter code: 570656

Important Qualification

Not all anxiety is created equal. If your test anxiety is causing major issues in your life beyond the classroom or testing center, or if you are experiencing troubling physical symptoms related to your anxiety, it may be a sign of a serious physiological or psychological condition. If this sounds like your situation, we strongly encourage you to seek professional help.

Thank You

We at Mometrix would like to extend our heartfelt thanks to you, our friend and patron, for allowing us to play a part in your journey. It is a privilege to serve people from all walks of life who are unified in their commitment to building the best future they can for themselves.

The preparation you devote to these important testing milestones may be the most valuable educational opportunity you have for making a real difference in your life. We encourage you to put your heart into it—that feeling of succeeding, overcoming, and yes, conquering will be well worth the hours you've invested.

We want to hear your story, your struggles and your successes, and if you see any opportunities for us to improve our materials so we can help others even more effectively in the future, please share that with us as well. **The team at Mometrix would be absolutely thrilled to hear from you!** So please, send us an email (support@mometrix.com) and let's stay in touch.

> If you'd like some additional help, check out these other resources we offer for your exam:
> http://mometrixflashcards.com/MoGEA

Additional Bonus Material

Due to our efforts to try to keep this book to a manageable length, we've created a link that will give you access to all of your additional bonus material:

mometrix.com/bonus948/mogea081